R.I.P.D.™

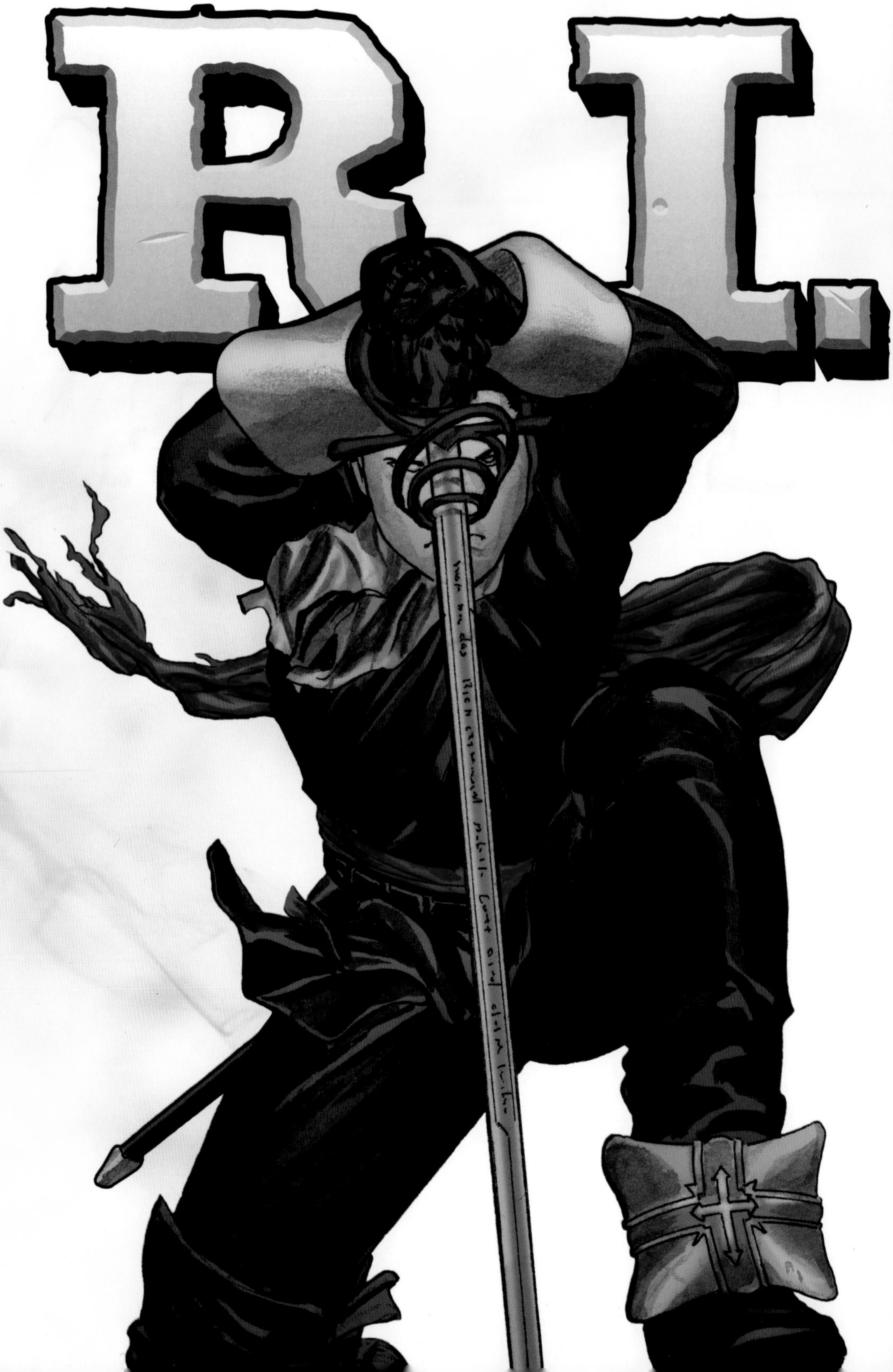
R.I.

P.D.™

VOLUME TWO
CITY OF THE DAMNED

story **JEREMY BARLOW**

line art **TONY PARKER**

colors **MICHELLE MADSEN**

letters **RICHARD STARKINGS and COMICRAFT**

chapter break art **DAVE WILKINS and TONY PARKER**

Based on the characters created by Peter M. Lenkov

 DARK HORSE BOOKS

Publisher **Mike Richardson**

Designer **Amy Arendts**

Digital Production **Christianne Goudreau**

Assistant Editor **Everett Patterson**

Editor **Patrick Thorpe**

Special thanks to Annie Gullion and Lia Ribacchi.

This volume collects issues #1–#4 of Dark Horse Comics' miniseries
R.I.P.D.: City of the Damned.

Published by
Dark Horse Books
A division of Dark Horse Comics, Inc.
10956 SE Main Street
Milwaukie, OR 97222

DarkHorse.com

To find a comics shop in your area, call the Comic Shop Locator Service toll-free at 1-888-266-4226. International Licensing: (503) 905-2377.

First edition: May 2013
ISBN 978-1-61655-113-1
10 9 8 7 6 5 4 3 2 1
Printed in China

MIKE RICHARDSON President and Publisher NEIL HANKERSON Executive Vice President TOM WEDDLE Chief Financial Officer RANDY STRADLEY Vice President of Publishing MICHAEL MARTENS Vice President of Book Trade Sales ANITA NELSON Vice President of Business Affairs SCOTT ALLIE Editor in Chief MATT PARKINSON Vice President of Marketing DAVID SCROGGY Vice President of Product Development DALE LAFOUNTAIN Vice President of Information Technology DARLENE VOGEL Senior Director of Print, Design, and Production KEN LIZZI General Counsel DAVEY ESTRADA Editorial Director CHRIS WARNER Senior Books Editor DIANA SCHUTZ Executive Editor CARY GRAZZINI Director of Print and Development LIA RIBACCHI Art Director CARA NIECE Director of Scheduling TIM WIESCH Director of International Licensing MARK BERNARDI Director of Digital Publishing

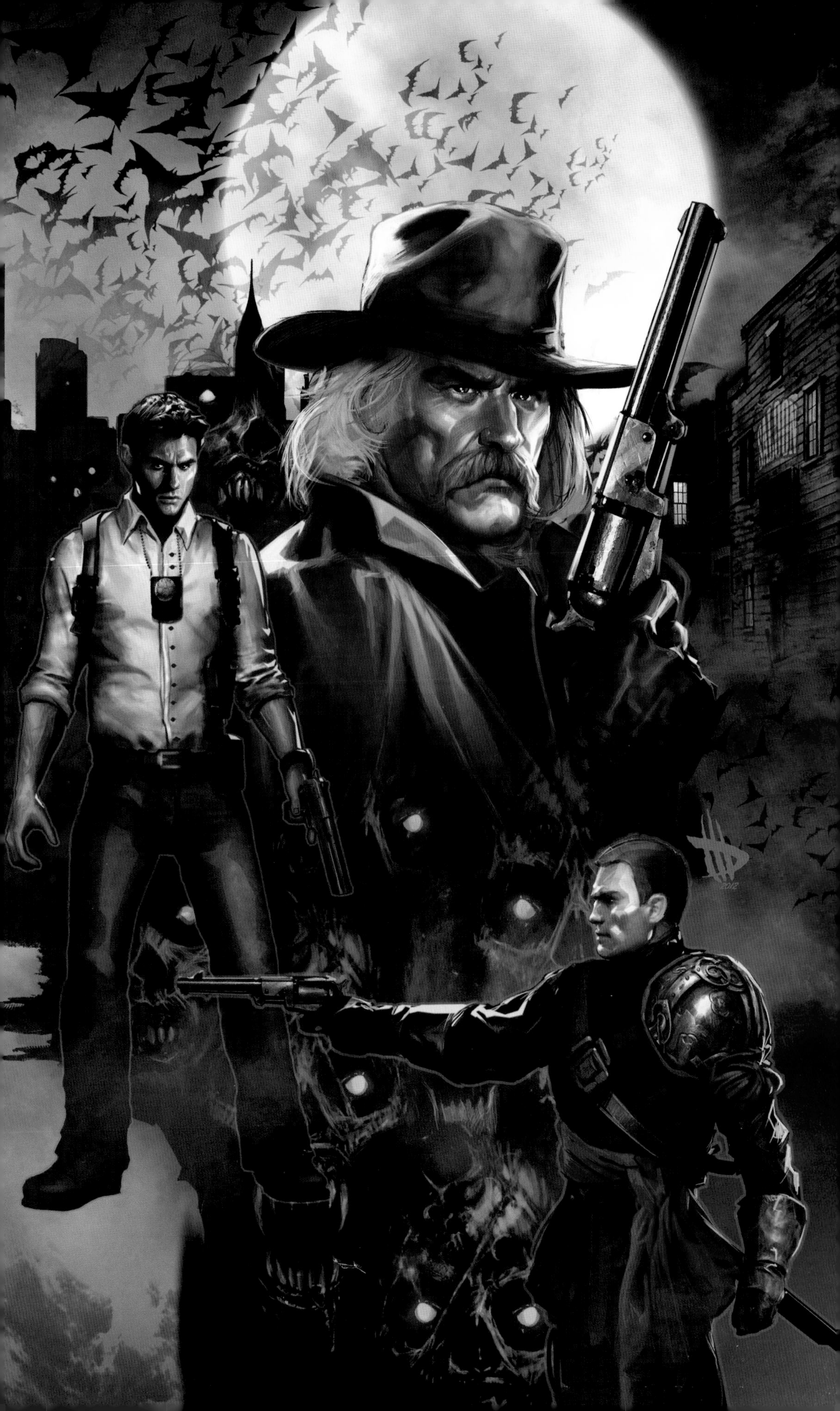

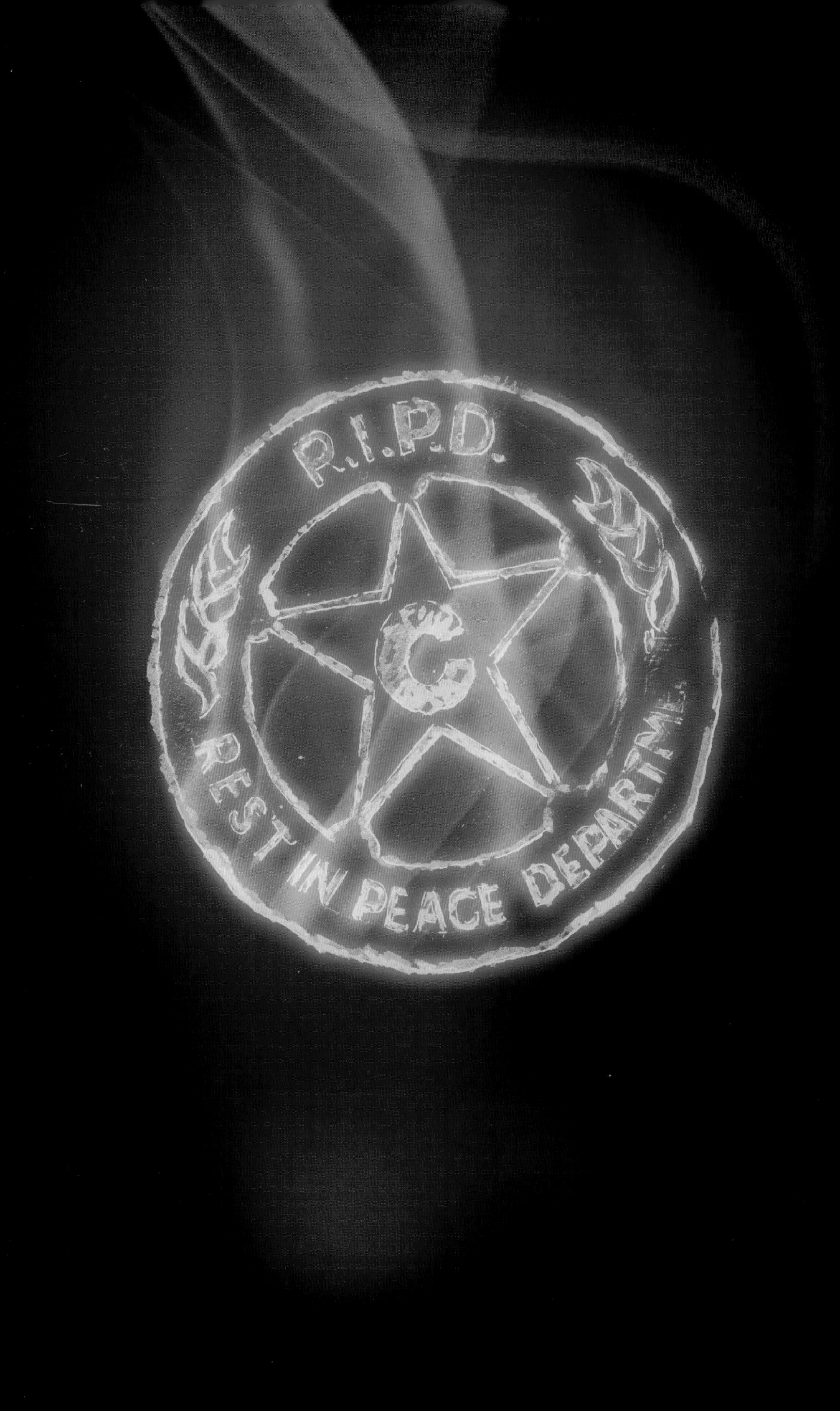
R.I.P.D.
C
REST IN PEACE DEPARTMENT

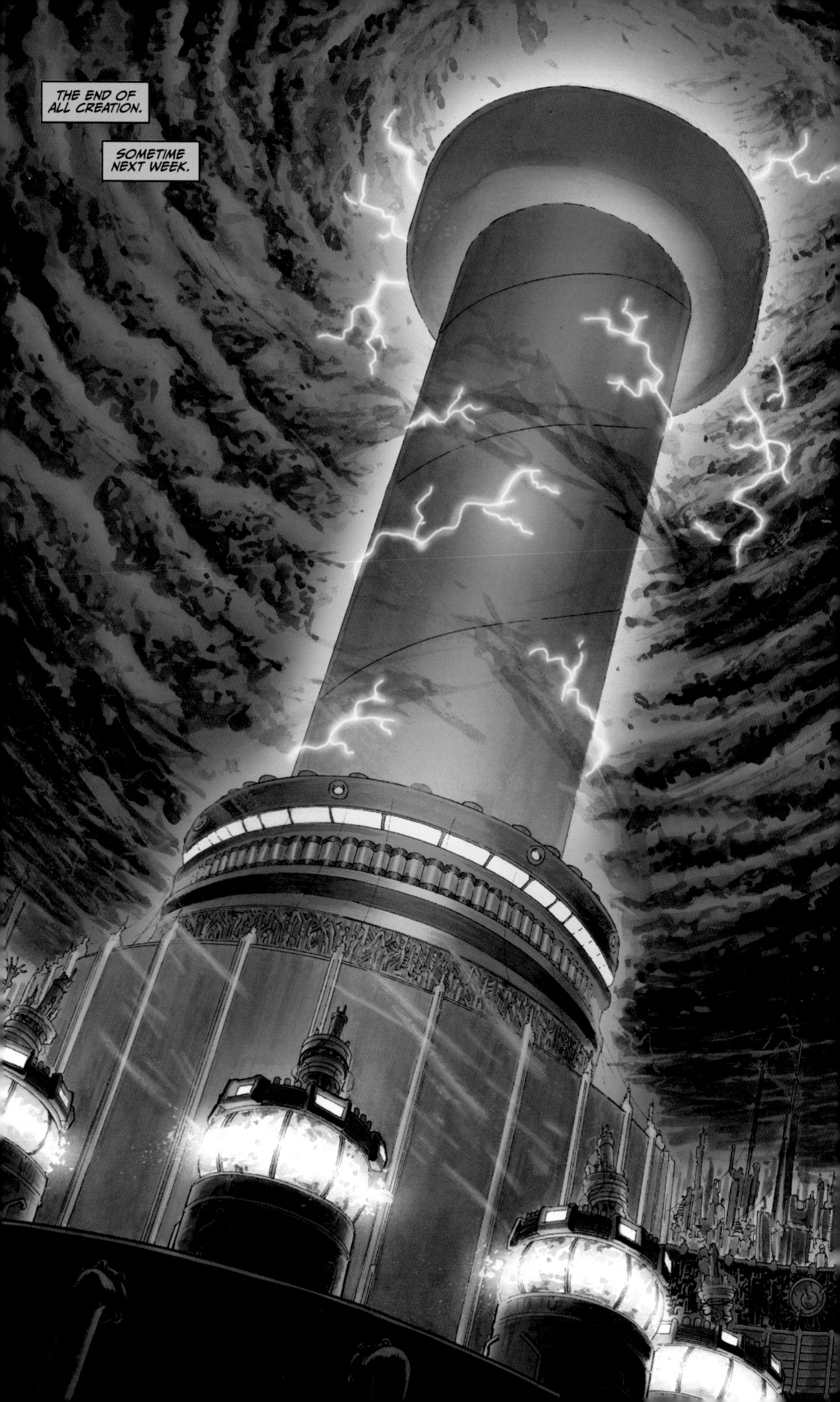
THE END OF ALL CREATION.
SOMETIME NEXT WEEK.

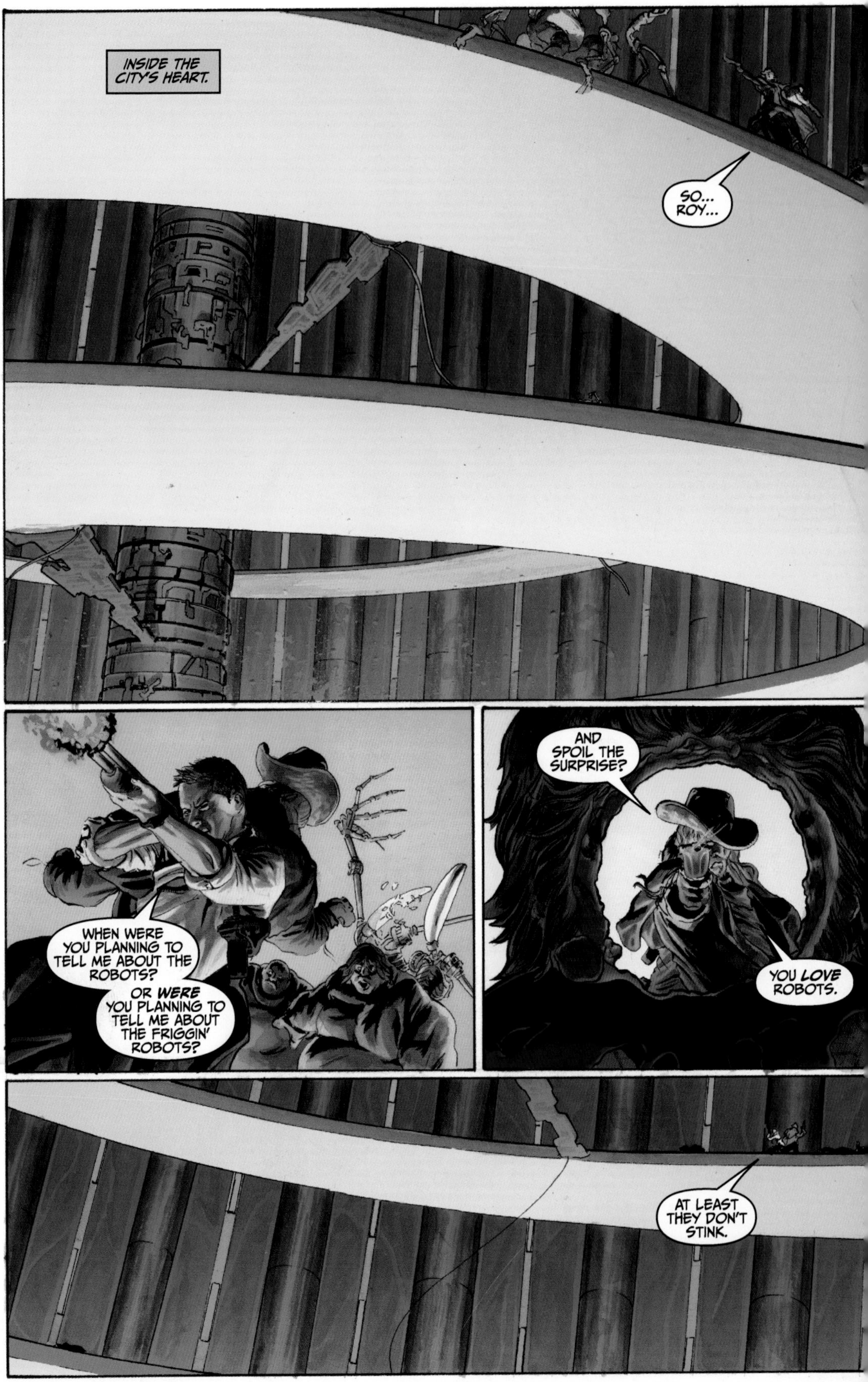
INSIDE THE CITY'S HEART.
SO... ROY...
WHEN WERE YOU PLANNING TO TELL ME ABOUT THE ROBOTS?
OR WERE YOU PLANNING TO TELL ME ABOUT THE FRIGGIN' ROBOTS?
AND SPOIL THE SURPRISE?
YOU LOVE ROBOTS.
AT LEAST THEY DON'T STINK.

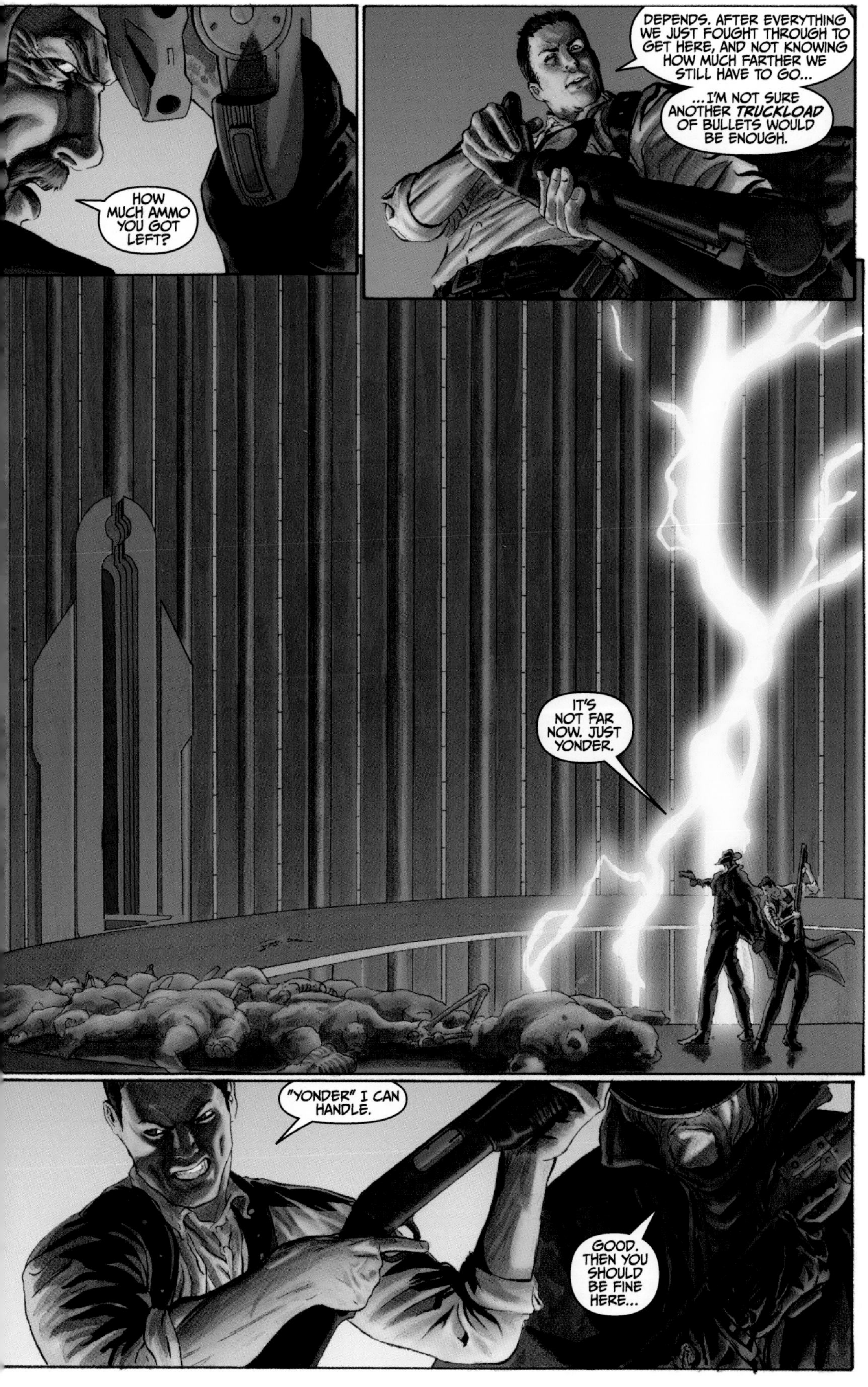
HOW MUCH AMMO YOU GOT LEFT?
DEPENDS. AFTER EVERYTHING WE JUST FOUGHT THROUGH TO GET HERE, AND NOT KNOWING HOW MUCH FARTHER WE STILL HAVE TO GO...
...I'M NOT SURE ANOTHER TRUCKLOAD OF BULLETS WOULD BE ENOUGH.
IT'S NOT FAR NOW. JUST YONDER.
"YONDER" I CAN HANDLE.
GOOD. THEN YOU SHOULD BE FINE HERE...

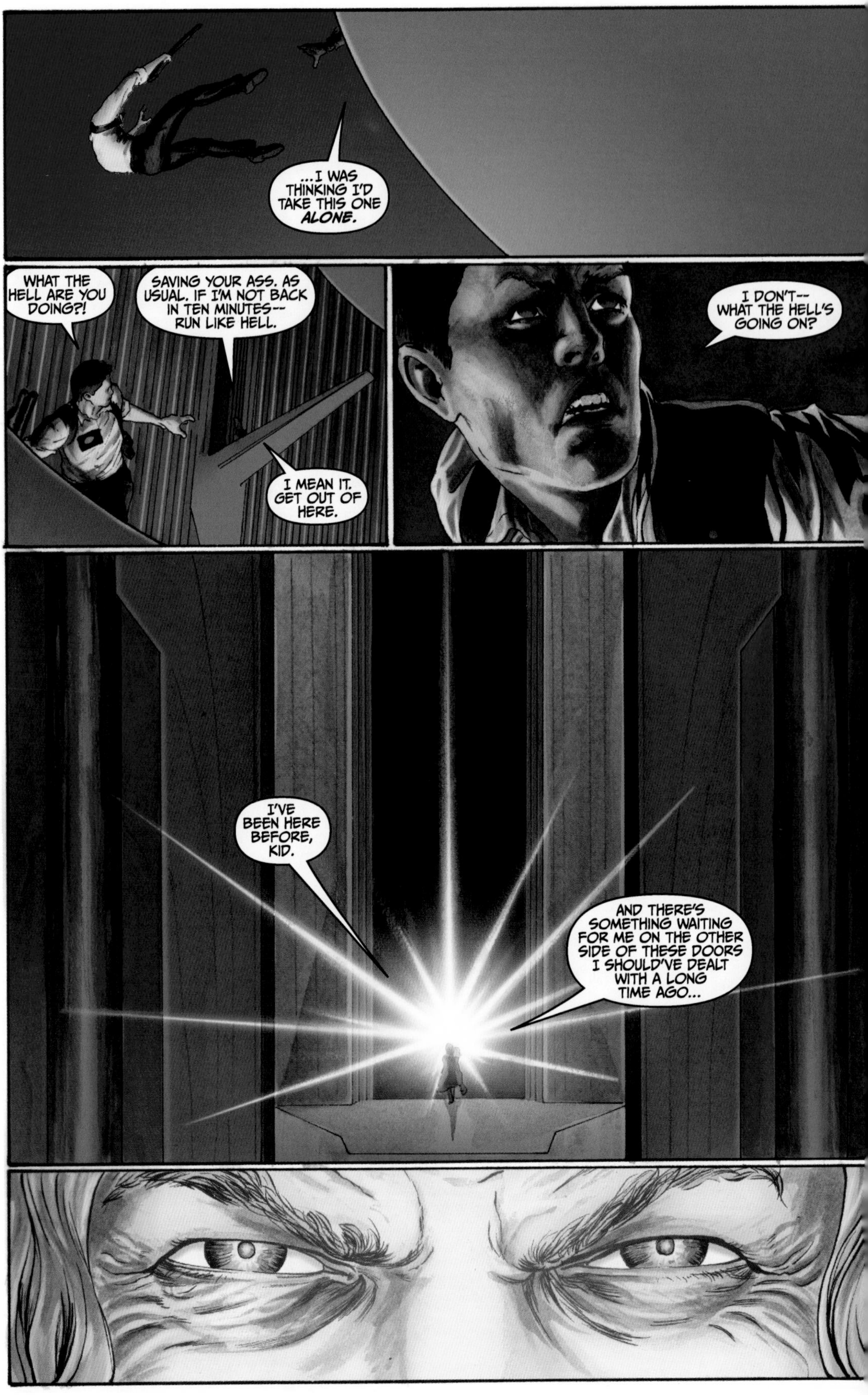
...I WAS THINKING I'D TAKE THIS ONE ALONE.
WHAT THE HELL ARE YOU DOING?!
SAVING YOUR ASS. AS USUAL. IF I'M NOT BACK IN TEN MINUTES-- RUN LIKE HELL.
I MEAN IT. GET OUT OF HERE.
I DON'T-- WHAT THE HELL'S GOING ON?
I'VE BEEN HERE BEFORE, KID.
AND THERE'S SOMETHING WAITING FOR ME ON THE OTHER SIDE OF THESE DOORS I SHOULD'VE DEALT WITH A LONG TIME AGO...

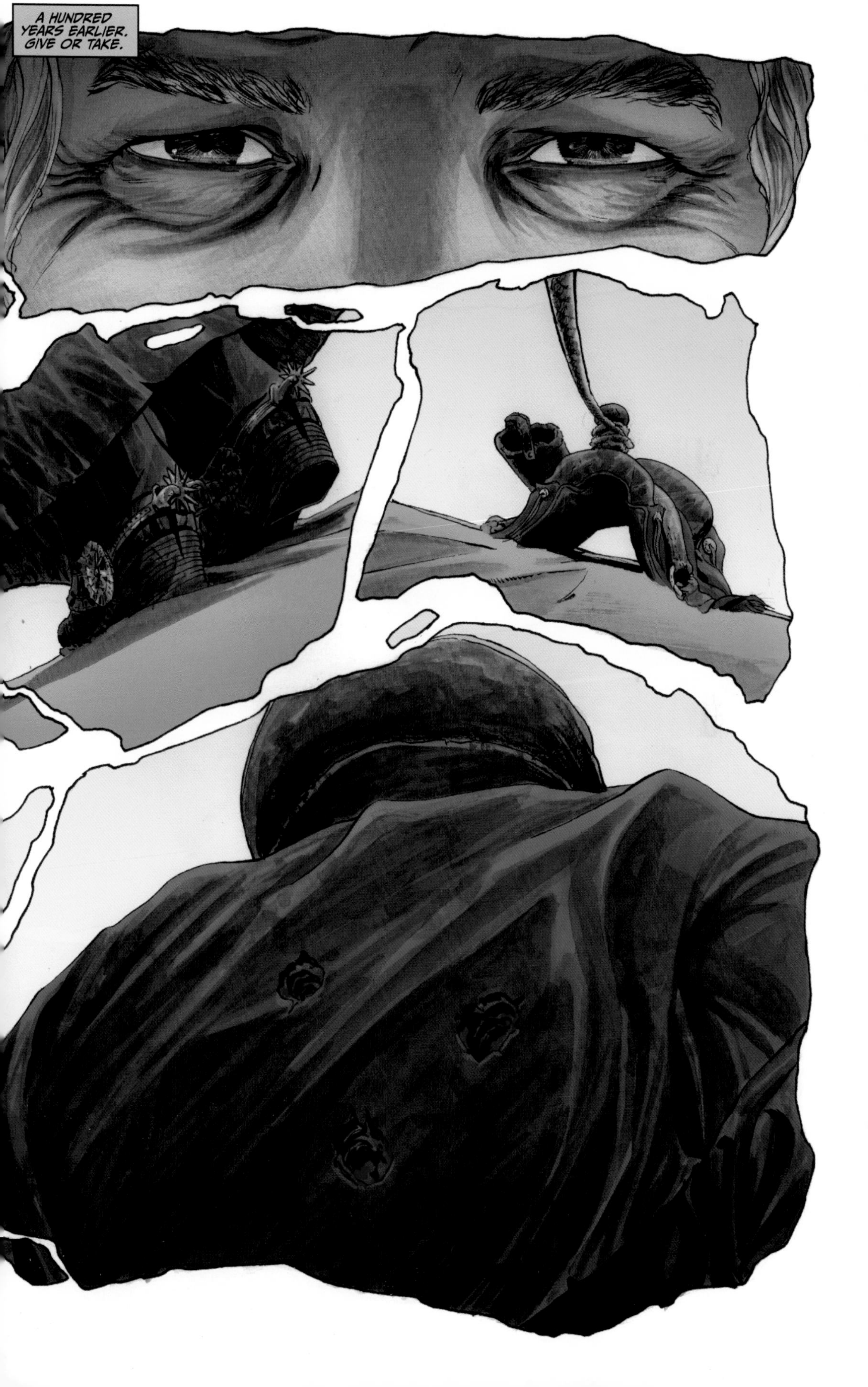
A HUNDRED YEARS EARLIER. GIVE OR TAKE.

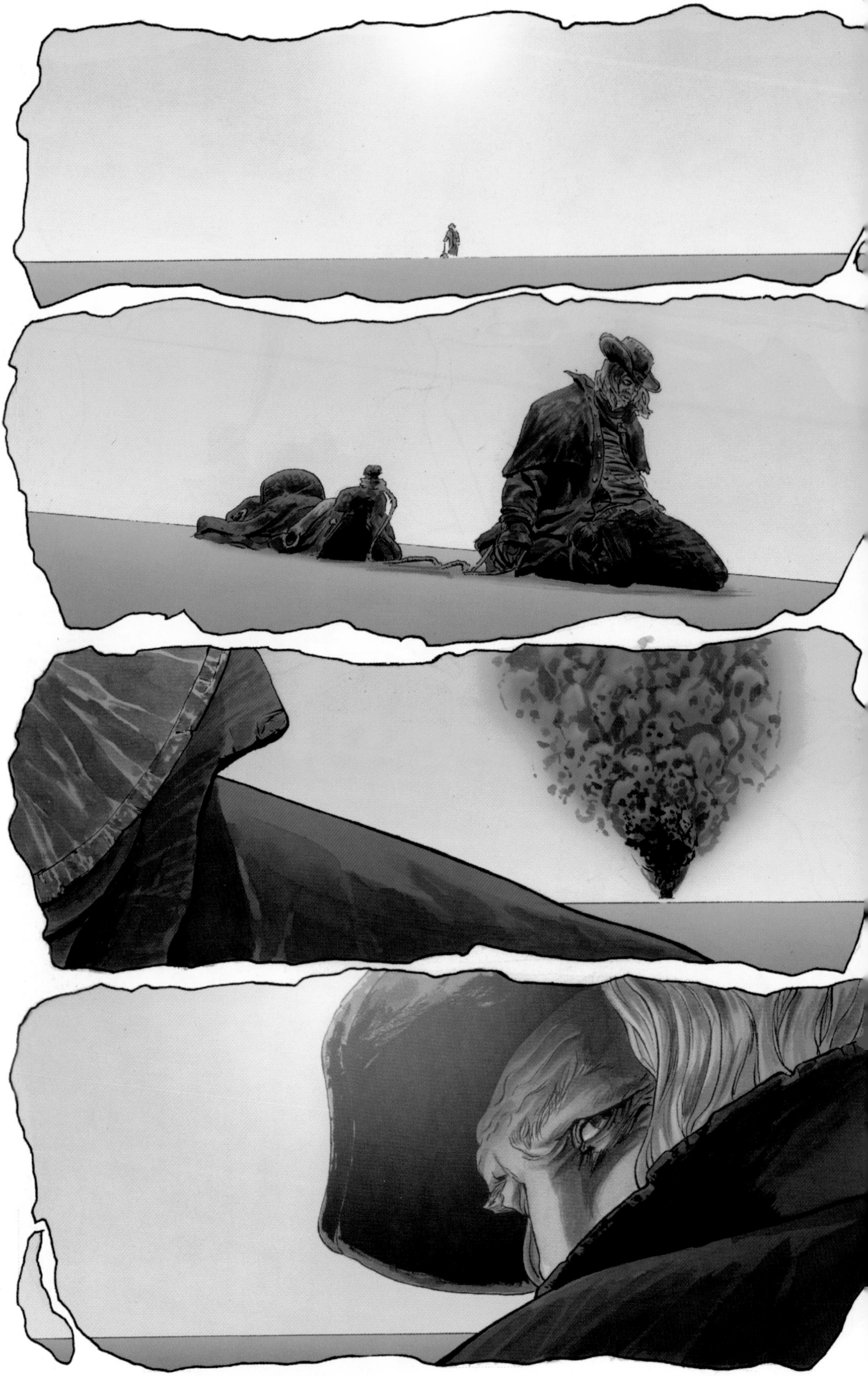

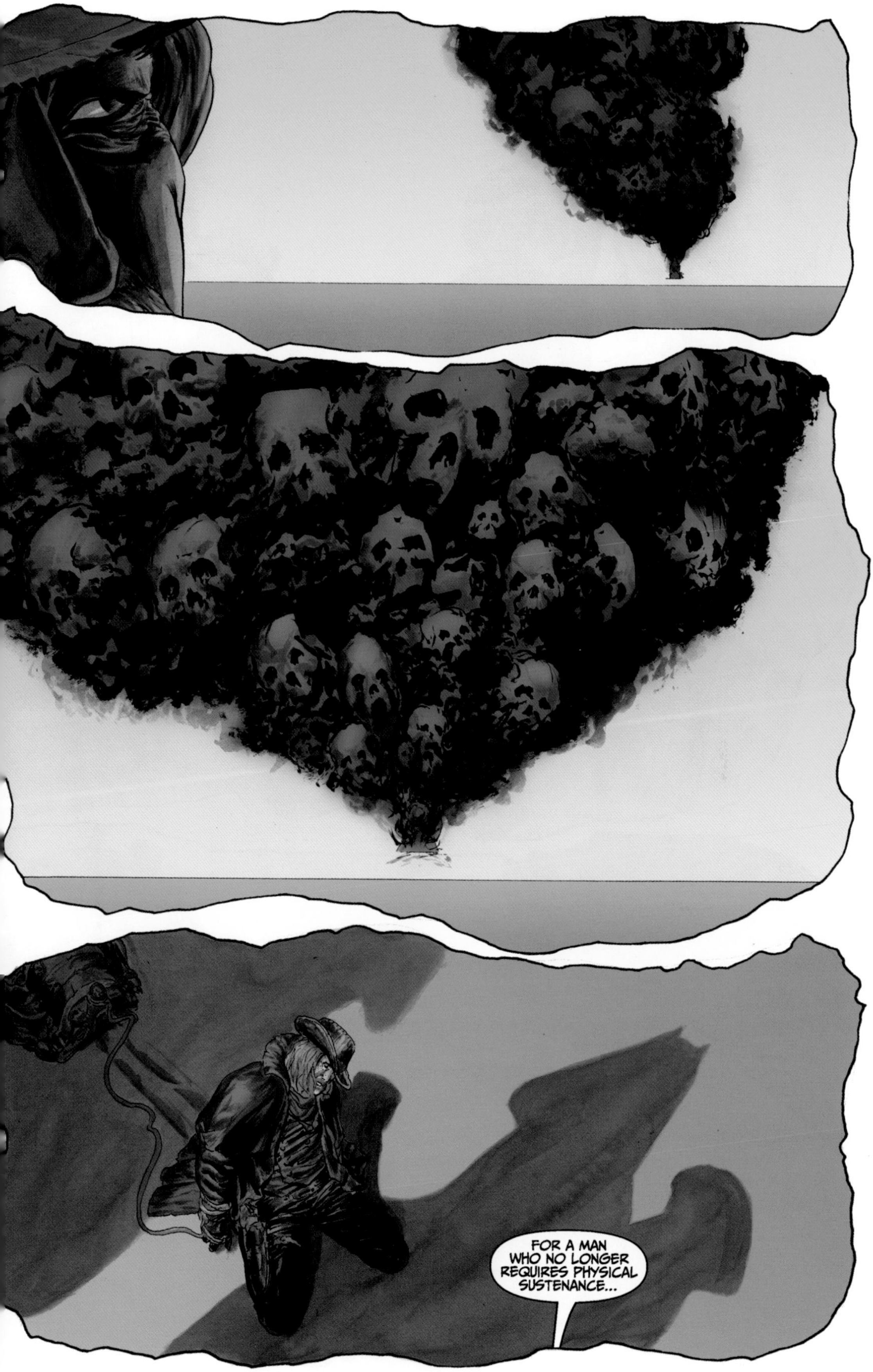
FOR A MAN WHO NO LONGER REQUIRES PHYSICAL SUSTENANCE...

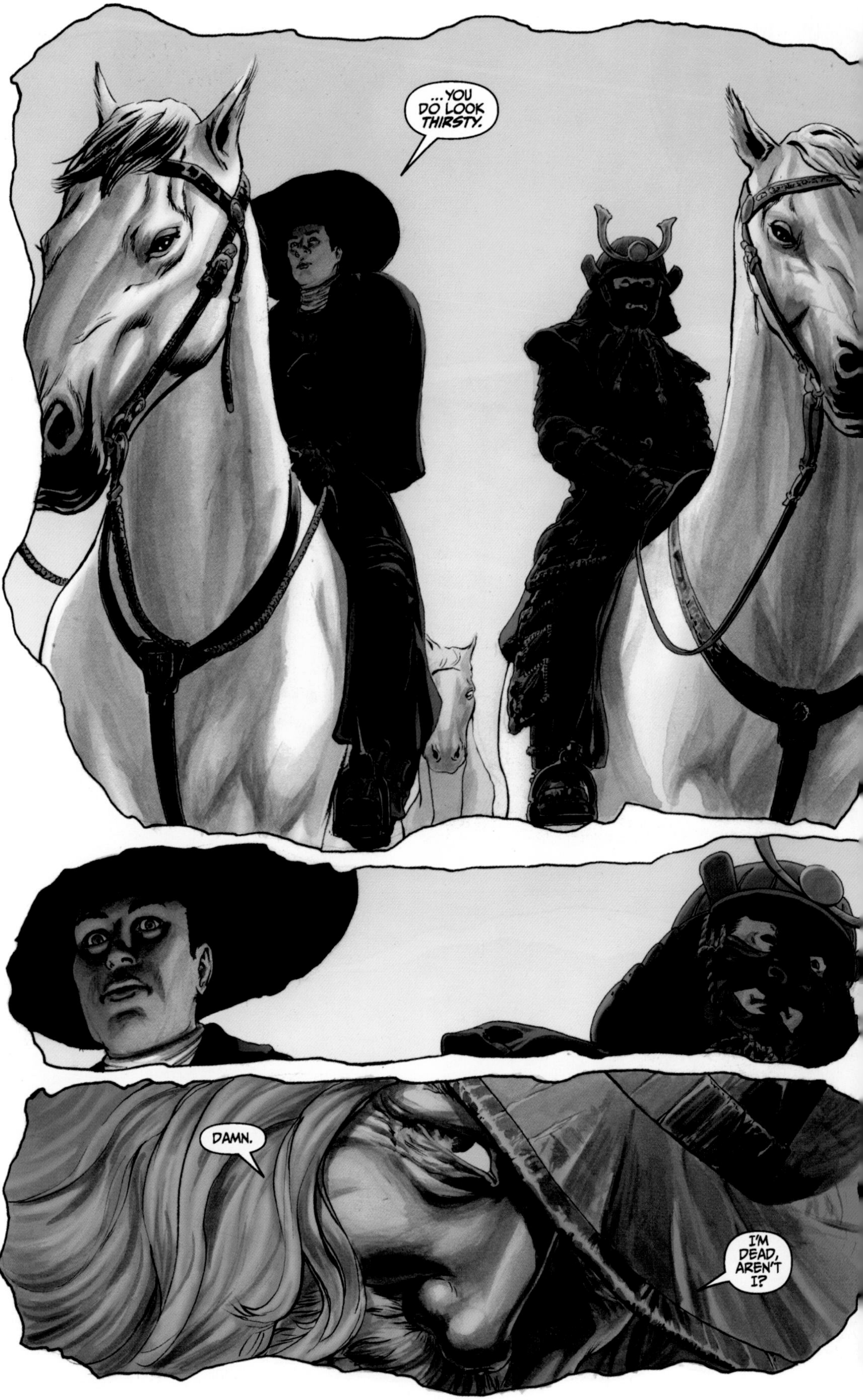
...YOU DO LOOK THIRSTY.
DAMN.
I'M DEAD, AREN'T I?

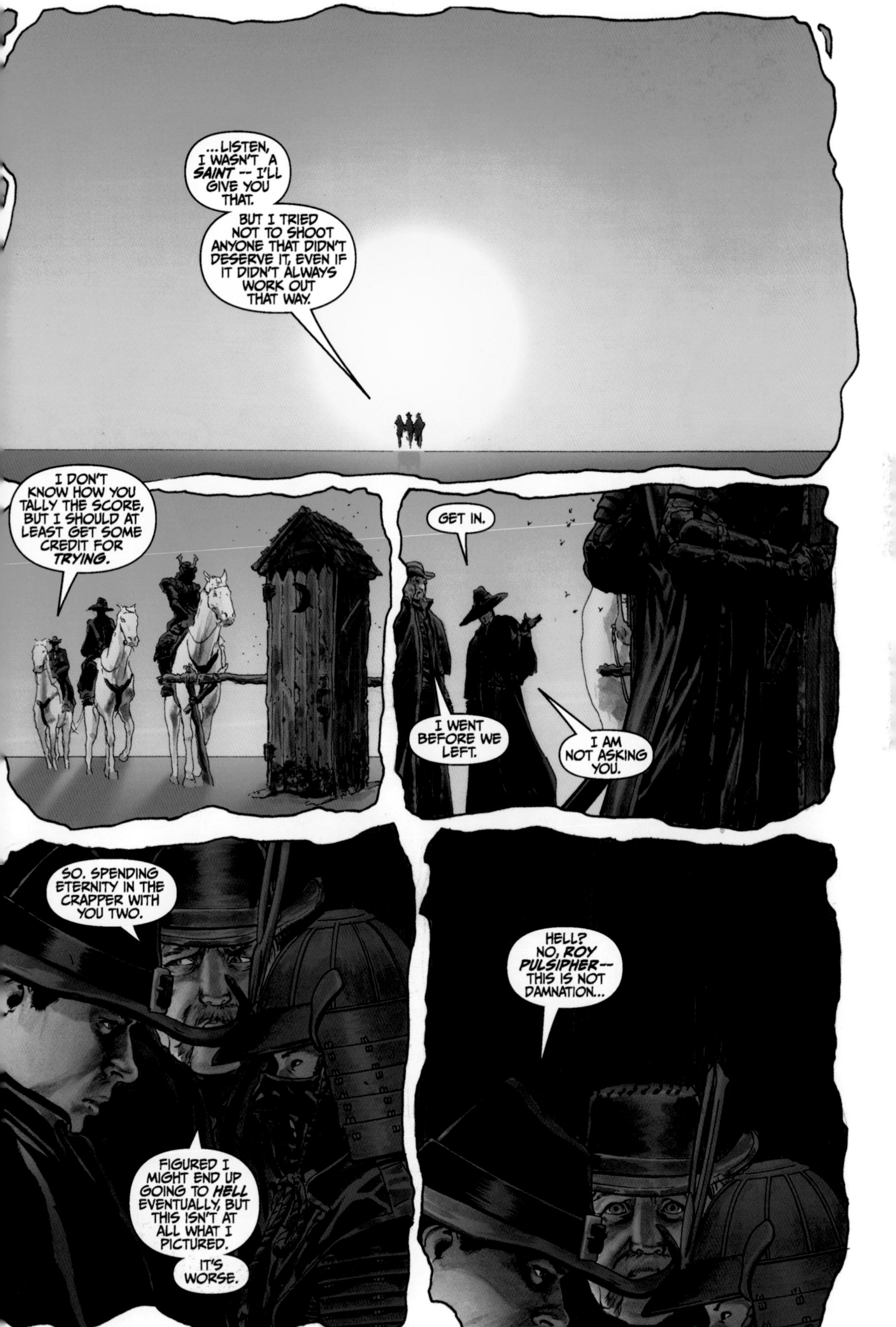
...LISTEN, I WASN'T A SAINT -- I'LL GIVE YOU THAT.
BUT I TRIED NOT TO SHOOT ANYONE THAT DIDN'T DESERVE IT, EVEN IF IT DIDN'T ALWAYS WORK OUT THAT WAY.
I DON'T KNOW HOW YOU TALLY THE SCORE, BUT I SHOULD AT LEAST GET SOME CREDIT FOR TRYING.
GET IN.
I WENT BEFORE WE LEFT.
I AM NOT ASKING YOU.
SO. SPENDING ETERNITY IN THE CRAPPER WITH YOU TWO.
FIGURED I MIGHT END UP GOING TO HELL EVENTUALLY, BUT THIS ISN'T AT ALL WHAT I PICTURED.
IT'S WORSE.
HELL? NO, ROY PULSIPHER-- THIS IS NOT DAMNATION...

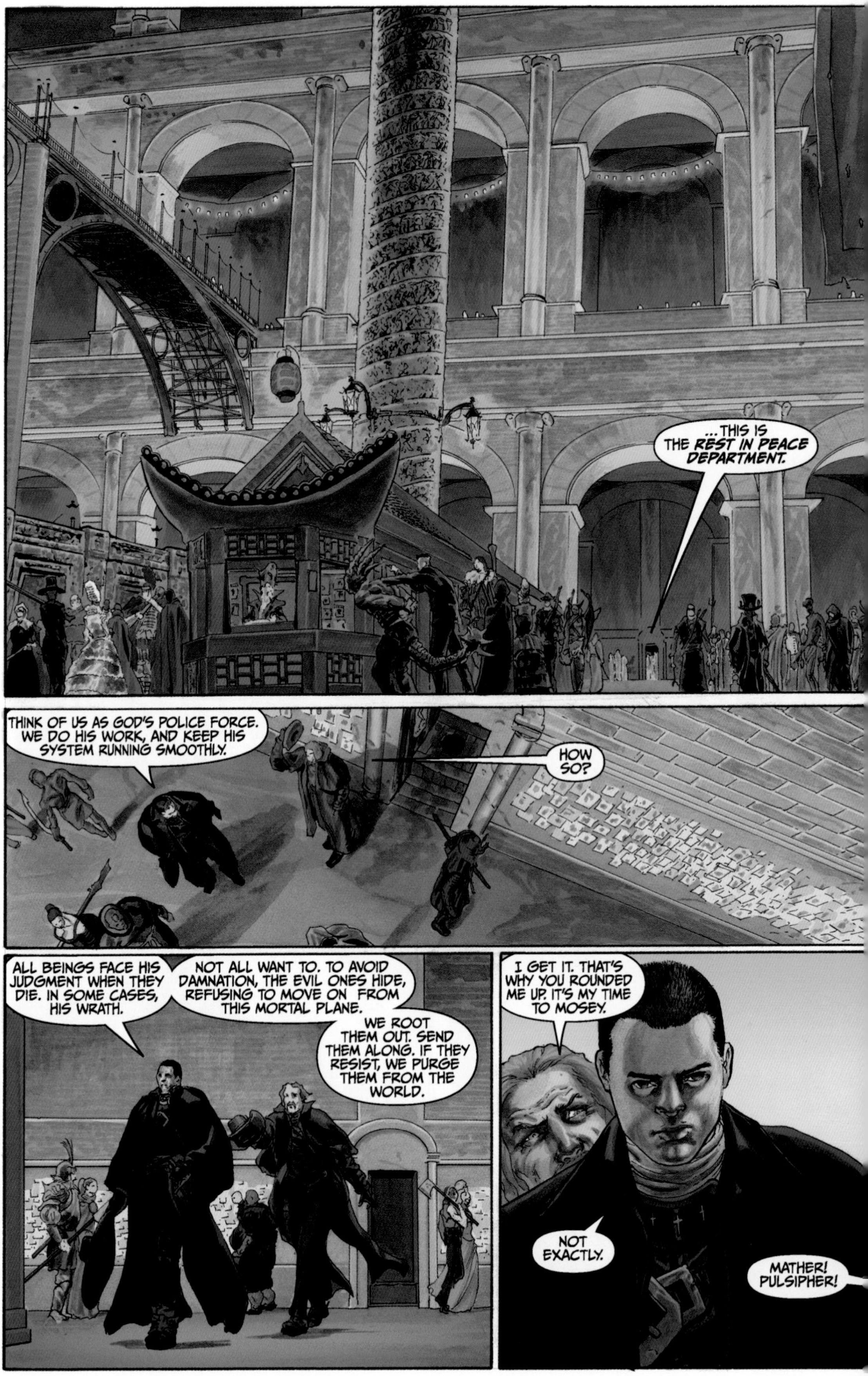
...THIS IS THE REST IN PEACE DEPARTMENT.
THINK OF US AS GOD'S POLICE FORCE. WE DO HIS WORK, AND KEEP HIS SYSTEM RUNNING SMOOTHLY.
HOW SO?
ALL BEINGS FACE HIS JUDGMENT WHEN THEY DIE. IN SOME CASES, HIS WRATH.
NOT ALL WANT TO. TO AVOID DAMNATION, THE EVIL ONES HIDE, REFUSING TO MOVE ON FROM THIS MORTAL PLANE.
WE ROOT THEM OUT. SEND THEM ALONG. IF THEY RESIST, WE PURGE THEM FROM THE WORLD.
I GET IT. THAT'S WHY YOU ROUNDED ME UP. IT'S MY TIME TO MOSEY.
NOT EXACTLY.
MATHER! PULSIPHER!

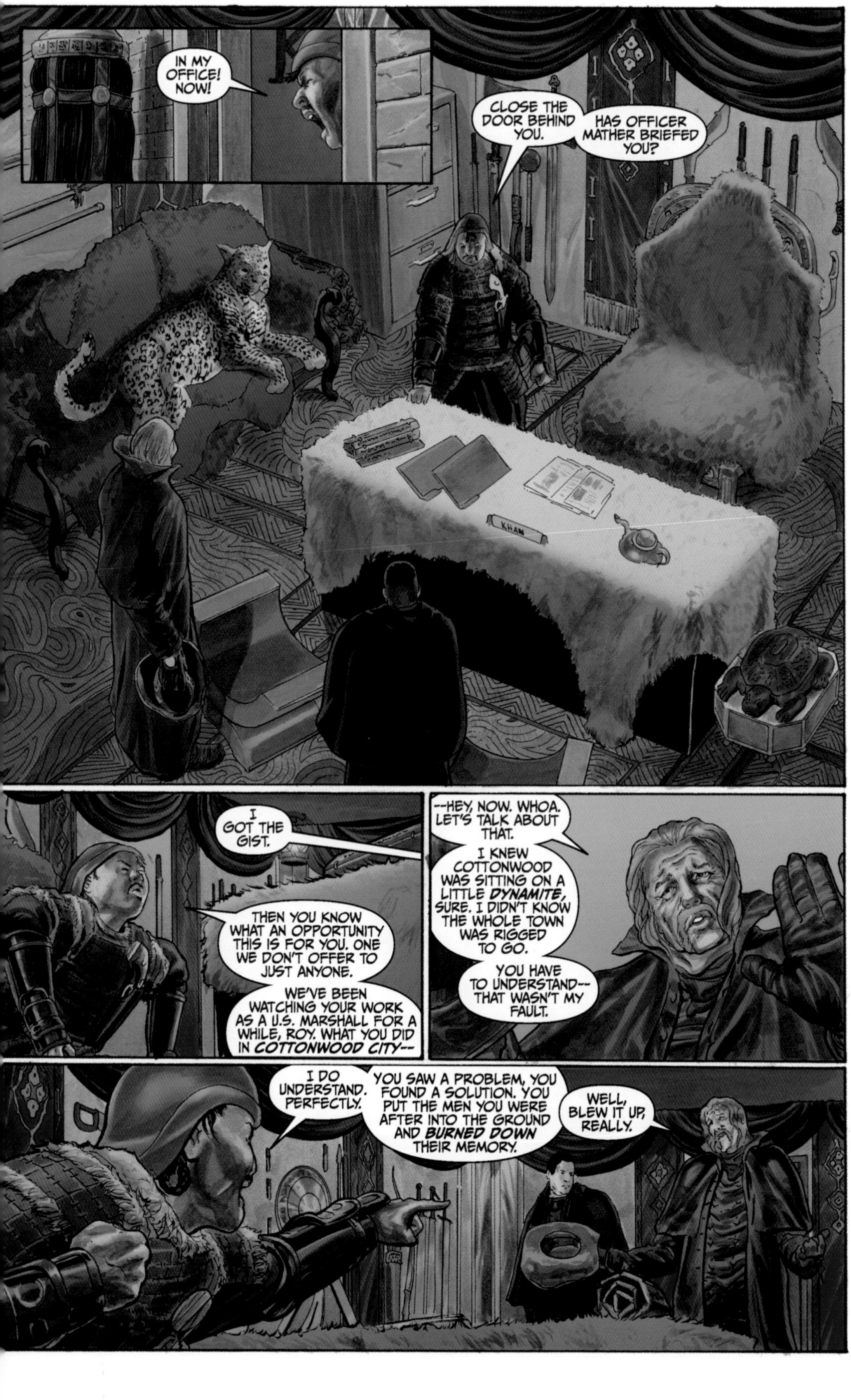
IN MY OFFICE! NOW!
CLOSE THE DOOR BEHIND YOU.
HAS OFFICER MATHER BRIEFED YOU?
KHAM
I GOT THE GIST.
THEN YOU KNOW WHAT AN OPPORTUNITY THIS IS FOR YOU. ONE WE DON'T OFFER TO JUST ANYONE.
WE'VE BEEN WATCHING YOUR WORK AS A U.S. MARSHALL FOR A WHILE, ROY. WHAT YOU DID IN COTTONWOOD CITY--
--HEY, NOW. WHOA. LET'S TALK ABOUT THAT.
I KNEW COTTONWOOD WAS SITTING ON A LITTLE DYNAMITE, SURE. I DIDN'T KNOW THE WHOLE TOWN WAS RIGGED TO GO.
YOU HAVE TO UNDERSTAND-- THAT WASN'T MY FAULT.
I DO UNDERSTAND. PERFECTLY.
YOU SAW A PROBLEM, YOU FOUND A SOLUTION. YOU PUT THE MEN YOU WERE AFTER INTO THE GROUND AND BURNED DOWN THEIR MEMORY.
WELL, BLEW IT UP, REALLY.

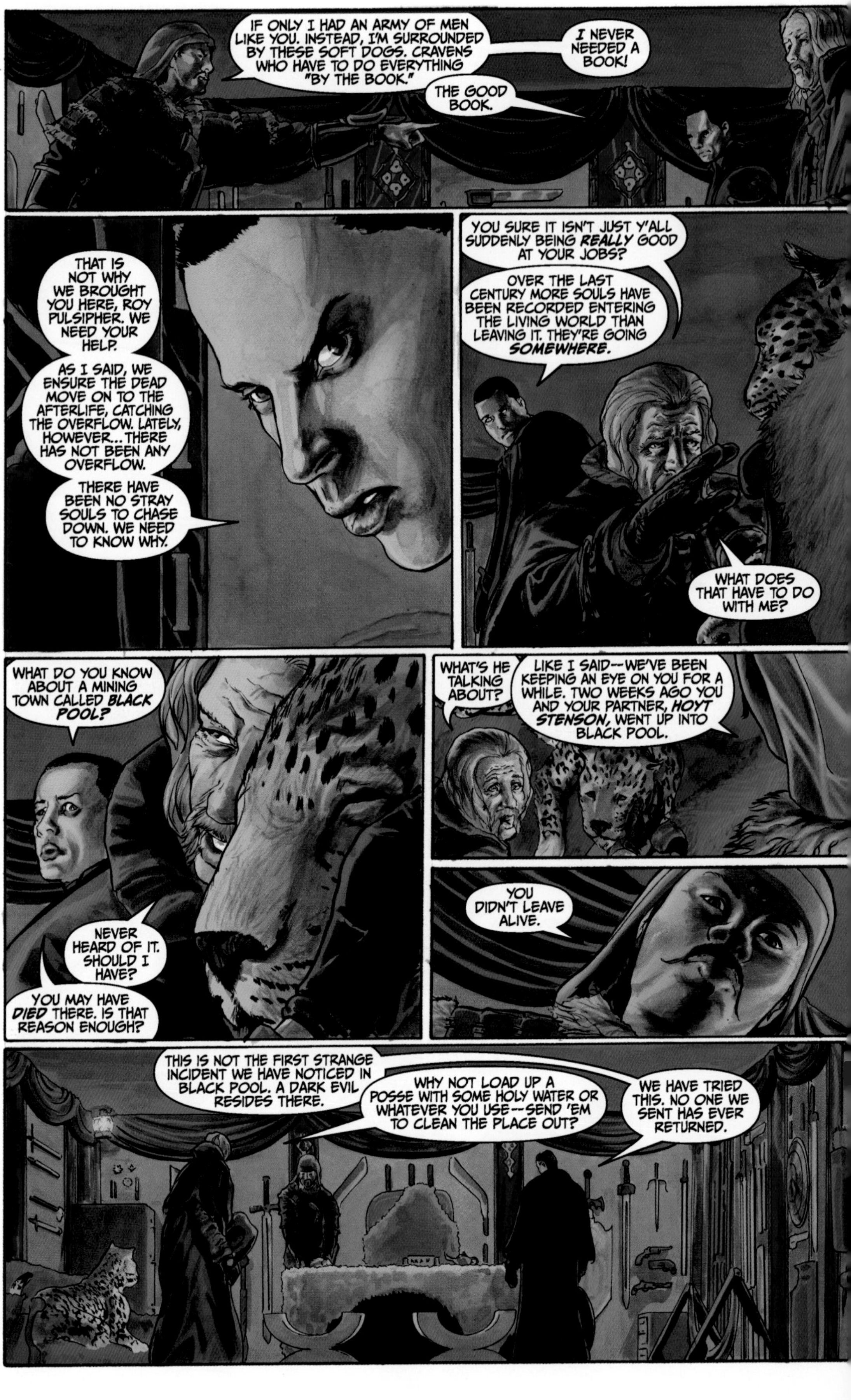

IF ONLY I HAD AN ARMY OF MEN LIKE YOU. INSTEAD, I'M SURROUNDED BY THESE SOFT DOGS. CRAVENS WHO HAVE TO DO EVERYTHING "BY THE BOOK."
THE GOOD BOOK.
I NEVER NEEDED A BOOK!
THAT IS NOT WHY WE BROUGHT YOU HERE, ROY PULSIPHER. WE NEED YOUR HELP.
AS I SAID, WE ENSURE THE DEAD MOVE ON TO THE AFTERLIFE, CATCHING THE OVERFLOW. LATELY, HOWEVER... THERE HAS NOT BEEN ANY OVERFLOW.
THERE HAVE BEEN NO STRAY SOULS TO CHASE DOWN. WE NEED TO KNOW WHY.
YOU SURE IT ISN'T JUST Y'ALL SUDDENLY BEING REALLY GOOD AT YOUR JOBS?
OVER THE LAST CENTURY MORE SOULS HAVE BEEN RECORDED ENTERING THE LIVING WORLD THAN LEAVING IT. THEY'RE GOING SOMEWHERE.
WHAT DOES THAT HAVE TO DO WITH ME?
WHAT DO YOU KNOW ABOUT A MINING TOWN CALLED BLACK POOL?
NEVER HEARD OF IT. SHOULD I HAVE?
YOU MAY HAVE DIED THERE. IS THAT REASON ENOUGH?
WHAT'S HE TALKING ABOUT?
LIKE I SAID--WE'VE BEEN KEEPING AN EYE ON YOU FOR A WHILE. TWO WEEKS AGO YOU AND YOUR PARTNER, HOYT STENSON, WENT UP INTO BLACK POOL.
YOU DIDN'T LEAVE ALIVE.
THIS IS NOT THE FIRST STRANGE INCIDENT WE HAVE NOTICED IN BLACK POOL. A DARK EVIL RESIDES THERE.
WHY NOT LOAD UP A POSSE WITH SOME HOLY WATER OR WHATEVER YOU USE--SEND 'EM TO CLEAN THE PLACE OUT?
WE HAVE TRIED THIS. NO ONE WE SENT HAS EVER RETURNED.

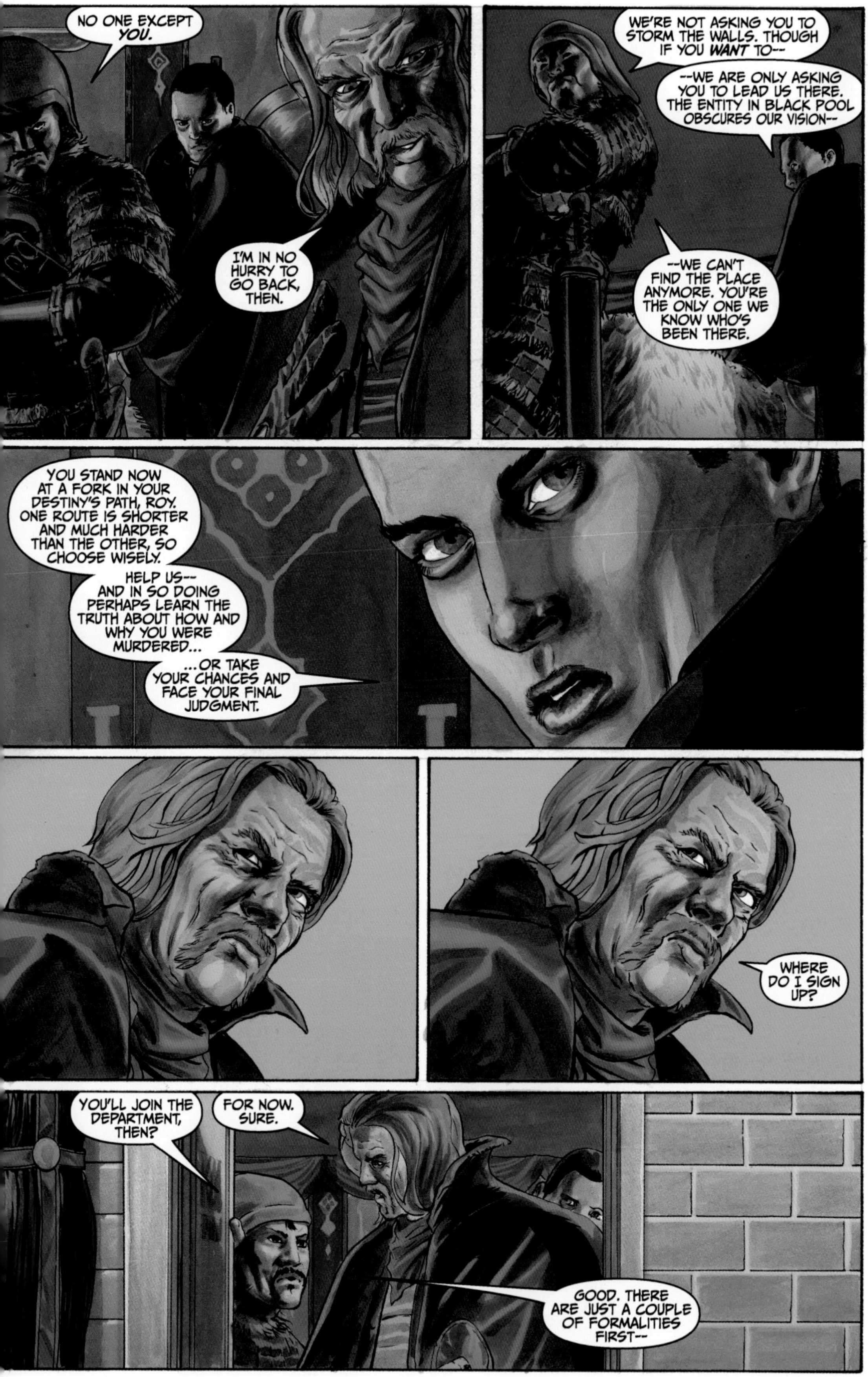
NO ONE EXCEPT YOU.
I'M IN NO HURRY TO GO BACK, THEN.
WE'RE NOT ASKING YOU TO STORM THE WALLS. THOUGH IF YOU WANT TO--
--WE ARE ONLY ASKING YOU TO LEAD US THERE. THE ENTITY IN BLACK POOL OBSCURES OUR VISION--
--WE CAN'T FIND THE PLACE ANYMORE. YOU'RE THE ONLY ONE WE KNOW WHO'S BEEN THERE.
YOU STAND NOW AT A FORK IN YOUR DESTINY'S PATH, ROY. ONE ROUTE IS SHORTER AND MUCH HARDER THAN THE OTHER, SO CHOOSE WISELY.
HELP US-- AND IN SO DOING PERHAPS LEARN THE TRUTH ABOUT HOW AND WHY YOU WERE MURDERED...
...OR TAKE YOUR CHANCES AND FACE YOUR FINAL JUDGMENT.
WHERE DO I SIGN UP?
YOU'LL JOIN THE DEPARTMENT, THEN?
FOR NOW. SURE.
GOOD. THERE ARE JUST A COUPLE OF FORMALITIES FIRST--

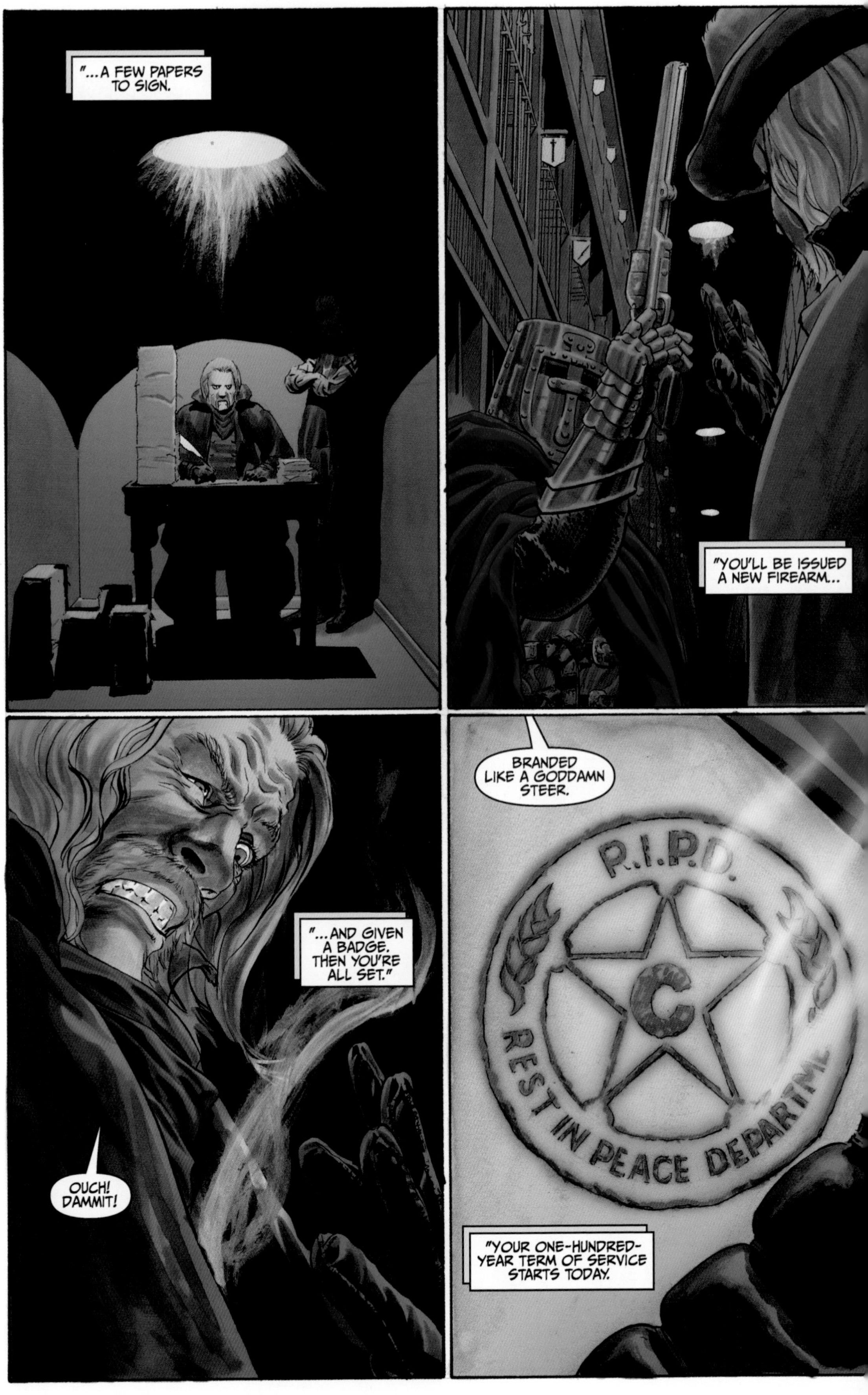
"...A FEW PAPERS TO SIGN.
"YOU'LL BE ISSUED A NEW FIREARM...
"...AND GIVEN A BADGE. THEN YOU'RE ALL SET."
OUCH! DAMMIT!
BRANDED LIKE A GODDAMN STEER.
P.I.P.D.
C
REST IN PEACE DEPARTME
"YOUR ONE-HUNDRED-YEAR TERM OF SERVICE STARTS TODAY.

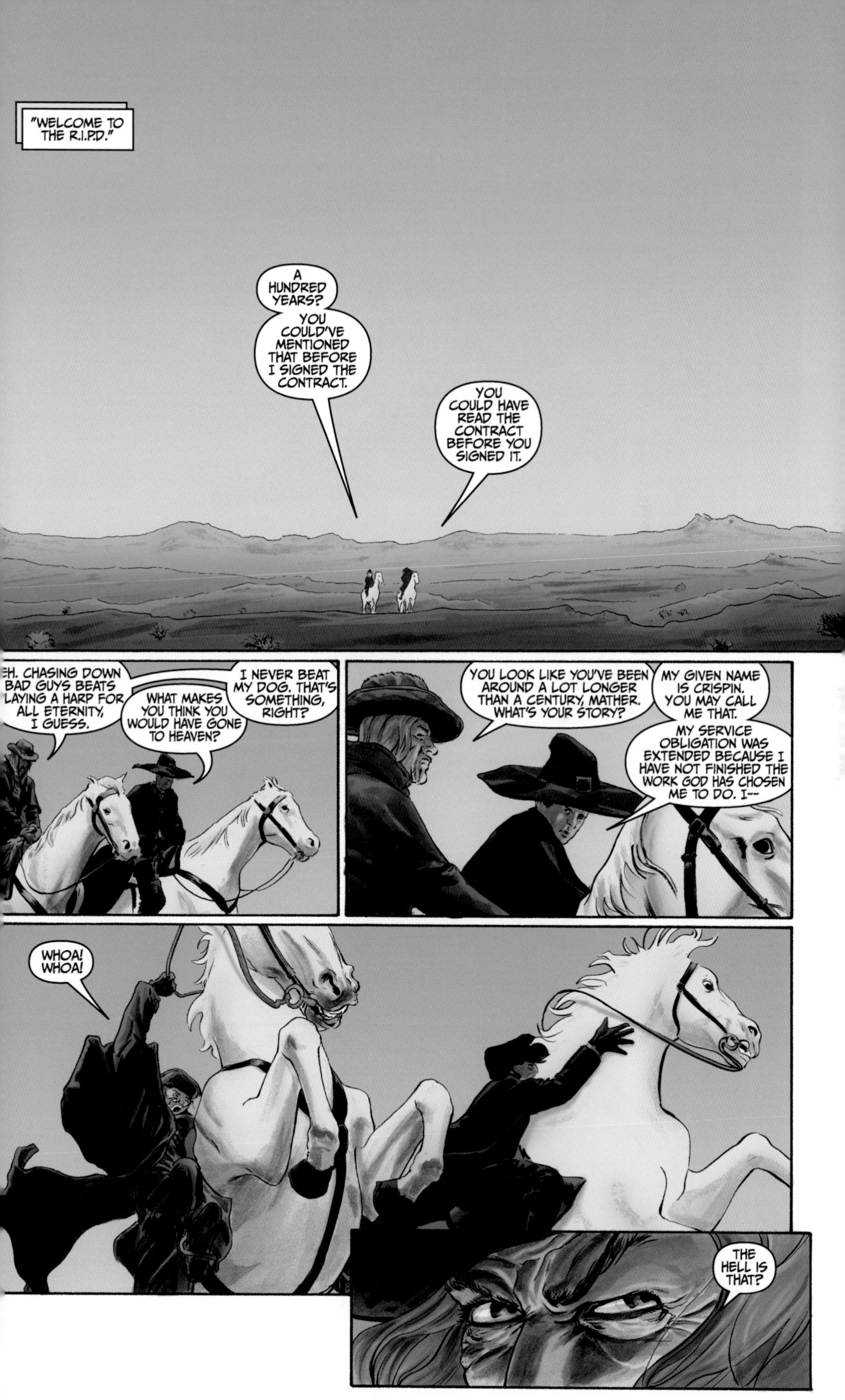
"WELCOME TO THE R.I.P.D."
A HUNDRED YEARS?
YOU COULD'VE MENTIONED THAT BEFORE I SIGNED THE CONTRACT.
YOU COULD HAVE READ THE CONTRACT BEFORE YOU SIGNED IT.
EH. CHASING DOWN BAD GUYS BEATS PLAYING A HARP FOR ALL ETERNITY, I GUESS.
WHAT MAKES YOU THINK YOU WOULD HAVE GONE TO HEAVEN?
I NEVER BEAT MY DOG. THAT'S SOMETHING, RIGHT?
YOU LOOK LIKE YOU'VE BEEN AROUND A LOT LONGER THAN A CENTURY, MATHER. WHAT'S YOUR STORY?
MY GIVEN NAME IS CRISPIN. YOU MAY CALL ME THAT.
MY SERVICE OBLIGATION WAS EXTENDED BECAUSE I HAVE NOT FINISHED THE WORK GOD HAS CHOSEN ME TO DO. I--
WHOA! WHOA!
THE HELL IS THAT?

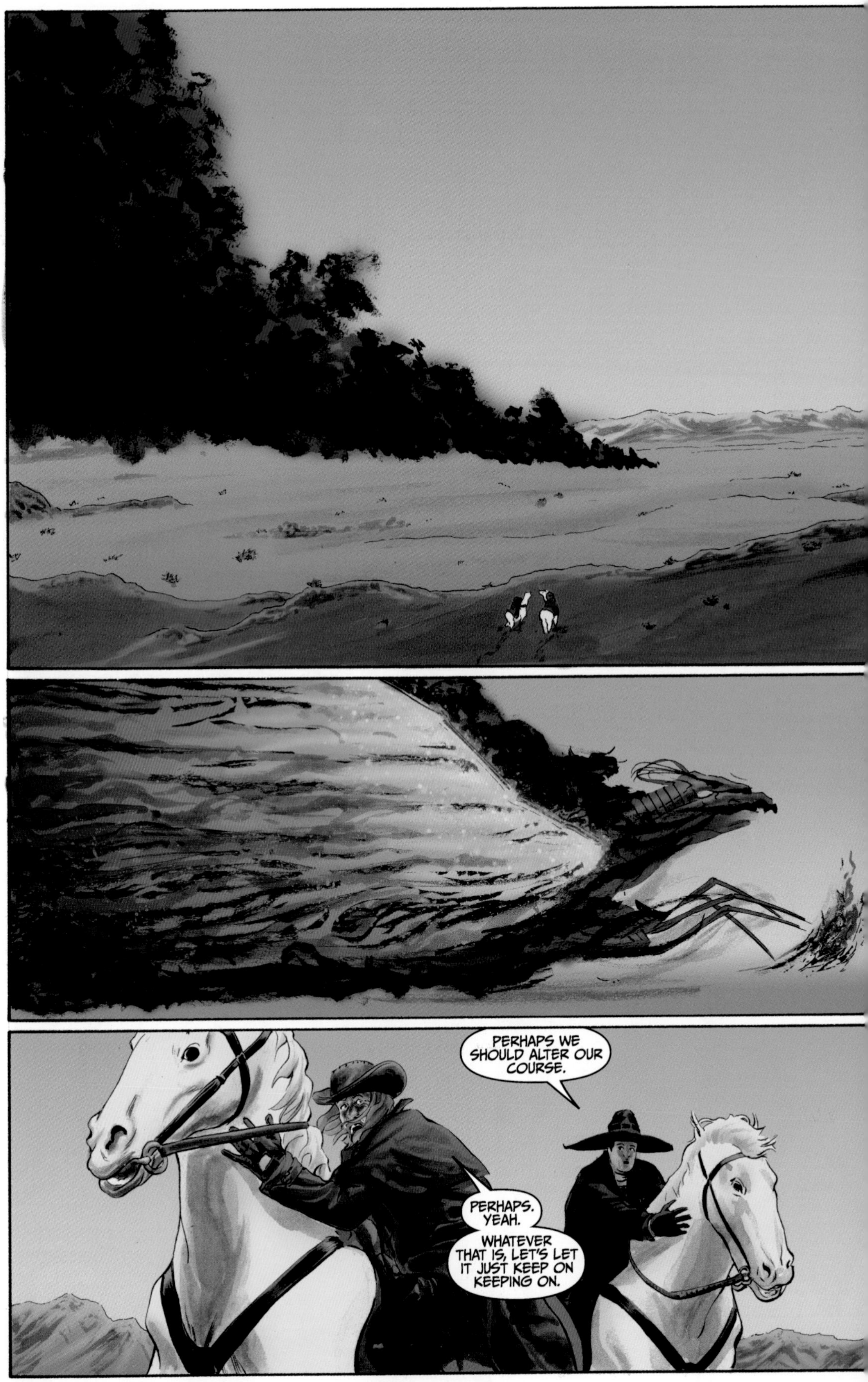
PERHAPS WE SHOULD ALTER OUR COURSE.
PERHAPS. YEAH.
WHATEVER THAT IS, LET'S LET IT JUST KEEP ON KEEPING ON.

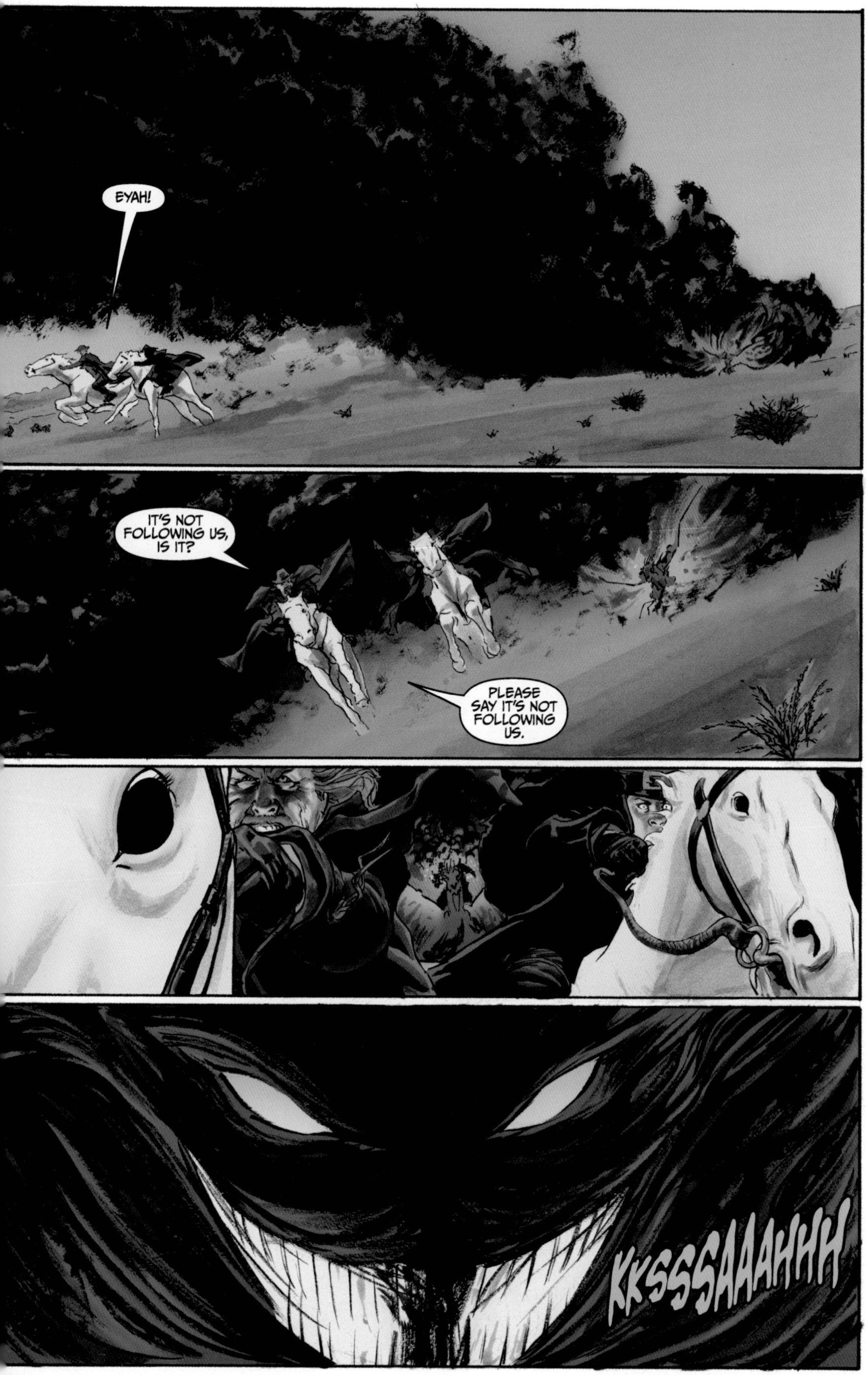

EYAH!
IT'S NOT FOLLOWING US, IS IT?
PLEASE SAY IT'S NOT FOLLOWING US.
KKSSSAAAHHH

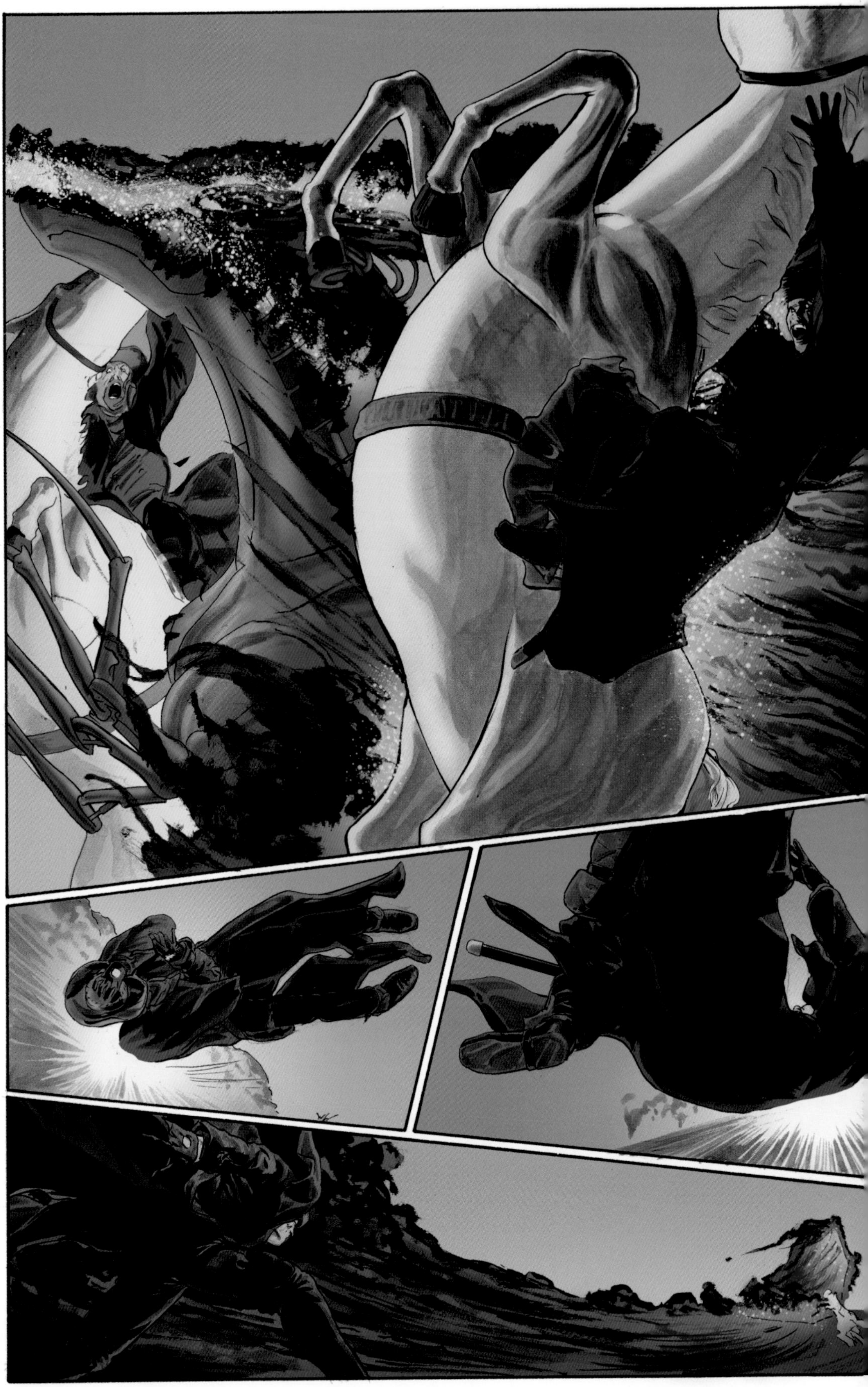

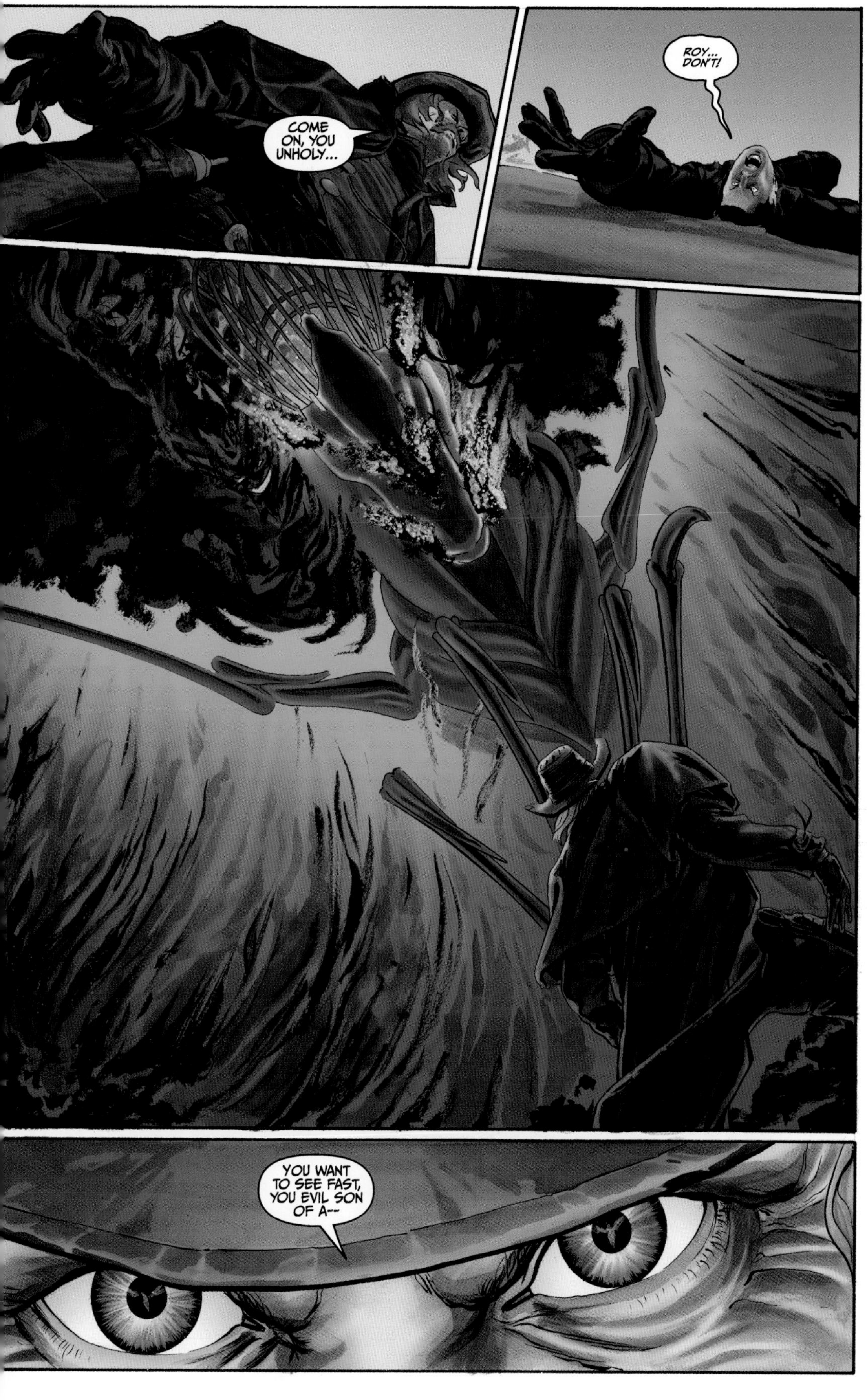
COME ON, YOU UNHOLY...
ROY... DON'T!
YOU WANT TO SEE FAST, YOU EVIL SON OF A--

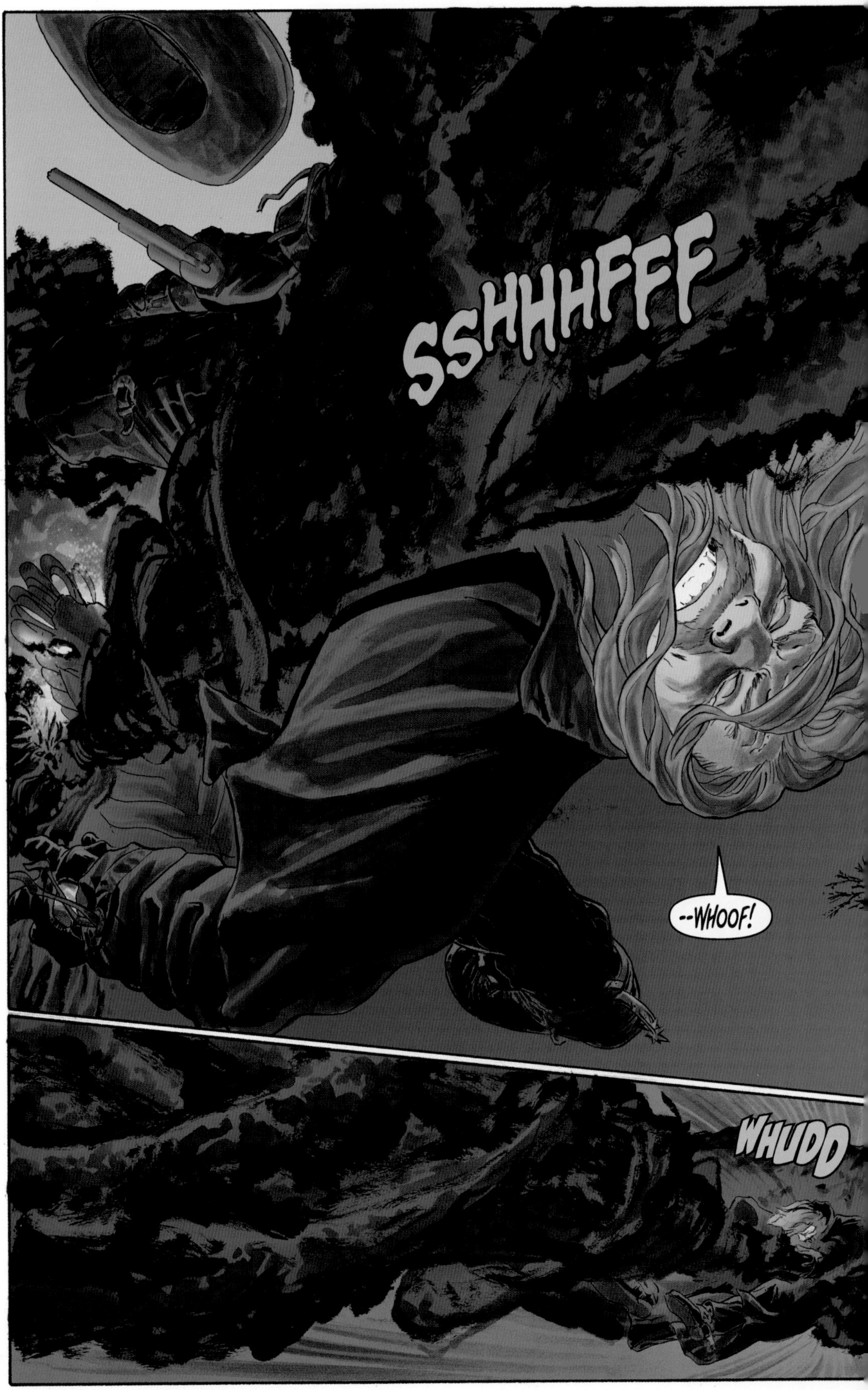
SSHHHFFF
--WHOOF!
WHUDD

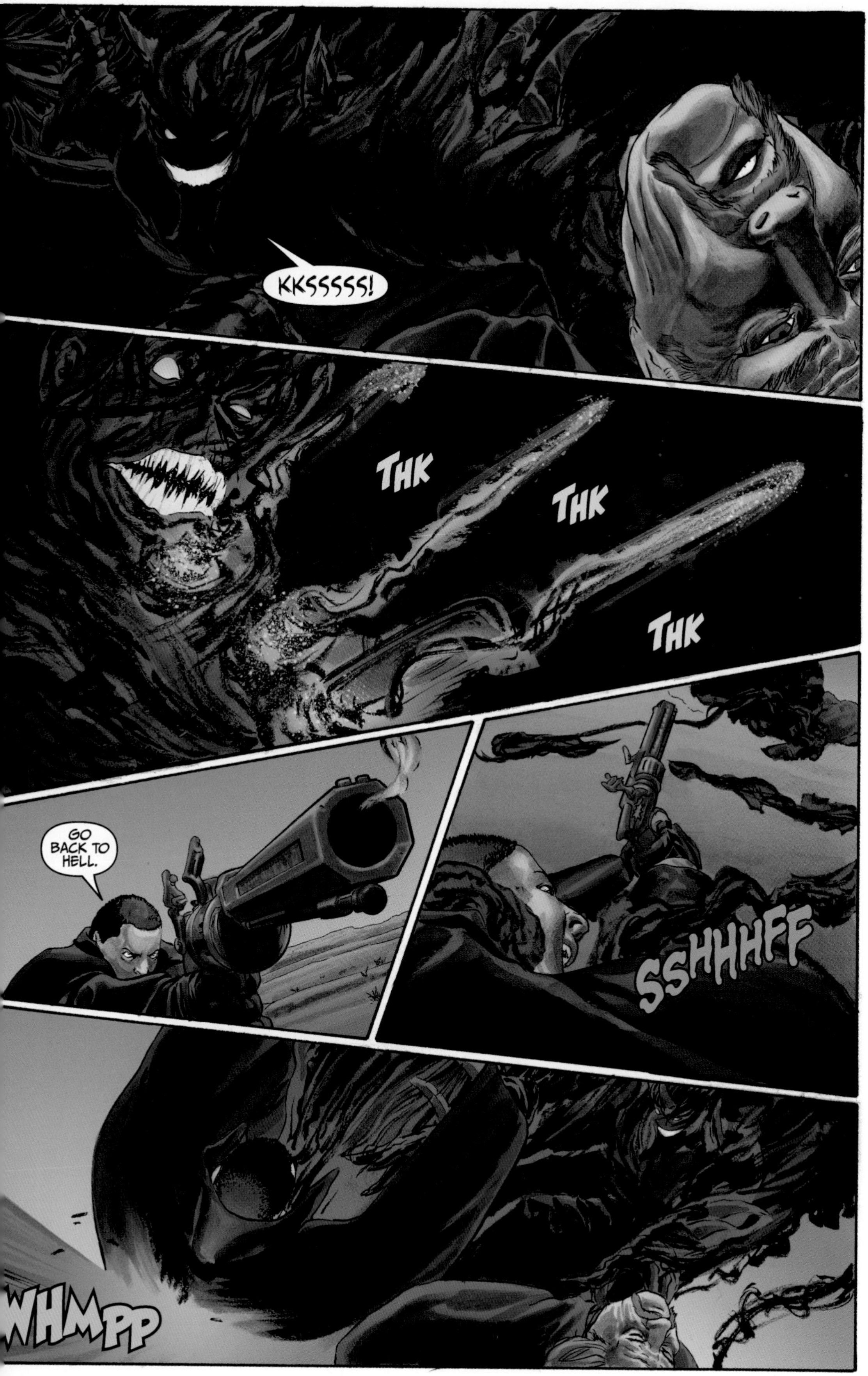
KKSSSSS!
THK
THK
THK
GO BACK TO HELL.
SSHHHFF
WHMPP

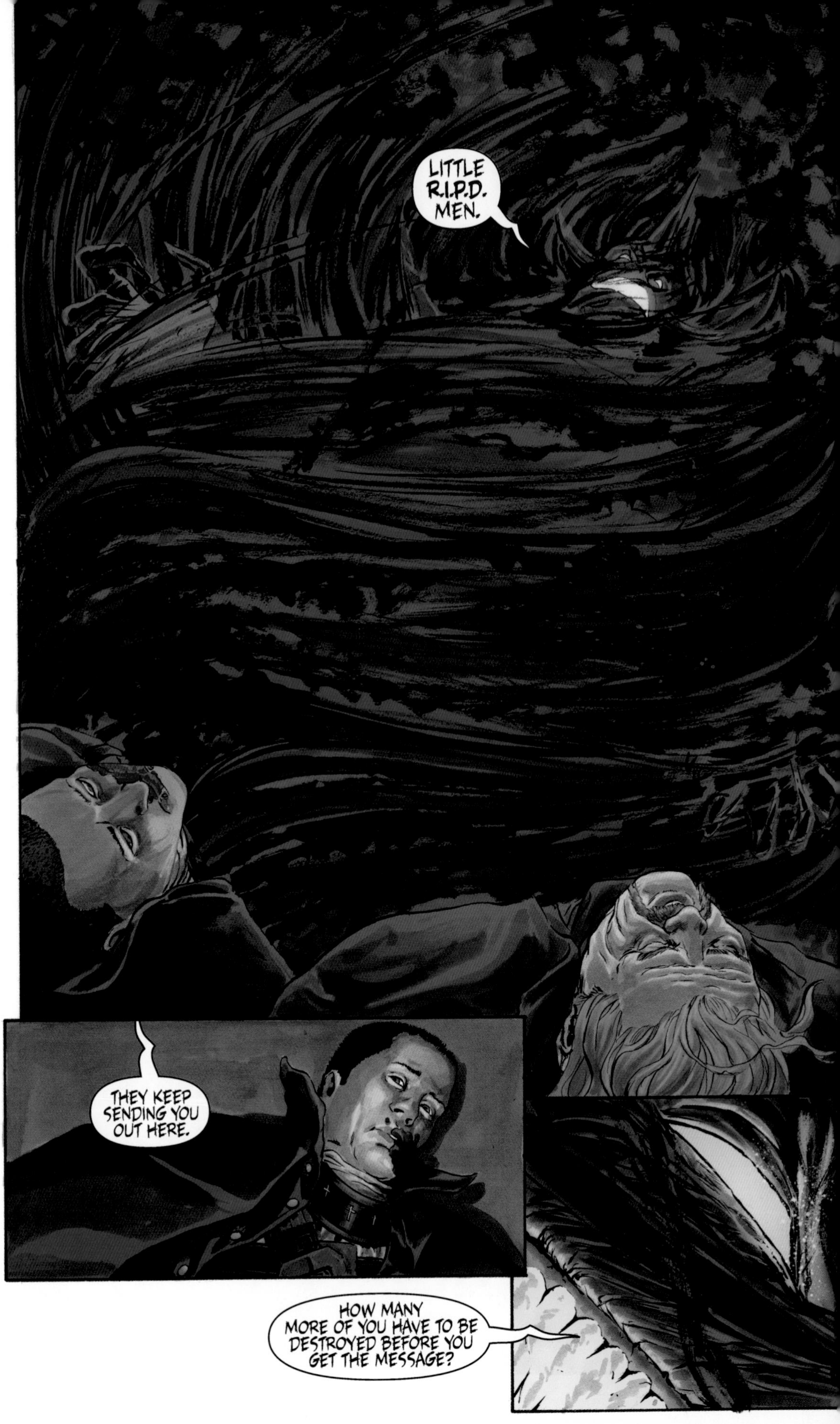
LITTLE R.I.P.D. MEN.
THEY KEEP SENDING YOU OUT HERE.
HOW MANY MORE OF YOU HAVE TO BE DESTROYED BEFORE YOU GET THE MESSAGE?

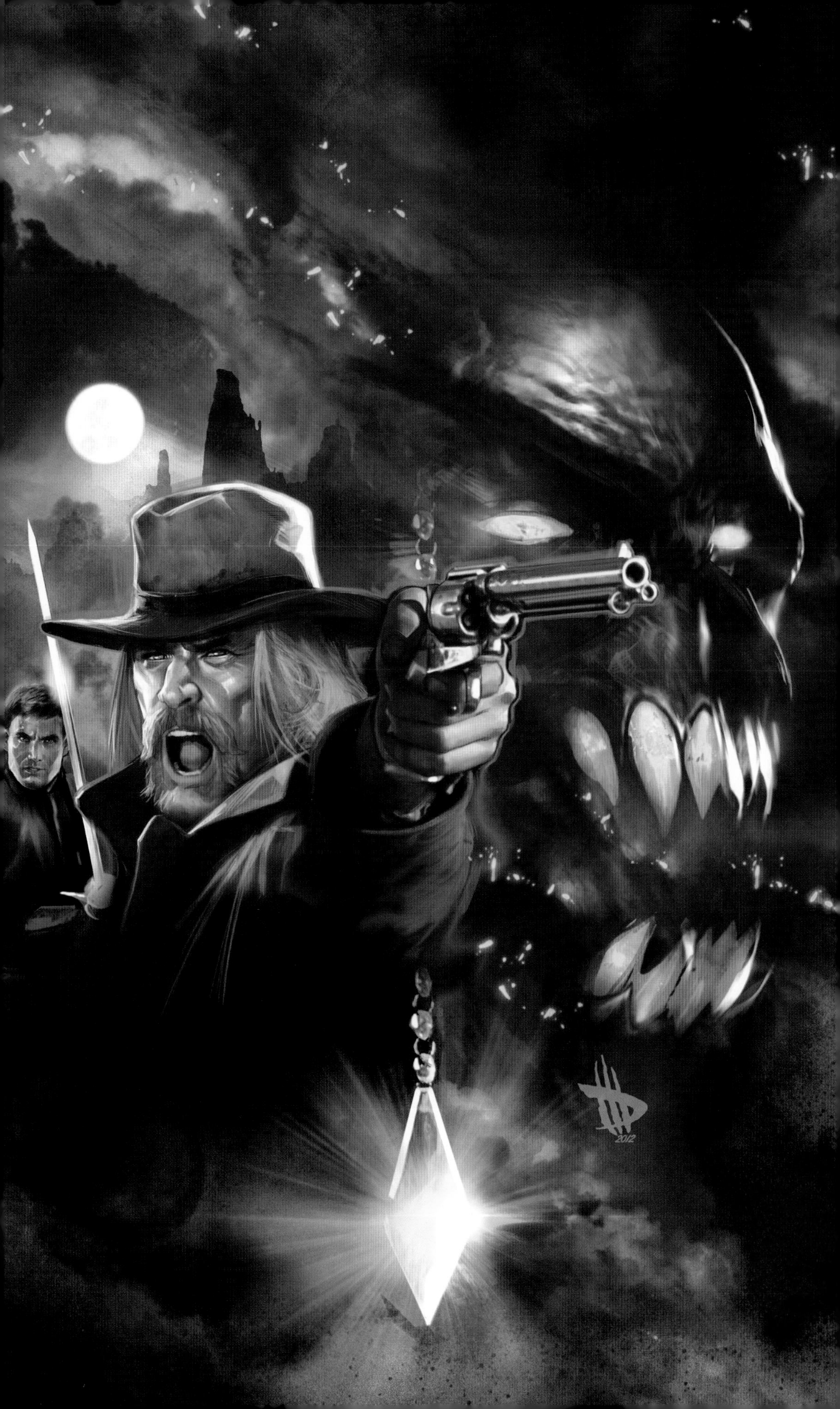

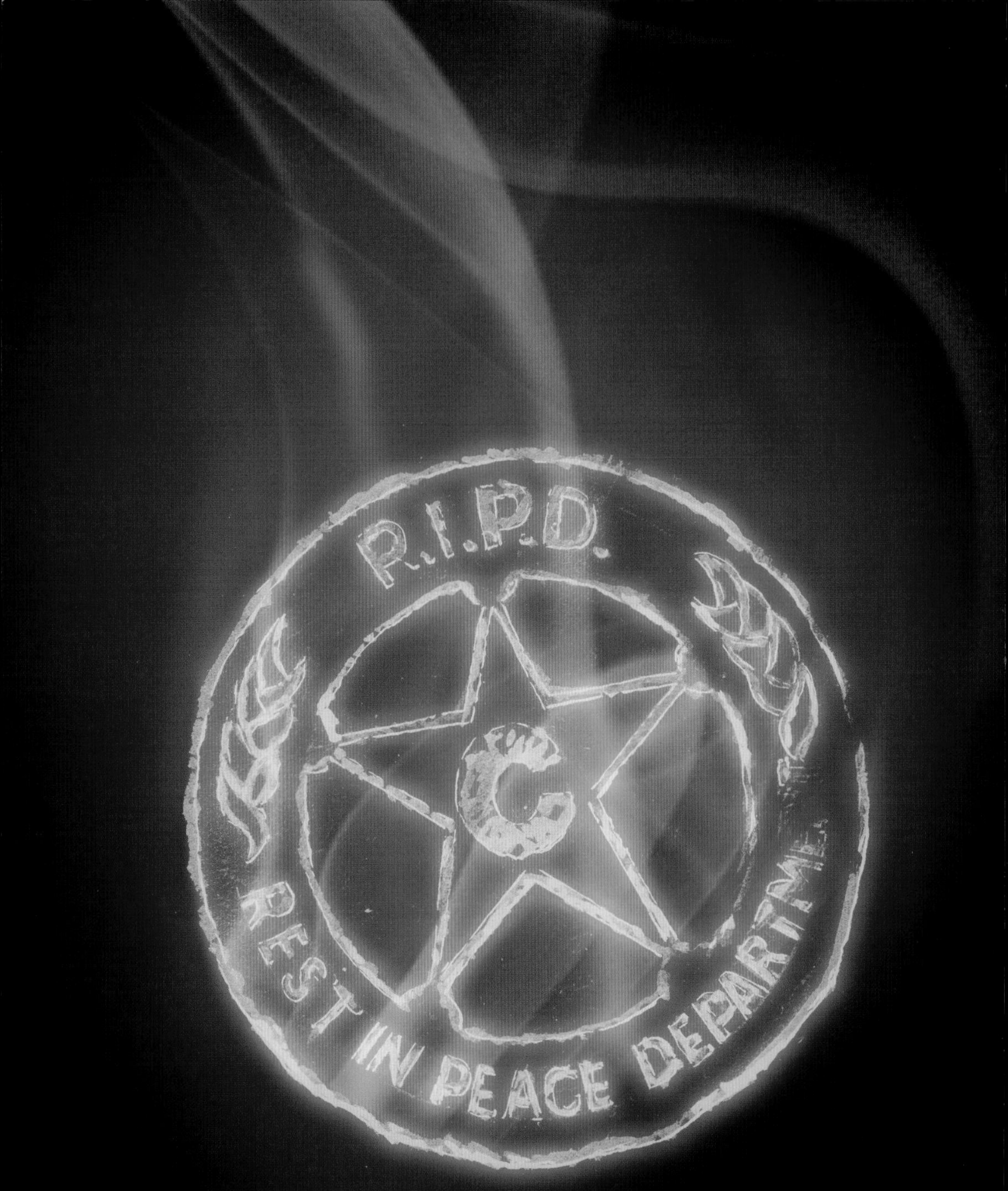
R.I.P.D.
C
REST IN PEACE DEPARTM

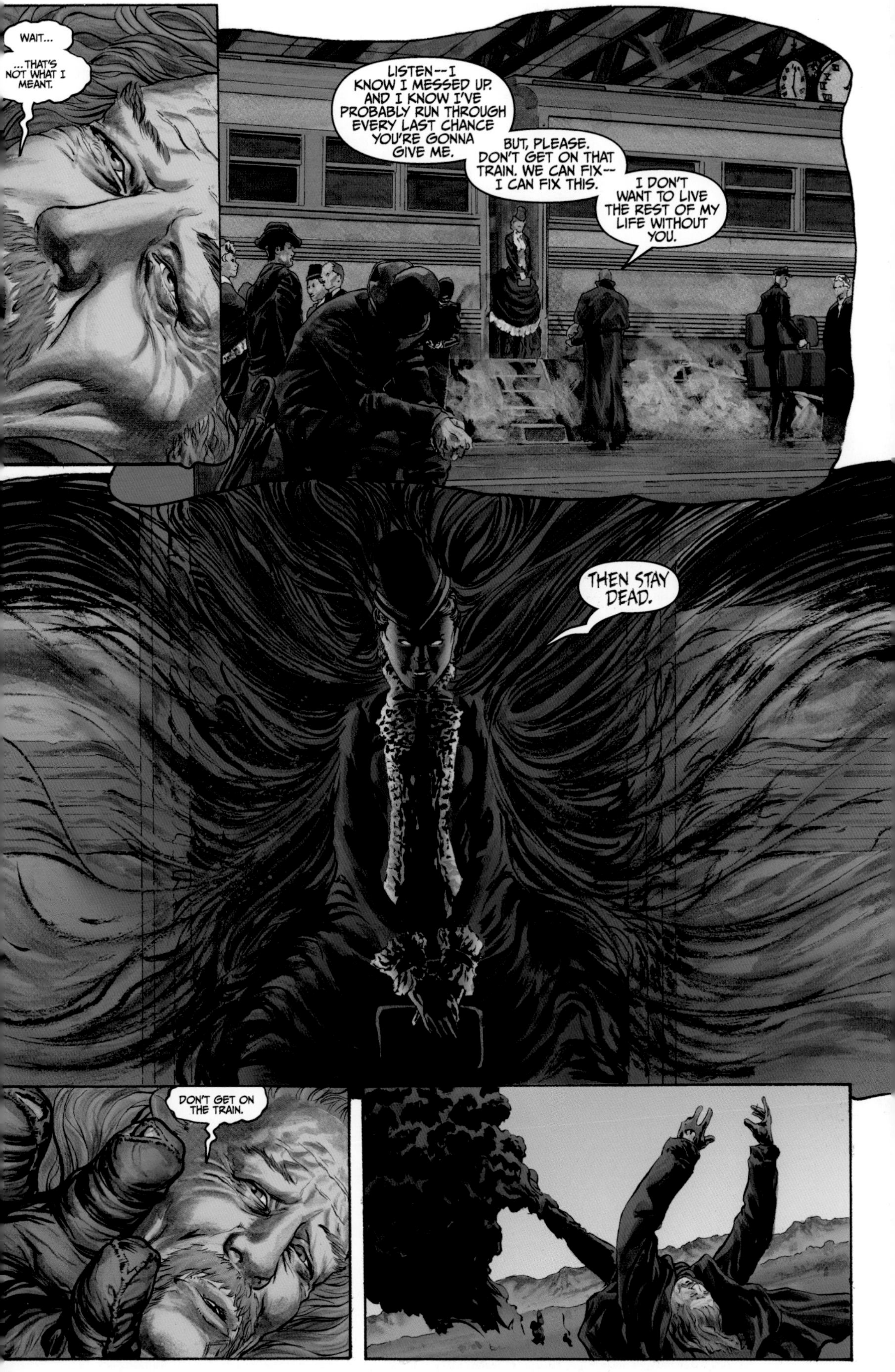
WAIT...
...THAT'S NOT WHAT I MEANT.
LISTEN--I KNOW I MESSED UP. AND I KNOW I'VE PROBABLY RUN THROUGH EVERY LAST CHANCE YOU'RE GONNA GIVE ME.
BUT, PLEASE. DON'T GET ON THAT TRAIN. WE CAN FIX-- I CAN FIX THIS.
I DON'T WANT TO LIVE THE REST OF MY LIFE WITHOUT YOU.
THEN STAY DEAD.
DON'T GET ON THE TRAIN.

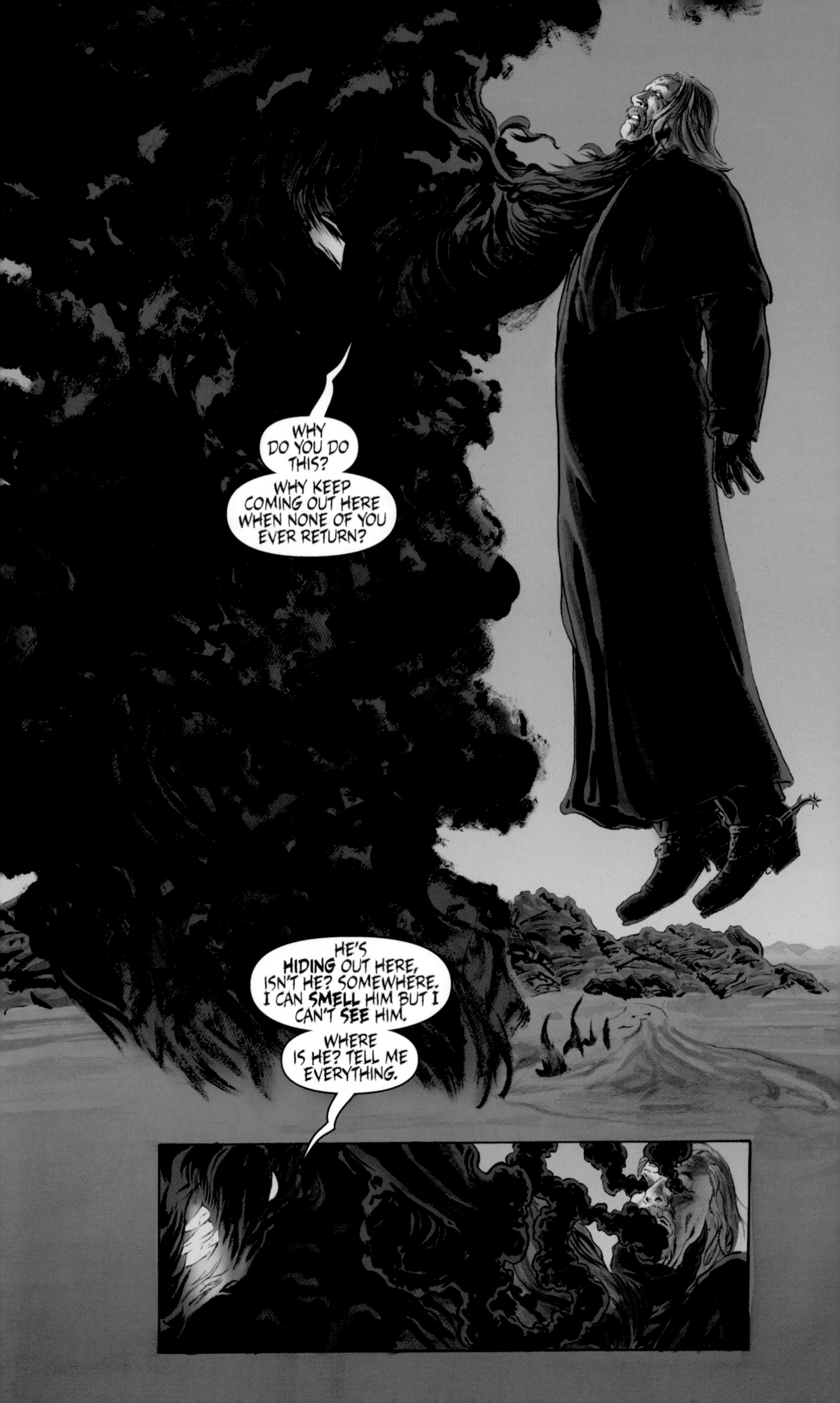
WHY DO YOU DO THIS?
WHY KEEP COMING OUT HERE WHEN NONE OF YOU EVER RETURN?
HE'S **HIDING** OUT HERE, ISN'T HE? SOMEWHERE. I CAN **SMELL** HIM BUT I CAN'T **SEE** HIM.
WHERE IS HE? TELL ME EVERYTHING.

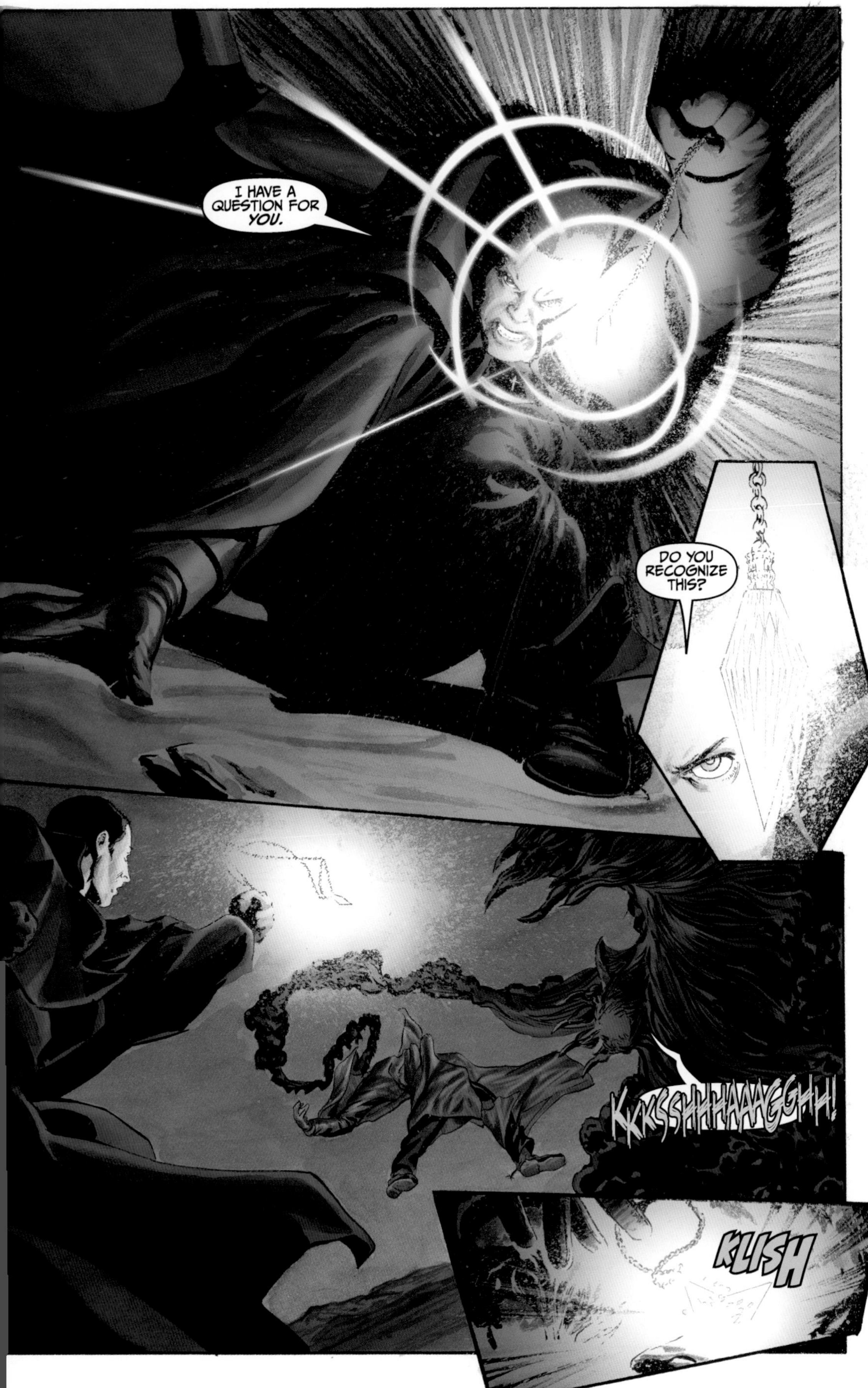

I HAVE A QUESTION FOR YOU.
DO YOU RECOGNIZE THIS?
KKKSSHHHAAAGGHH!
KLISH

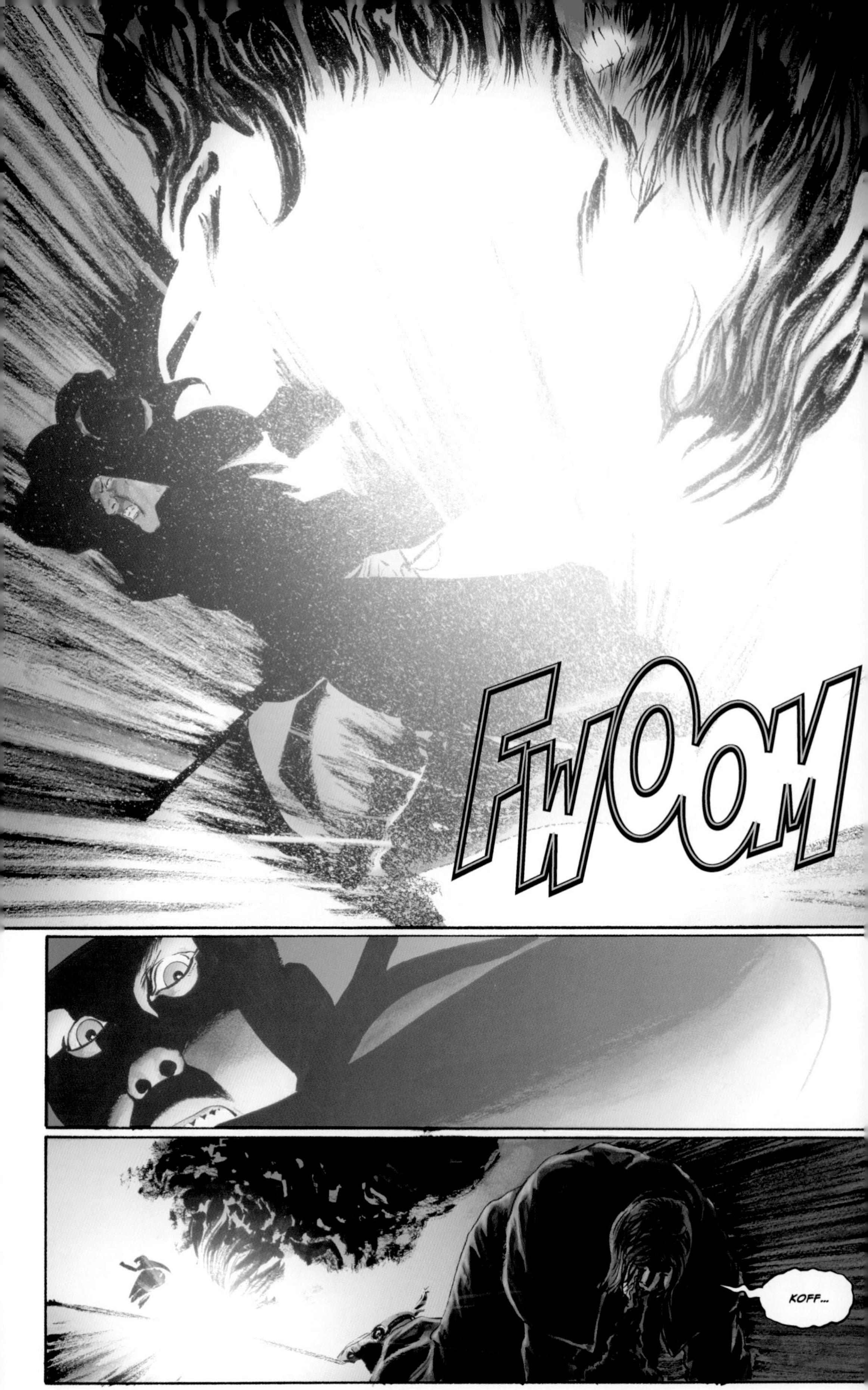
FWOOM
KOFF...

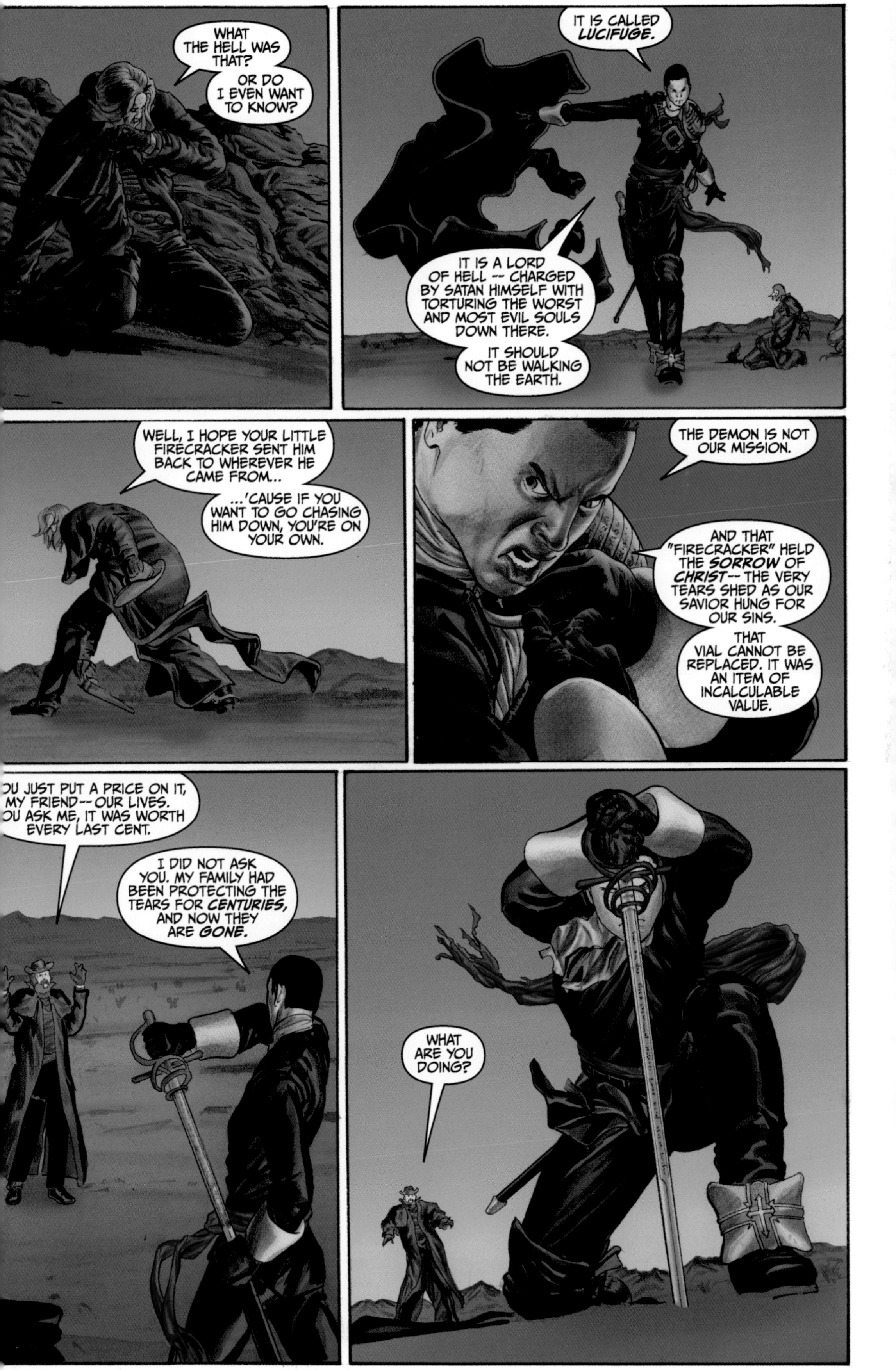
WHAT THE HELL WAS THAT?
OR DO I EVEN WANT TO KNOW?
IT IS CALLED *LUCIFUGE.*
IT IS A LORD OF HELL -- CHARGED BY SATAN HIMSELF WITH TORTURING THE WORST AND MOST EVIL SOULS DOWN THERE.
IT SHOULD NOT BE WALKING THE EARTH.
WELL, I HOPE YOUR LITTLE FIRECRACKER SENT HIM BACK TO WHEREVER HE CAME FROM...
...'CAUSE IF YOU WANT TO GO CHASING HIM DOWN, YOU'RE ON YOUR OWN.
THE DEMON IS NOT OUR MISSION.
AND THAT "FIRECRACKER" HELD THE *SORROW* OF *CHRIST*-- THE VERY TEARS SHED AS OUR SAVIOR HUNG FOR OUR SINS.
THAT VIAL CANNOT BE REPLACED. IT WAS AN ITEM OF INCALCULABLE VALUE.
OU JUST PUT A PRICE ON IT, MY FRIEND-- OUR LIVES. OU ASK ME, IT WAS WORTH EVERY LAST CENT.
I DID NOT ASK YOU. MY FAMILY HAD BEEN PROTECTING THE TEARS FOR *CENTURIES,* AND NOW THEY ARE *GONE.*
WHAT ARE YOU DOING?

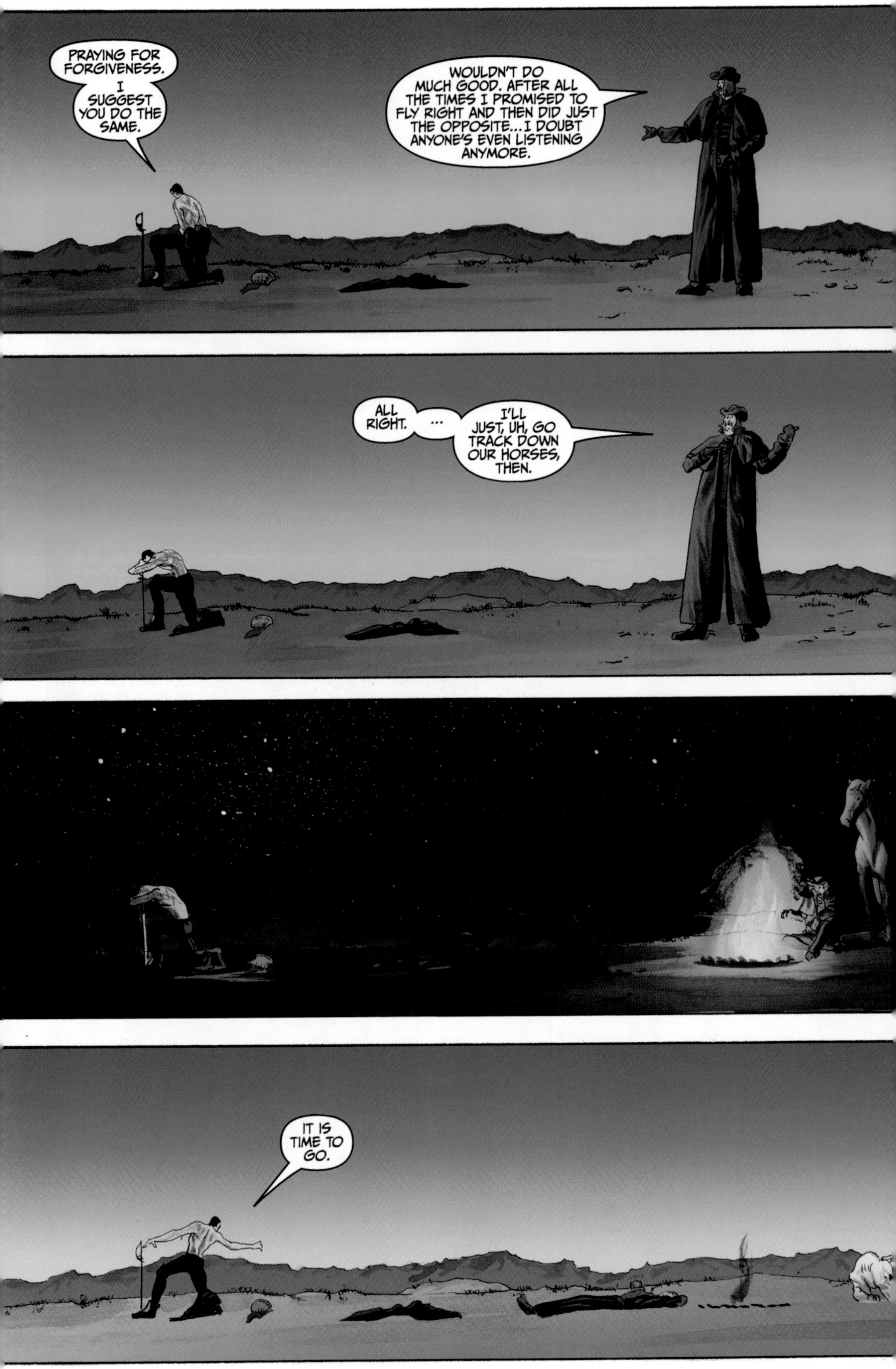
PRAYING FOR FORGIVENESS.
I SUGGEST YOU DO THE SAME.
WOULDN'T DO MUCH GOOD. AFTER ALL THE TIMES I PROMISED TO FLY RIGHT AND THEN DID JUST THE OPPOSITE...I DOUBT ANYONE'S EVEN LISTENING ANYMORE.
ALL RIGHT.
...
I'LL JUST, UH, GO TRACK DOWN OUR HORSES, THEN.
IT IS TIME TO GO.

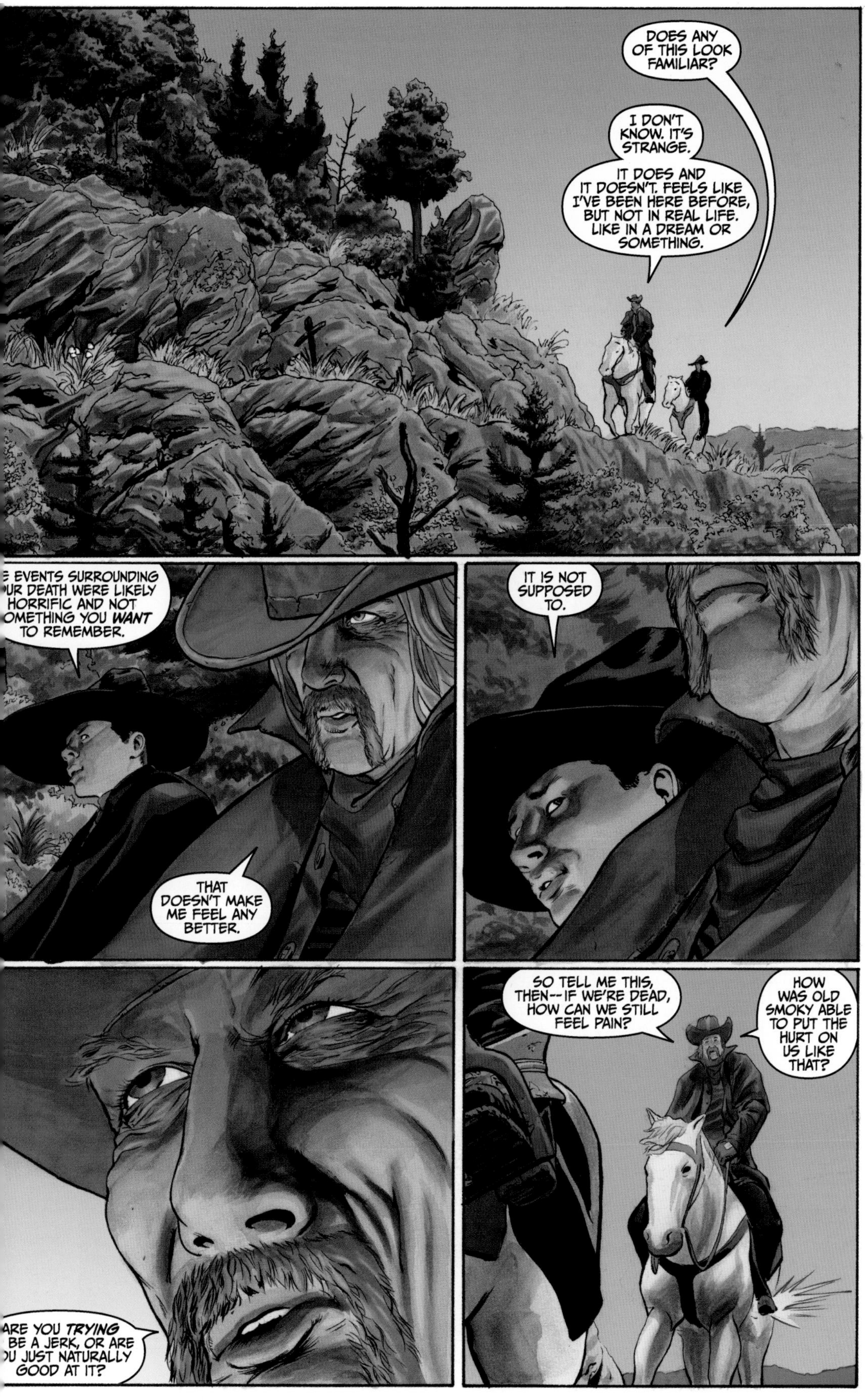
DOES ANY OF THIS LOOK FAMILIAR?
I DON'T KNOW. IT'S STRANGE.
IT DOES AND IT DOESN'T. FEELS LIKE I'VE BEEN HERE BEFORE, BUT NOT IN REAL LIFE. LIKE IN A DREAM OR SOMETHING.
E EVENTS SURROUNDING UR DEATH WERE LIKELY HORRIFIC AND NOT OMETHING YOU *WANT* TO REMEMBER.
THAT DOESN'T MAKE ME FEEL ANY BETTER.
IT IS NOT SUPPOSED TO.
ARE YOU *TRYING* BE A JERK, OR ARE U JUST NATURALLY GOOD AT IT?
SO TELL ME THIS, THEN--IF WE'RE DEAD, HOW CAN WE STILL FEEL PAIN?
HOW WAS OLD SMOKY ABLE TO PUT THE HURT ON US LIKE THAT?

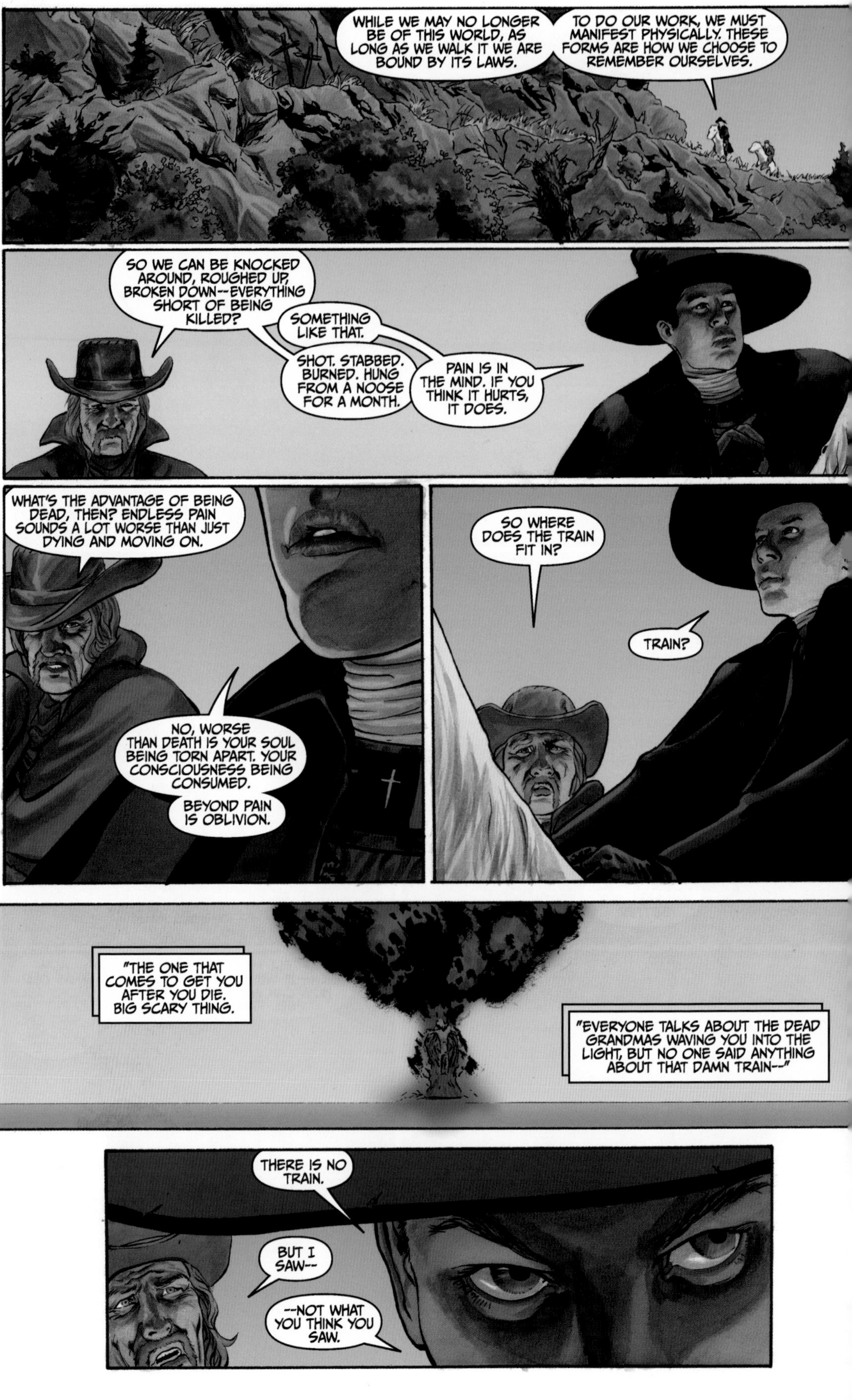
WHILE WE MAY NO LONGER BE OF THIS WORLD, AS LONG AS WE WALK IT WE ARE BOUND BY ITS LAWS.
TO DO OUR WORK, WE MUST MANIFEST PHYSICALLY. THESE FORMS ARE HOW WE CHOOSE TO REMEMBER OURSELVES.
SO WE CAN BE KNOCKED AROUND, ROUGHED UP, BROKEN DOWN--EVERYTHING SHORT OF BEING KILLED?
SOMETHING LIKE THAT.
SHOT. STABBED. BURNED. HUNG FROM A NOOSE FOR A MONTH.
PAIN IS IN THE MIND. IF YOU THINK IT HURTS, IT DOES.
WHAT'S THE ADVANTAGE OF BEING DEAD, THEN? ENDLESS PAIN SOUNDS A LOT WORSE THAN JUST DYING AND MOVING ON.
NO, WORSE THAN DEATH IS YOUR SOUL BEING TORN APART. YOUR CONSCIOUSNESS BEING CONSUMED.
BEYOND PAIN IS OBLIVION.
SO WHERE DOES THE TRAIN FIT IN?
TRAIN?
"THE ONE THAT COMES TO GET YOU AFTER YOU DIE. BIG SCARY THING.
"EVERYONE TALKS ABOUT THE DEAD GRANDMAS WAVING YOU INTO THE LIGHT, BUT NO ONE SAID ANYTHING ABOUT THAT DAMN TRAIN--"
THERE IS NO TRAIN.
BUT I SAW--
--NOT WHAT YOU THINK YOU SAW.

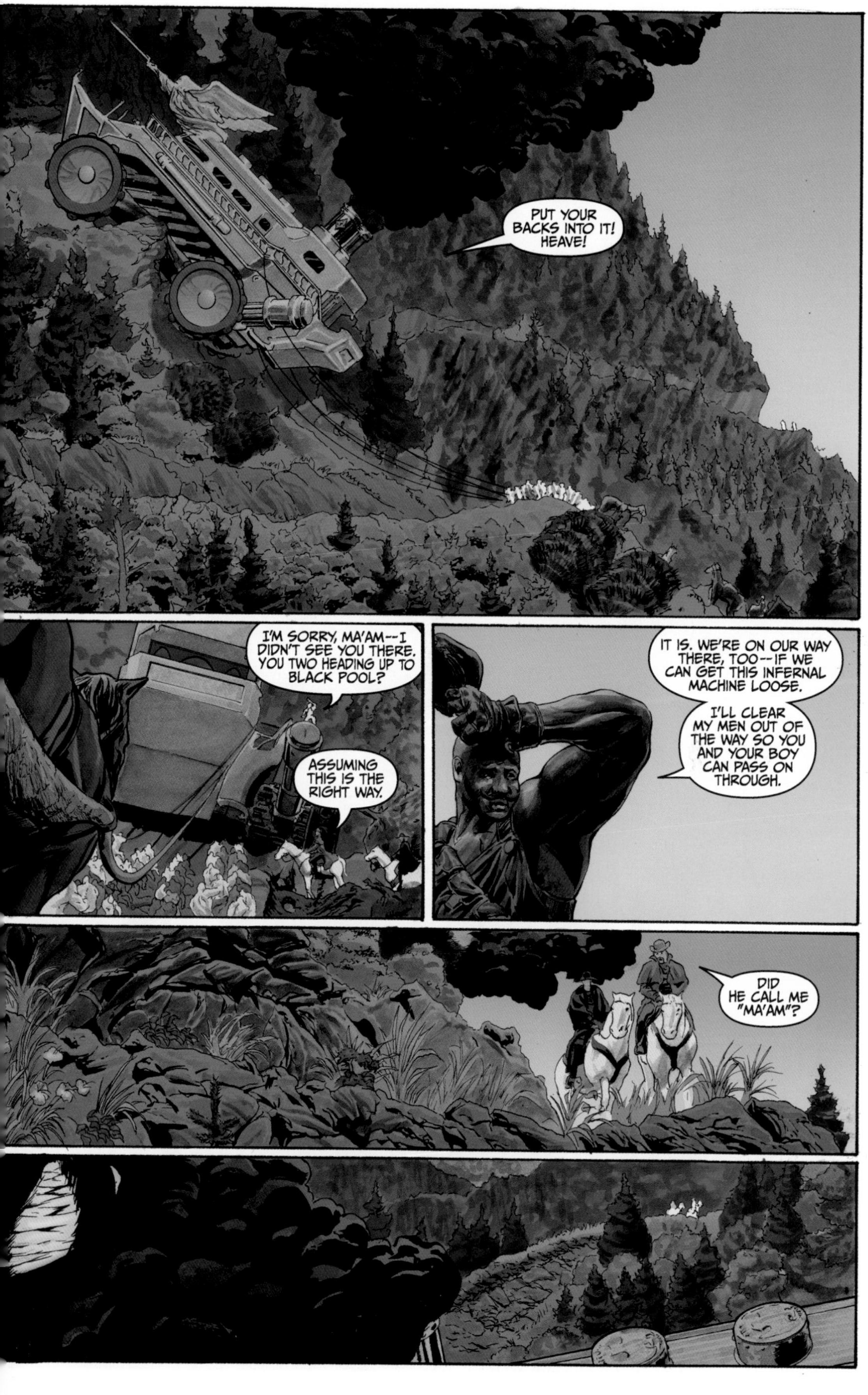

PUT YOUR BACKS INTO IT! HEAVE!
I'M SORRY, MA'AM--I DIDN'T SEE YOU THERE. YOU TWO HEADING UP TO BLACK POOL?
ASSUMING THIS IS THE RIGHT WAY.
IT IS. WE'RE ON OUR WAY THERE, TOO--IF WE CAN GET THIS INFERNAL MACHINE LOOSE.
I'LL CLEAR MY MEN OUT OF THE WAY SO YOU AND YOUR BOY CAN PASS ON THROUGH.
DID HE CALL ME "MA'AM"?

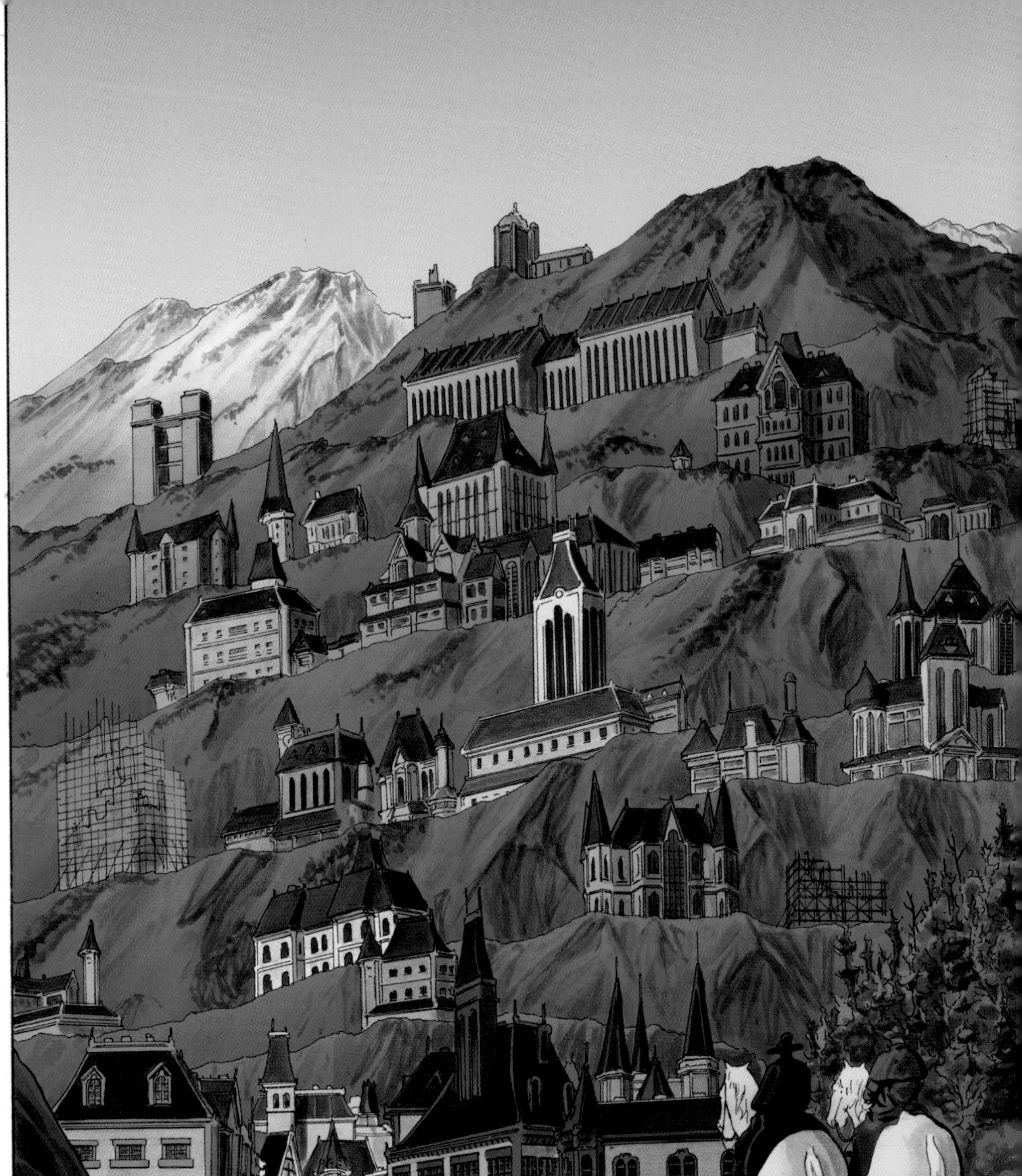

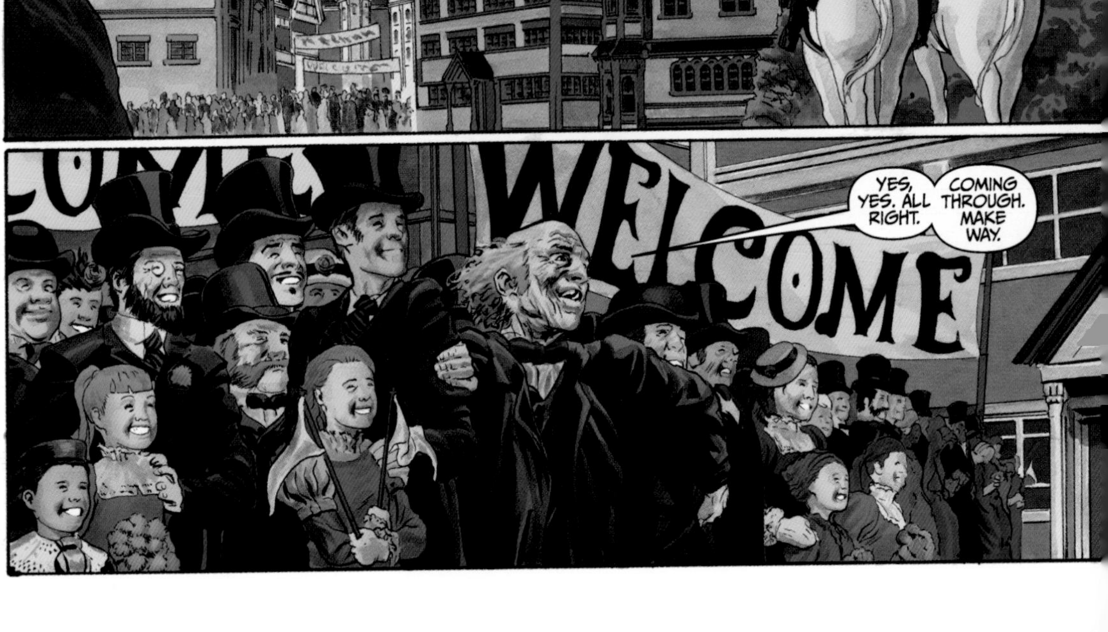
WELCOME
YES, YES. ALL RIGHT.
COMING THROUGH. MAKE WAY.

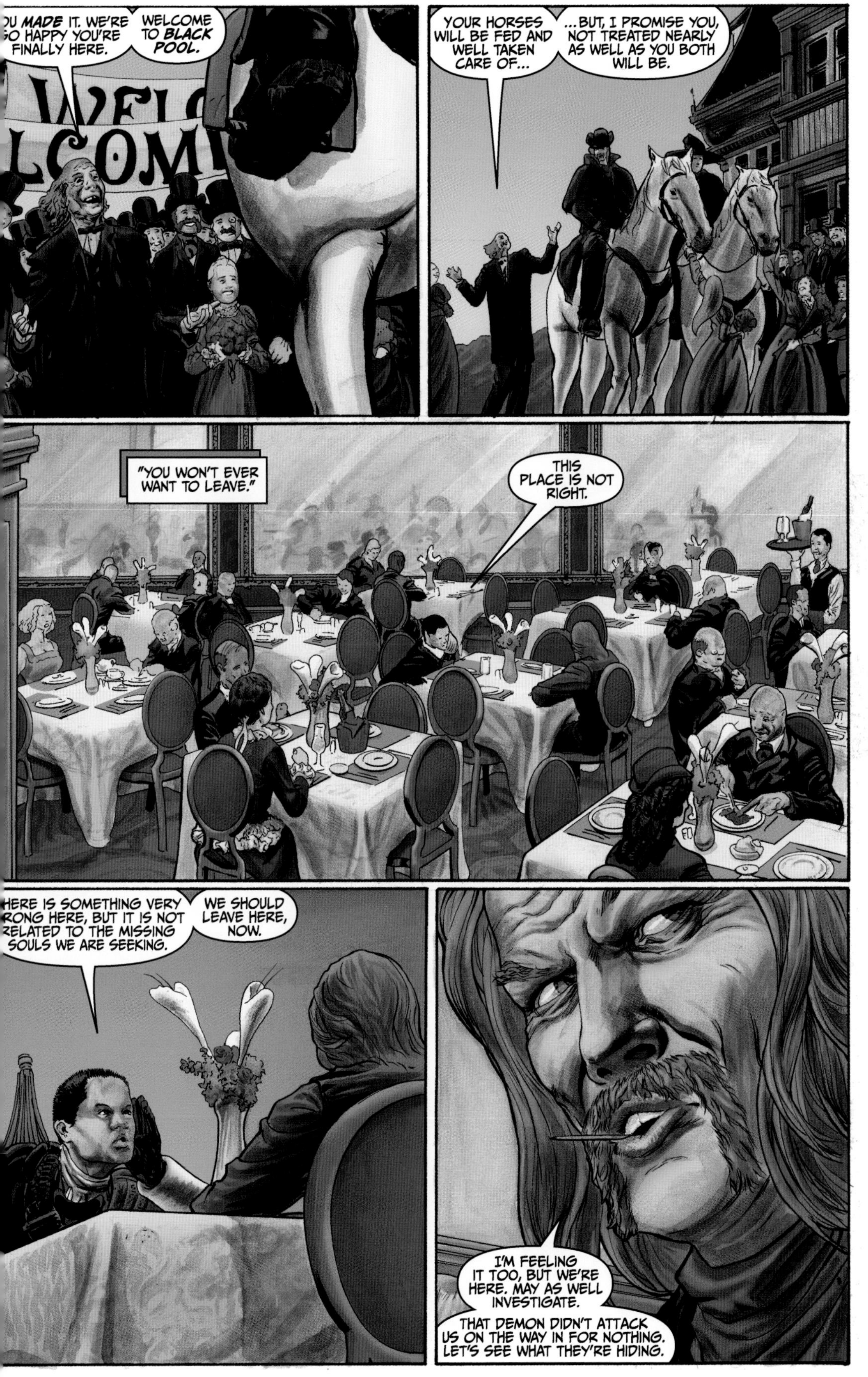

OU MADE IT. WE'RE SO HAPPY YOU'RE FINALLY HERE.
WELCOME TO BLACK POOL.
YOUR HORSES WILL BE FED AND WELL TAKEN CARE OF...
...BUT, I PROMISE YOU, NOT TREATED NEARLY AS WELL AS YOU BOTH WILL BE.
"YOU WON'T EVER WANT TO LEAVE."
THIS PLACE IS NOT RIGHT.
HERE IS SOMETHING VERY RONG HERE, BUT IT IS NOT RELATED TO THE MISSING SOULS WE ARE SEEKING.
WE SHOULD LEAVE HERE, NOW.
I'M FEELING IT TOO, BUT WE'RE HERE. MAY AS WELL INVESTIGATE.
THAT DEMON DIDN'T ATTACK US ON THE WAY IN FOR NOTHING. LET'S SEE WHAT THEY'RE HIDING.

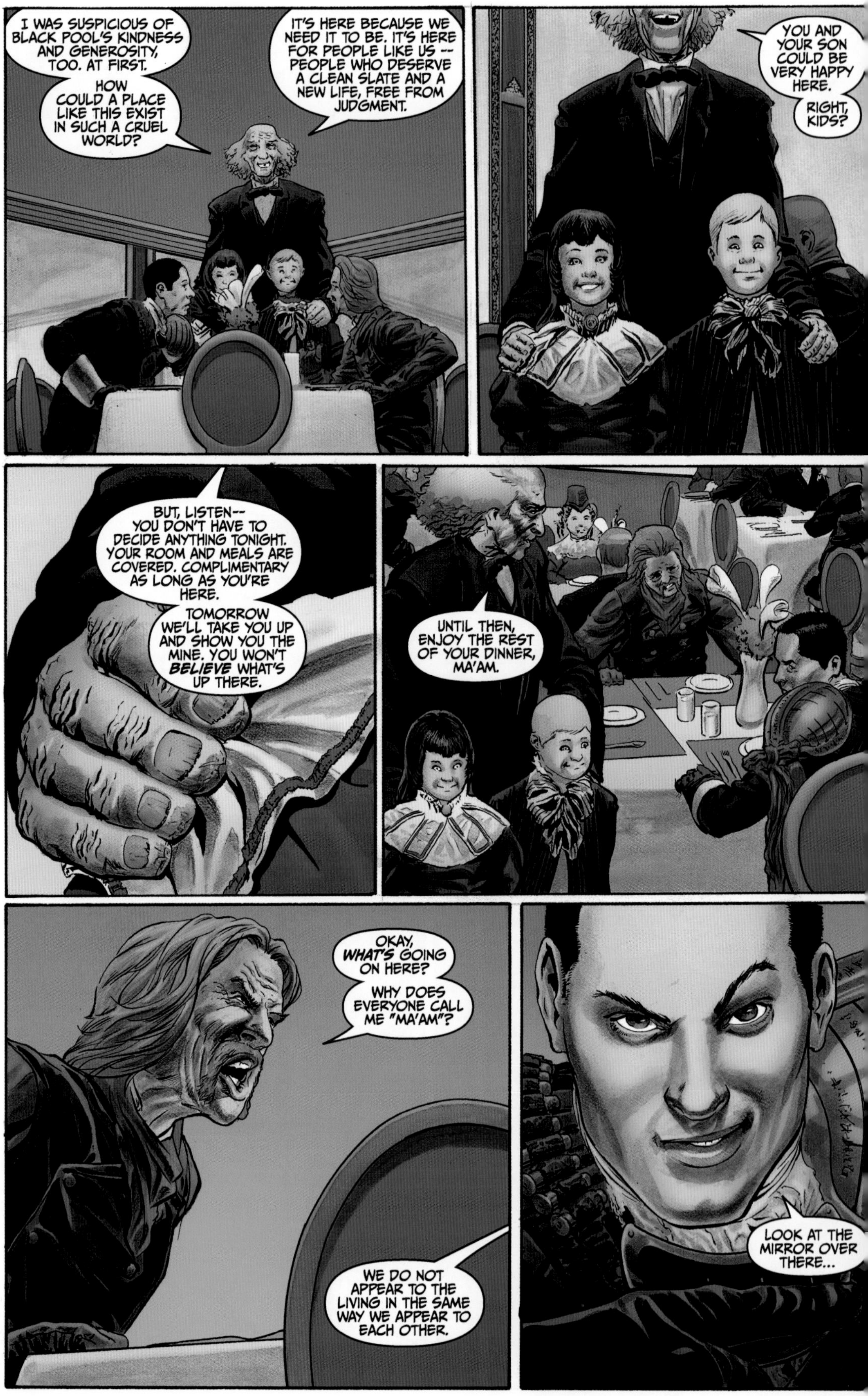
I WAS SUSPICIOUS OF BLACK POOL'S KINDNESS AND GENEROSITY, TOO. AT FIRST.
HOW COULD A PLACE LIKE THIS EXIST IN SUCH A CRUEL WORLD?
IT'S HERE BECAUSE WE NEED IT TO BE. IT'S HERE FOR PEOPLE LIKE US -- PEOPLE WHO DESERVE A CLEAN SLATE AND A NEW LIFE, FREE FROM JUDGMENT.
YOU AND YOUR SON COULD BE VERY HAPPY HERE.
RIGHT, KIDS?
BUT, LISTEN-- YOU DON'T HAVE TO DECIDE ANYTHING TONIGHT. YOUR ROOM AND MEALS ARE COVERED. COMPLIMENTARY AS LONG AS YOU'RE HERE.
TOMORROW WE'LL TAKE YOU UP AND SHOW YOU THE MINE. YOU WON'T *BELIEVE* WHAT'S UP THERE.
UNTIL THEN, ENJOY THE REST OF YOUR DINNER, MA'AM.
OKAY, *WHAT'S* GOING ON HERE?
WHY DOES EVERYONE CALL ME "MA'AM"?
WE DO NOT APPEAR TO THE LIVING IN THE SAME WAY WE APPEAR TO EACH OTHER.
LOOK AT THE MIRROR OVER THERE...

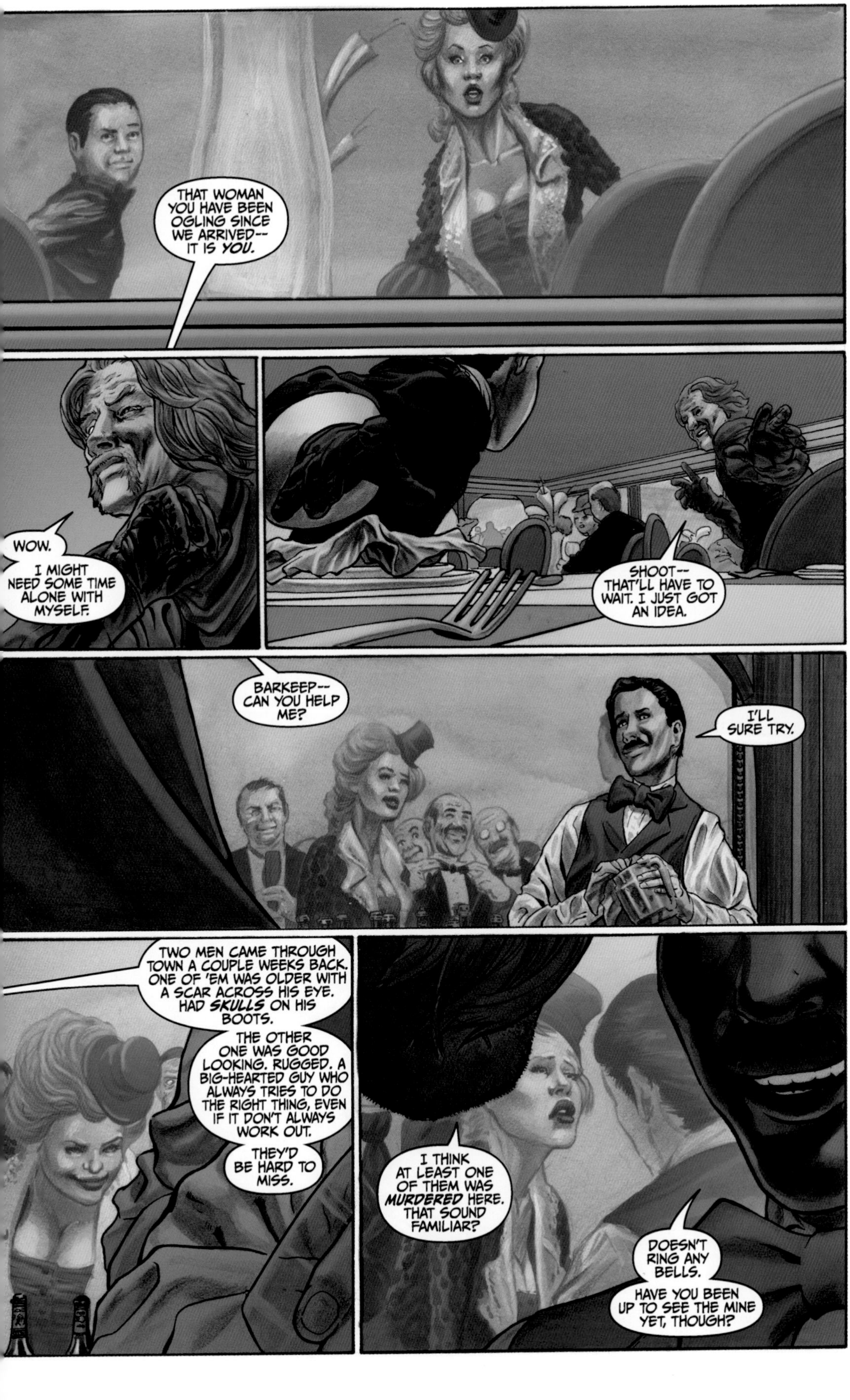
THAT WOMAN YOU HAVE BEEN OGLING SINCE WE ARRIVED-- IT IS *YOU.*
WOW.
I MIGHT NEED SOME TIME ALONE WITH MYSELF.
SHOOT-- THAT'LL HAVE TO WAIT. I JUST GOT AN IDEA.
BARKEEP-- CAN YOU HELP ME?
I'LL SURE TRY.
TWO MEN CAME THROUGH TOWN A COUPLE WEEKS BACK. ONE OF 'EM WAS OLDER WITH A SCAR ACROSS HIS EYE. HAD ***SKULLS*** ON HIS BOOTS.
THE OTHER ONE WAS GOOD LOOKING. RUGGED. A BIG-HEARTED GUY WHO ALWAYS TRIES TO DO THE RIGHT THING, EVEN IF IT DON'T ALWAYS WORK OUT.
THEY'D BE HARD TO MISS.
I THINK AT LEAST ONE OF THEM WAS ***MURDERED*** HERE. THAT SOUND FAMILIAR?
DOESN'T RING ANY BELLS.
HAVE YOU BEEN UP TO SEE THE MINE YET, THOUGH?

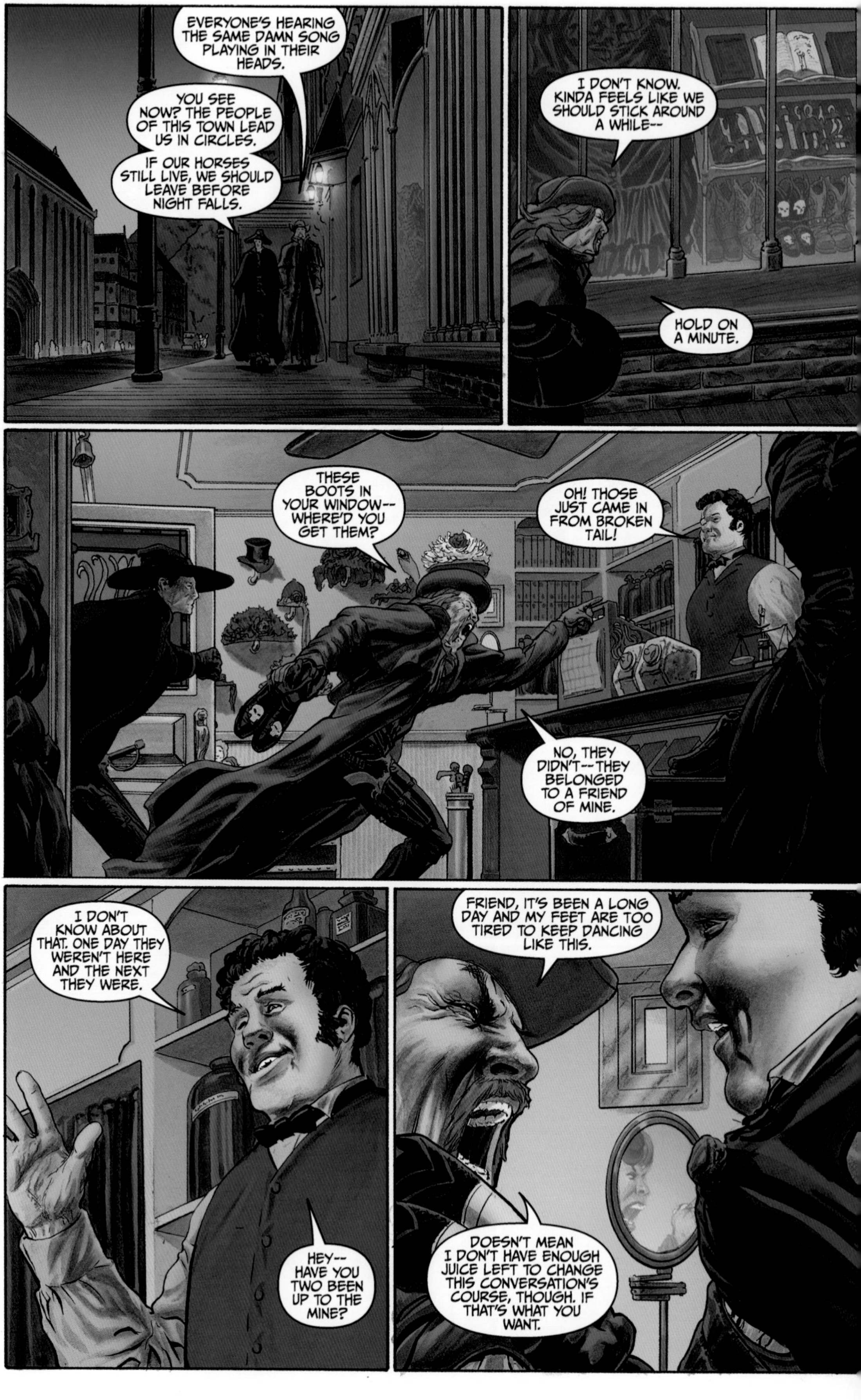
EVERYONE'S HEARING THE SAME DAMN SONG PLAYING IN THEIR HEADS.
YOU SEE NOW? THE PEOPLE OF THIS TOWN LEAD US IN CIRCLES.
IF OUR HORSES STILL LIVE, WE SHOULD LEAVE BEFORE NIGHT FALLS.
I DON'T KNOW. KINDA FEELS LIKE WE SHOULD STICK AROUND A WHILE--
HOLD ON A MINUTE.
THESE BOOTS IN YOUR WINDOW-- WHERE'D YOU GET THEM?
OH! THOSE JUST CAME IN FROM BROKEN TAIL!
NO, THEY DIDN'T--THEY BELONGED TO A FRIEND OF MINE.
I DON'T KNOW ABOUT THAT. ONE DAY THEY WEREN'T HERE AND THE NEXT THEY WERE.
HEY-- HAVE YOU TWO BEEN UP TO THE MINE?
FRIEND, IT'S BEEN A LONG DAY AND MY FEET ARE TOO TIRED TO KEEP DANCING LIKE THIS.
DOESN'T MEAN I DON'T HAVE ENOUGH JUICE LEFT TO CHANGE THIS CONVERSATION'S COURSE, THOUGH. IF THAT'S WHAT YOU WANT.

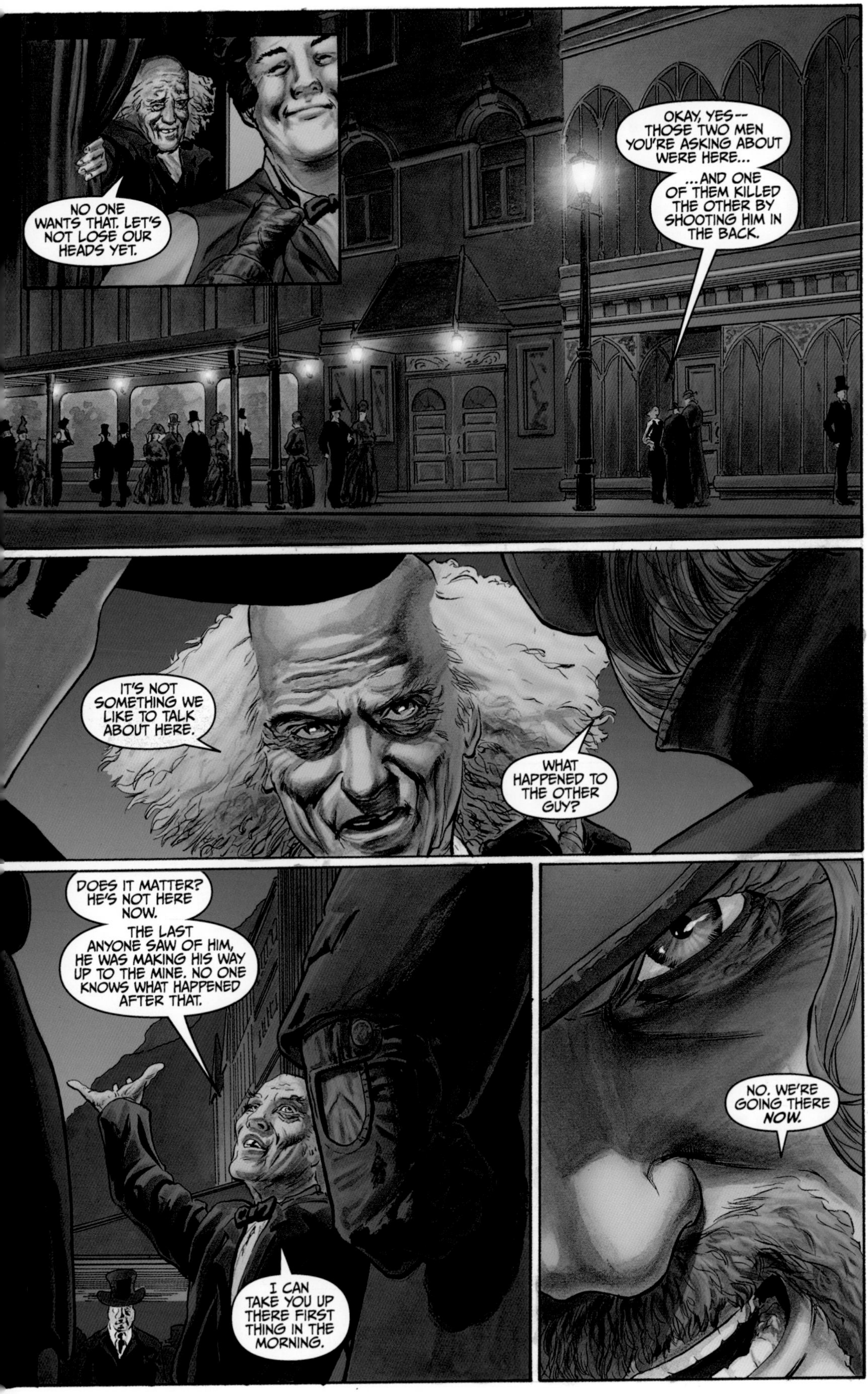
NO ONE WANTS THAT. LET'S NOT LOSE OUR HEADS YET.
OKAY, YES-- THOSE TWO MEN YOU'RE ASKING ABOUT WERE HERE...
...AND ONE OF THEM KILLED THE OTHER BY SHOOTING HIM IN THE BACK.
IT'S NOT SOMETHING WE LIKE TO TALK ABOUT HERE.
WHAT HAPPENED TO THE OTHER GUY?
DOES IT MATTER? HE'S NOT HERE NOW.
THE LAST ANYONE SAW OF HIM, HE WAS MAKING HIS WAY UP TO THE MINE. NO ONE KNOWS WHAT HAPPENED AFTER THAT.
I CAN TAKE YOU UP THERE FIRST THING IN THE MORNING.
NO. WE'RE GOING THERE *NOW.*

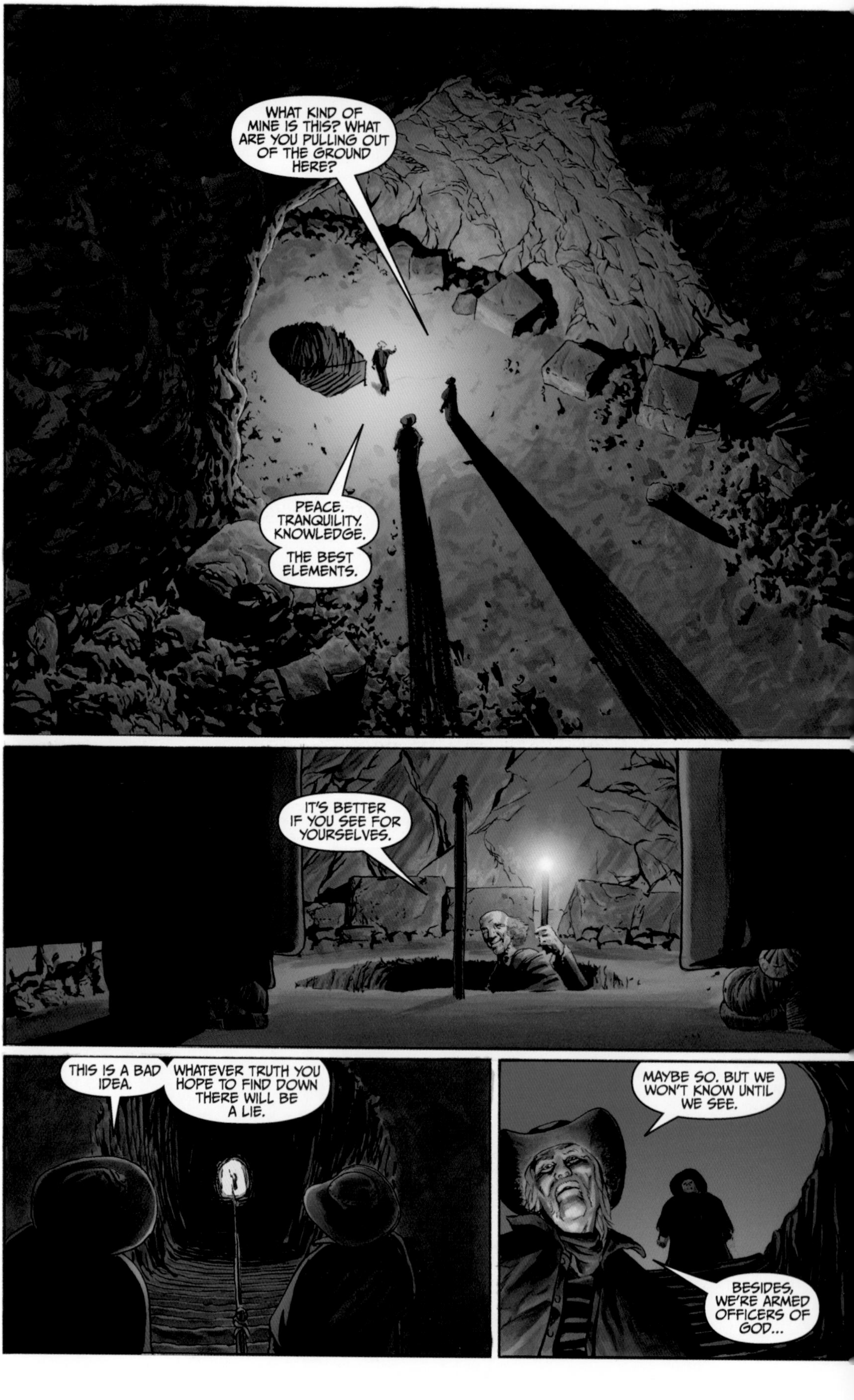
WHAT KIND OF MINE IS THIS? WHAT ARE YOU PULLING OUT OF THE GROUND HERE?
PEACE. TRANQUILITY. KNOWLEDGE.
THE BEST ELEMENTS.
IT'S BETTER IF YOU SEE FOR YOURSELVES.
THIS IS A BAD IDEA.
WHATEVER TRUTH YOU HOPE TO FIND DOWN THERE WILL BE A LIE.
MAYBE SO. BUT WE WON'T KNOW UNTIL WE SEE.
BESIDES, WE'RE ARMED OFFICERS OF GOD...

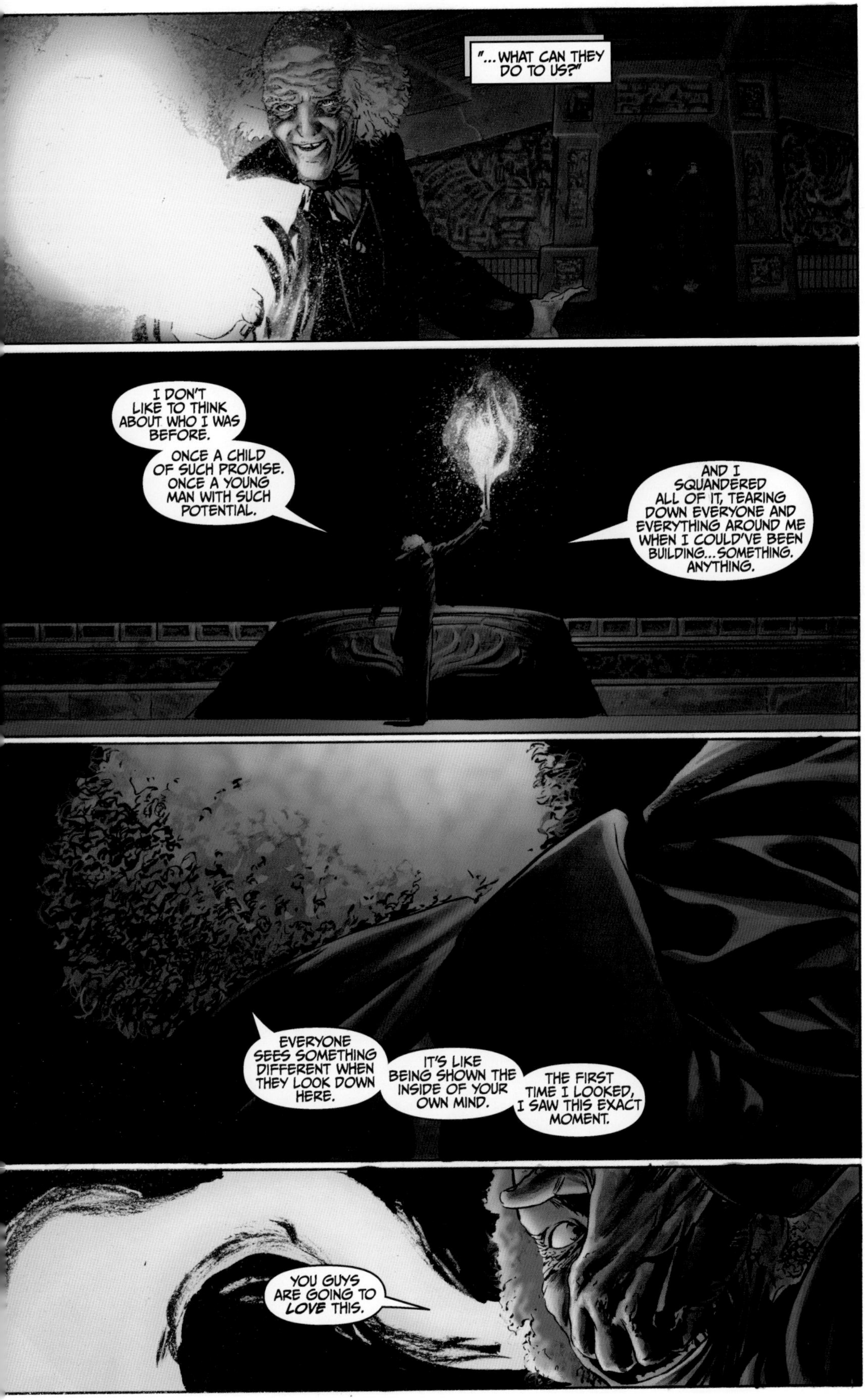
"...WHAT CAN THEY DO TO US?"
I DON'T LIKE TO THINK ABOUT WHO I WAS BEFORE.
ONCE A CHILD OF SUCH PROMISE. ONCE A YOUNG MAN WITH SUCH POTENTIAL.
AND I SQUANDERED ALL OF IT, TEARING DOWN EVERYONE AND EVERYTHING AROUND ME WHEN I COULD'VE BEEN BUILDING...SOMETHING. ANYTHING.
EVERYONE SEES SOMETHING DIFFERENT WHEN THEY LOOK DOWN HERE.
IT'S LIKE BEING SHOWN THE INSIDE OF YOUR OWN MIND.
THE FIRST TIME I LOOKED, I SAW THIS EXACT MOMENT.
YOU GUYS ARE GOING TO LOVE THIS.

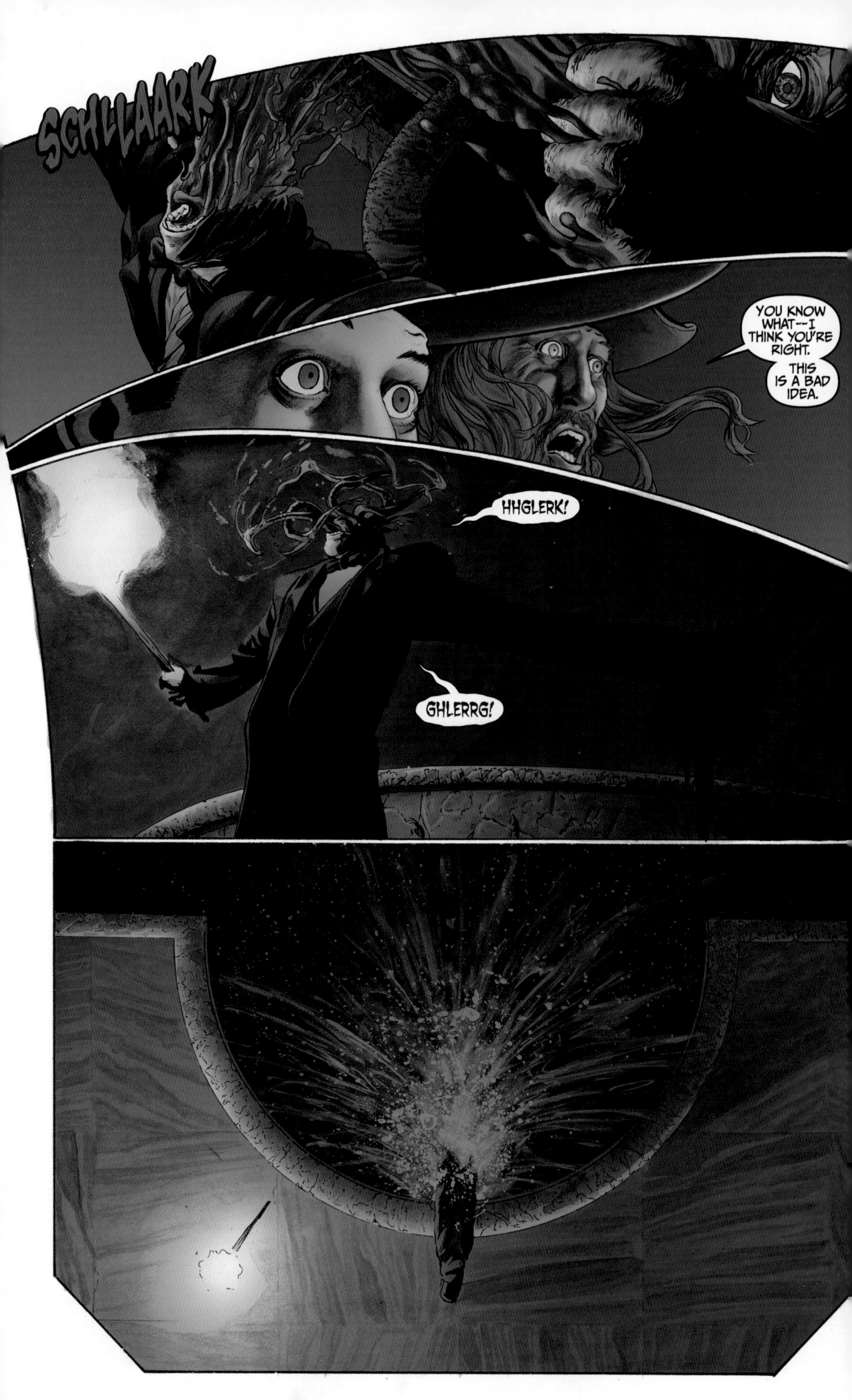
SCHLLAARK
YOU KNOW WHAT--I THINK YOU'RE RIGHT.
THIS IS A BAD IDEA.
HHGLERK!
GHLERRG!

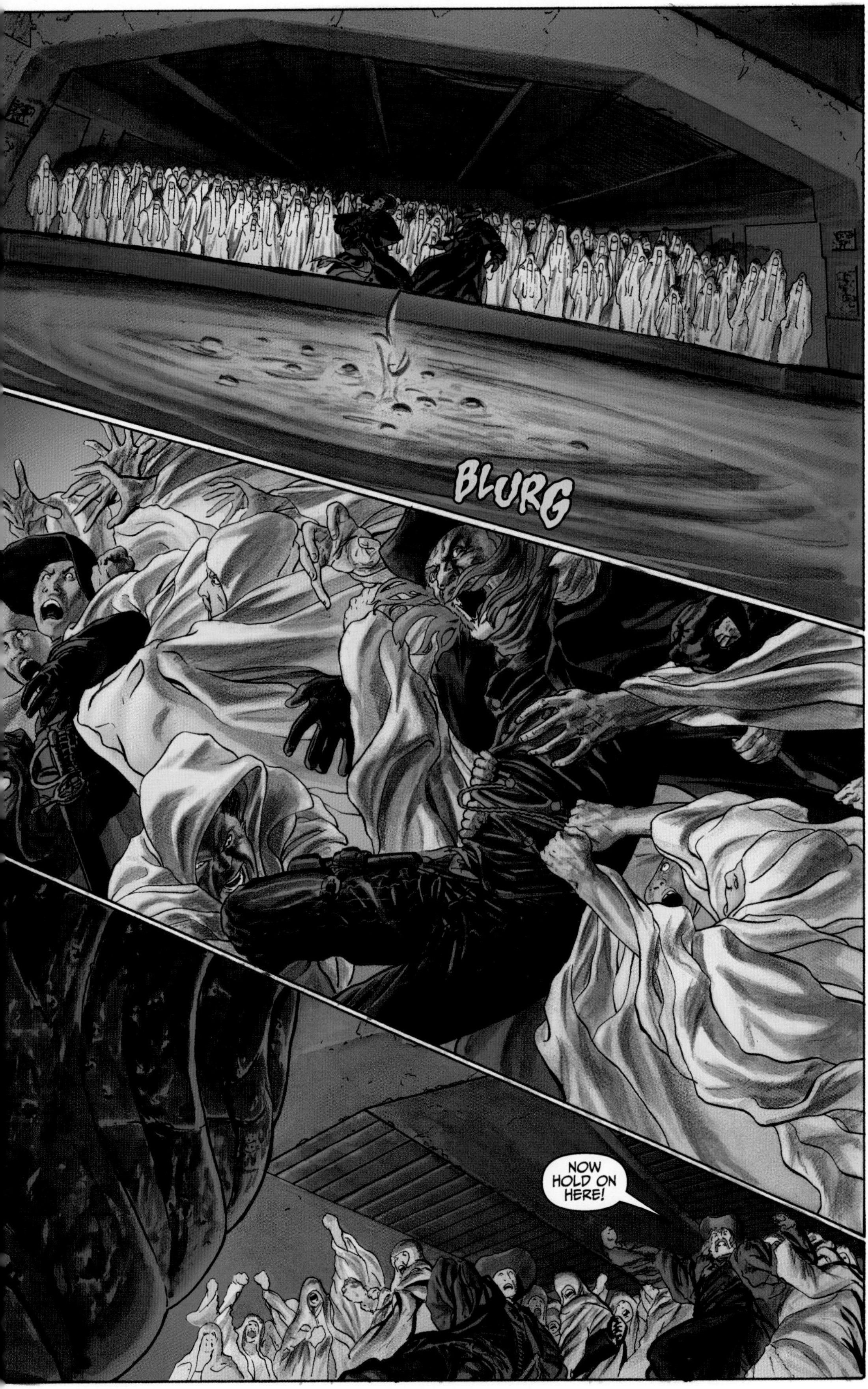
BLURG
NOW HOLD ON HERE!

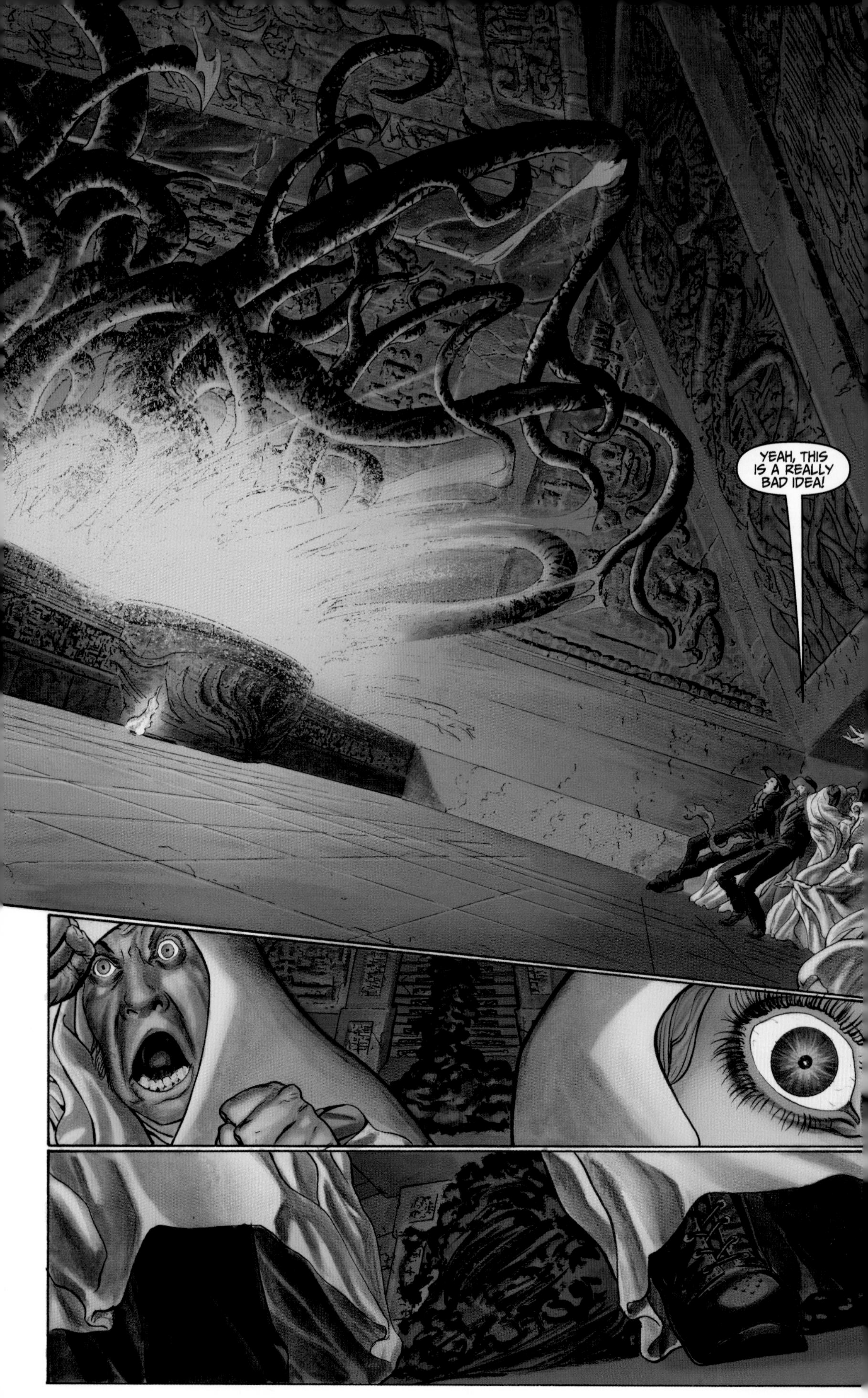
YEAH, THIS IS A REALLY BAD IDEA!

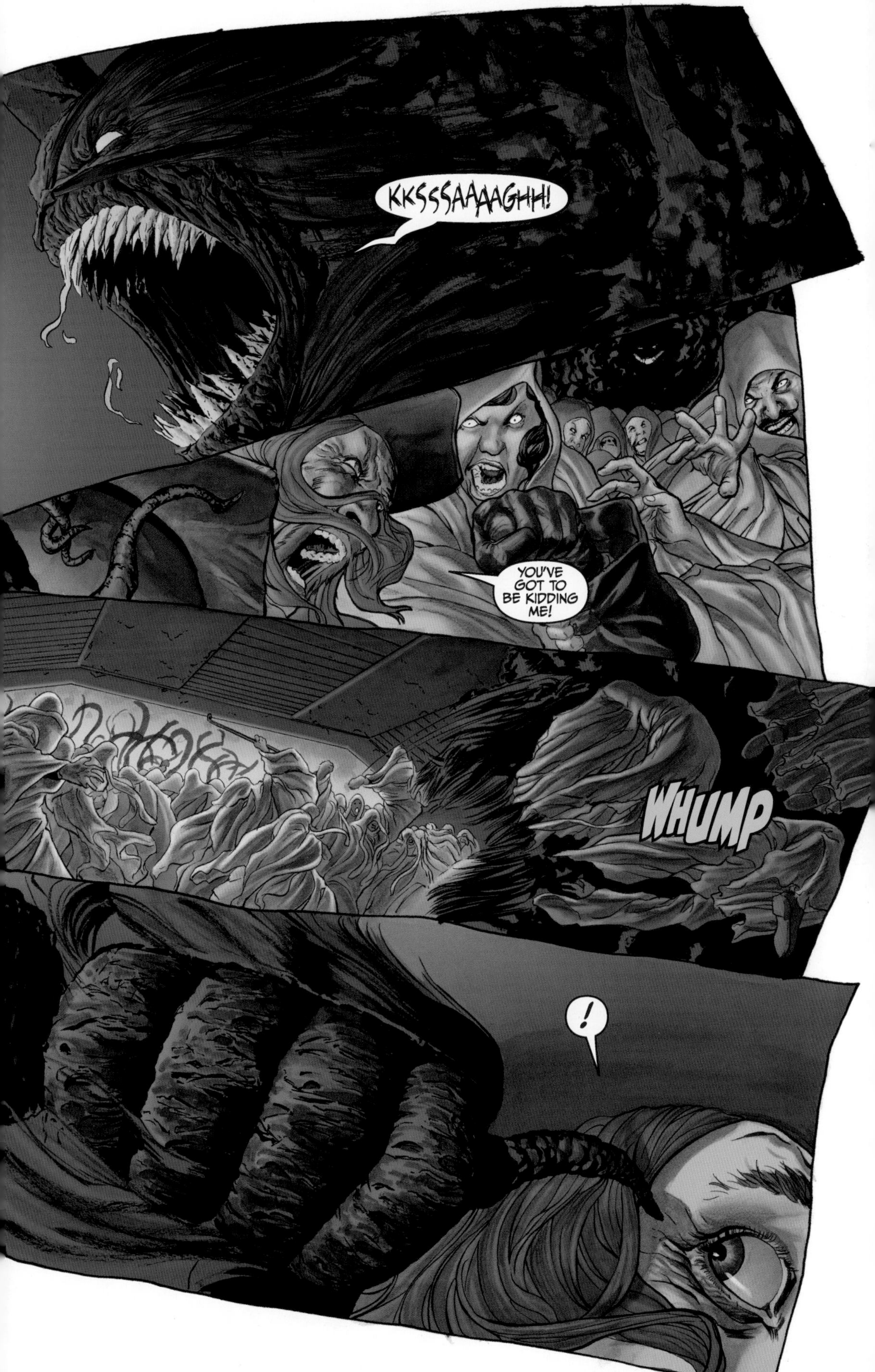
KKSSSAAAAAGHH!
YOU'VE GOT TO BE KIDDING ME!
WHUMP
!

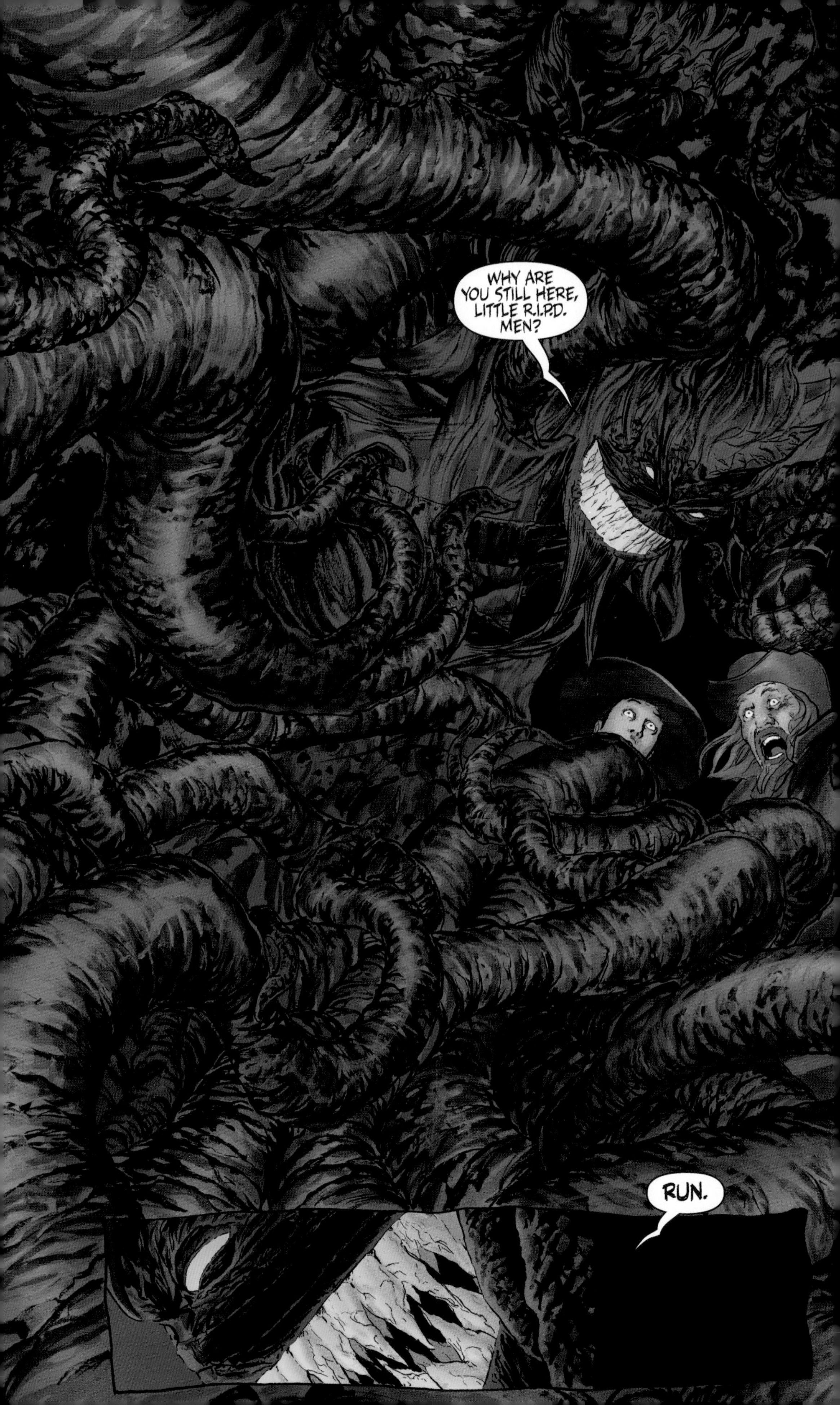
WHY ARE YOU STILL HERE, LITTLE R.I.P.D. MEN?
RUN.

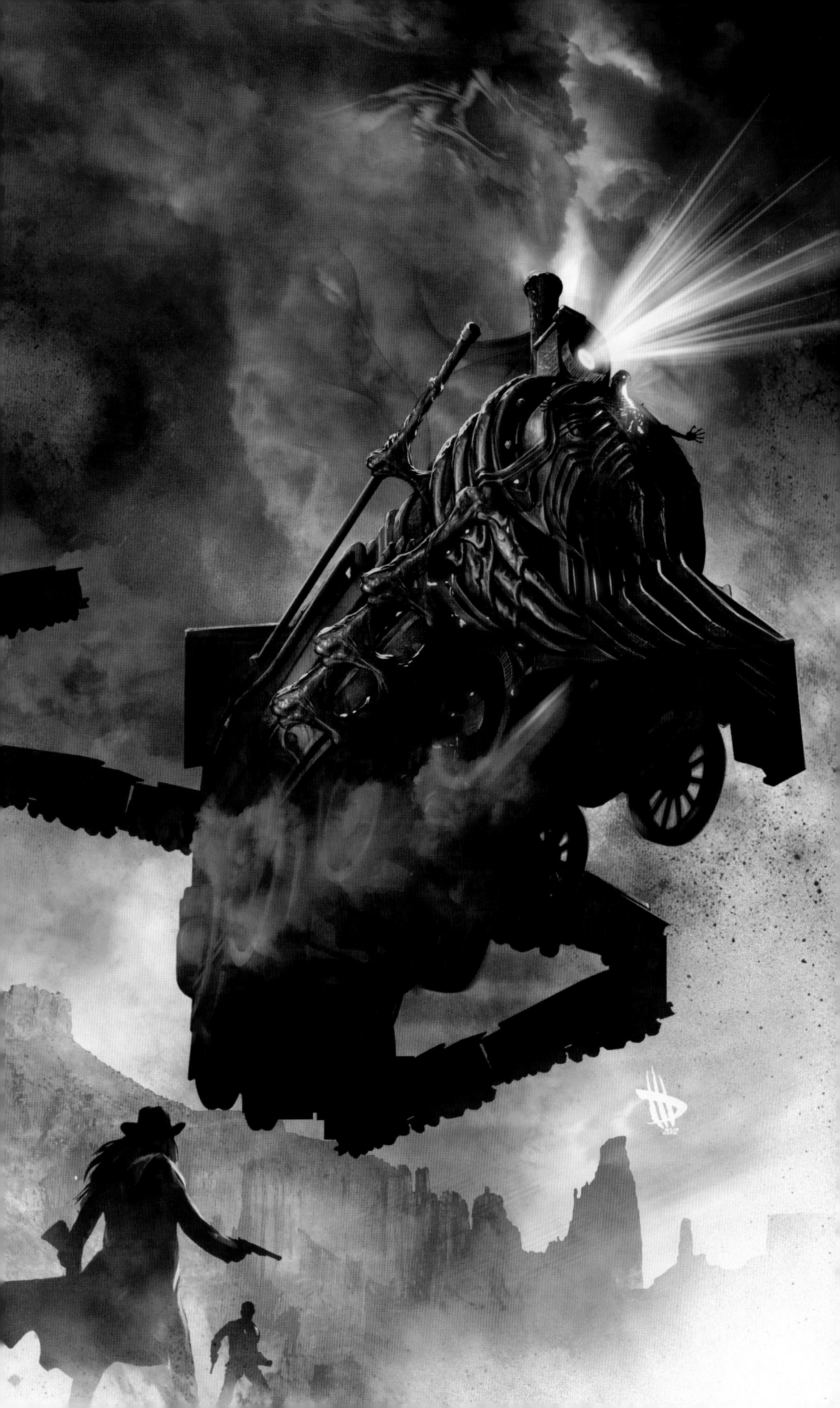

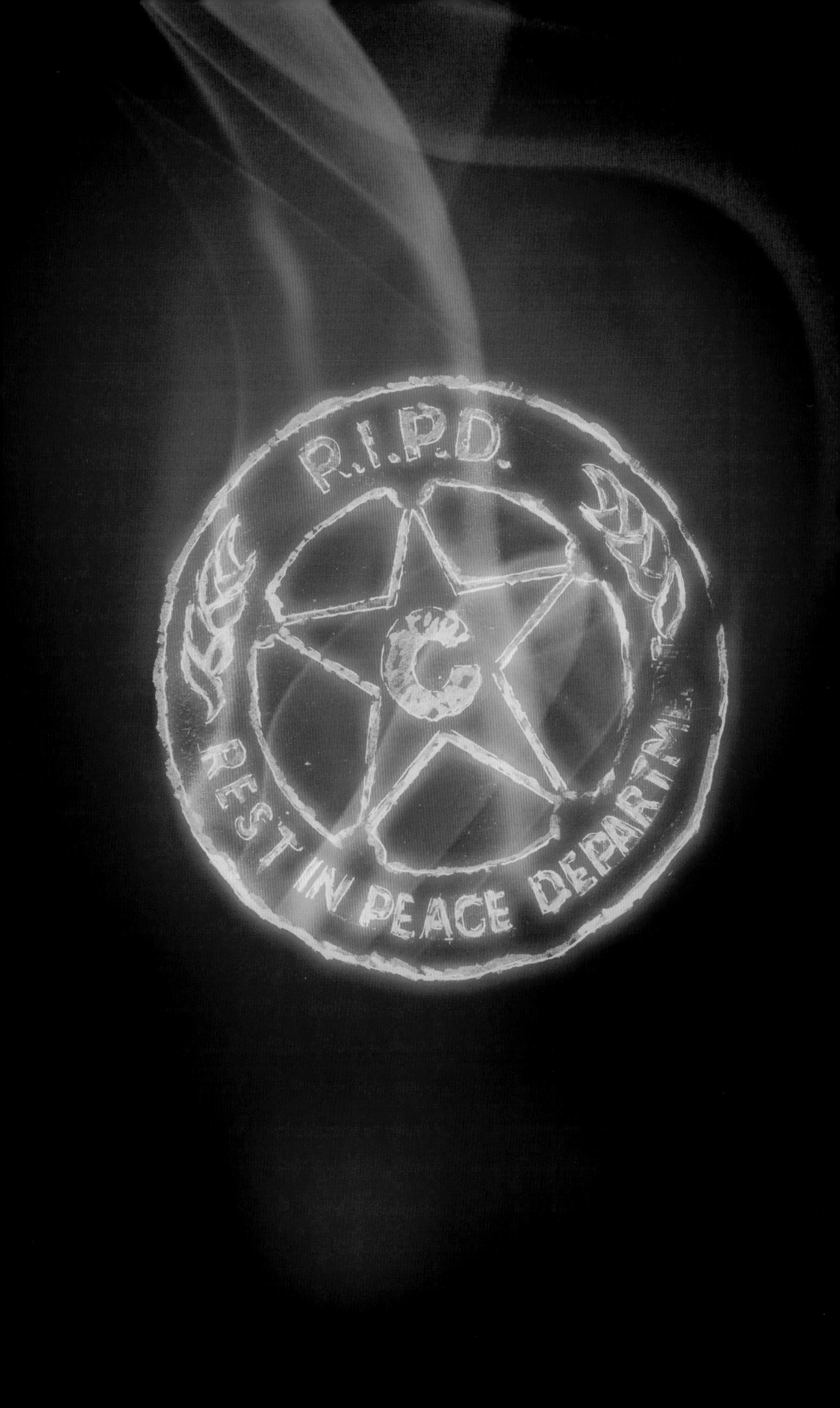
R.I.P.D.
C
REST IN PEACE DEPARTME

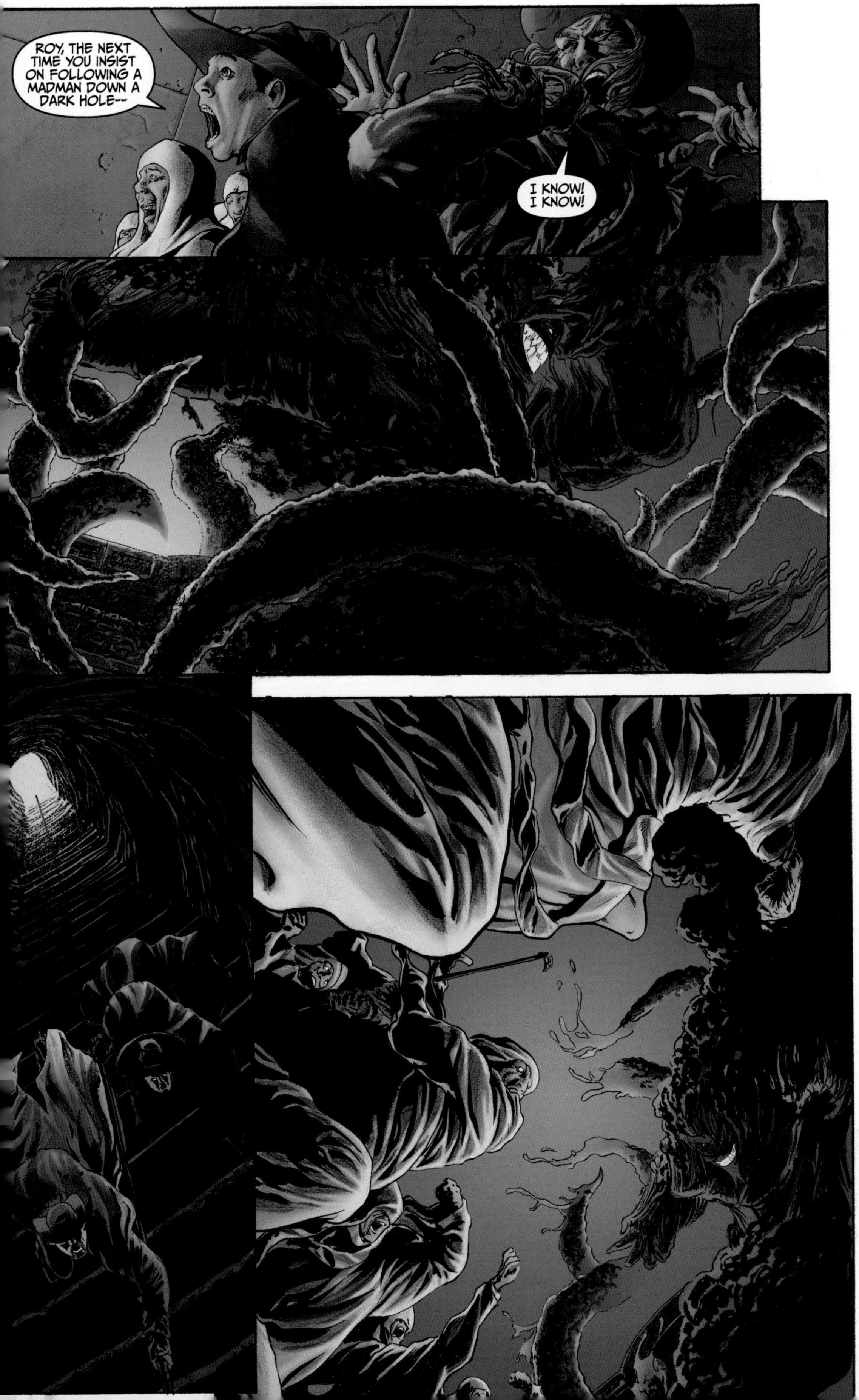
ROY, THE NEXT TIME YOU INSIST ON FOLLOWING A MADMAN DOWN A DARK HOLE--
I KNOW! I KNOW!

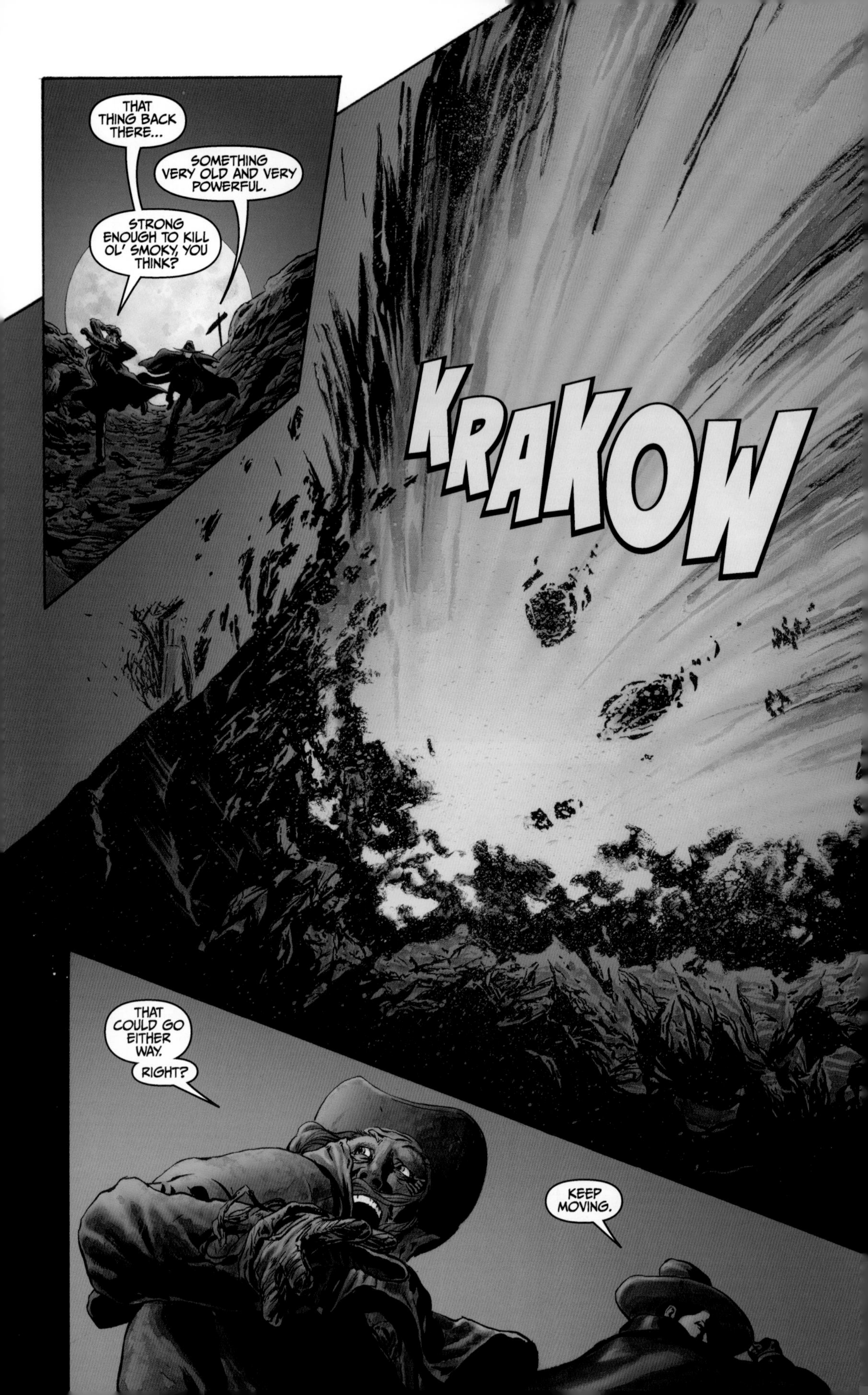
THAT THING BACK THERE...
SOMETHING VERY OLD AND VERY POWERFUL.
STRONG ENOUGH TO KILL OL' SMOKY, YOU THINK?
KRAKOW
THAT COULD GO EITHER WAY.
RIGHT?
KEEP MOVING.

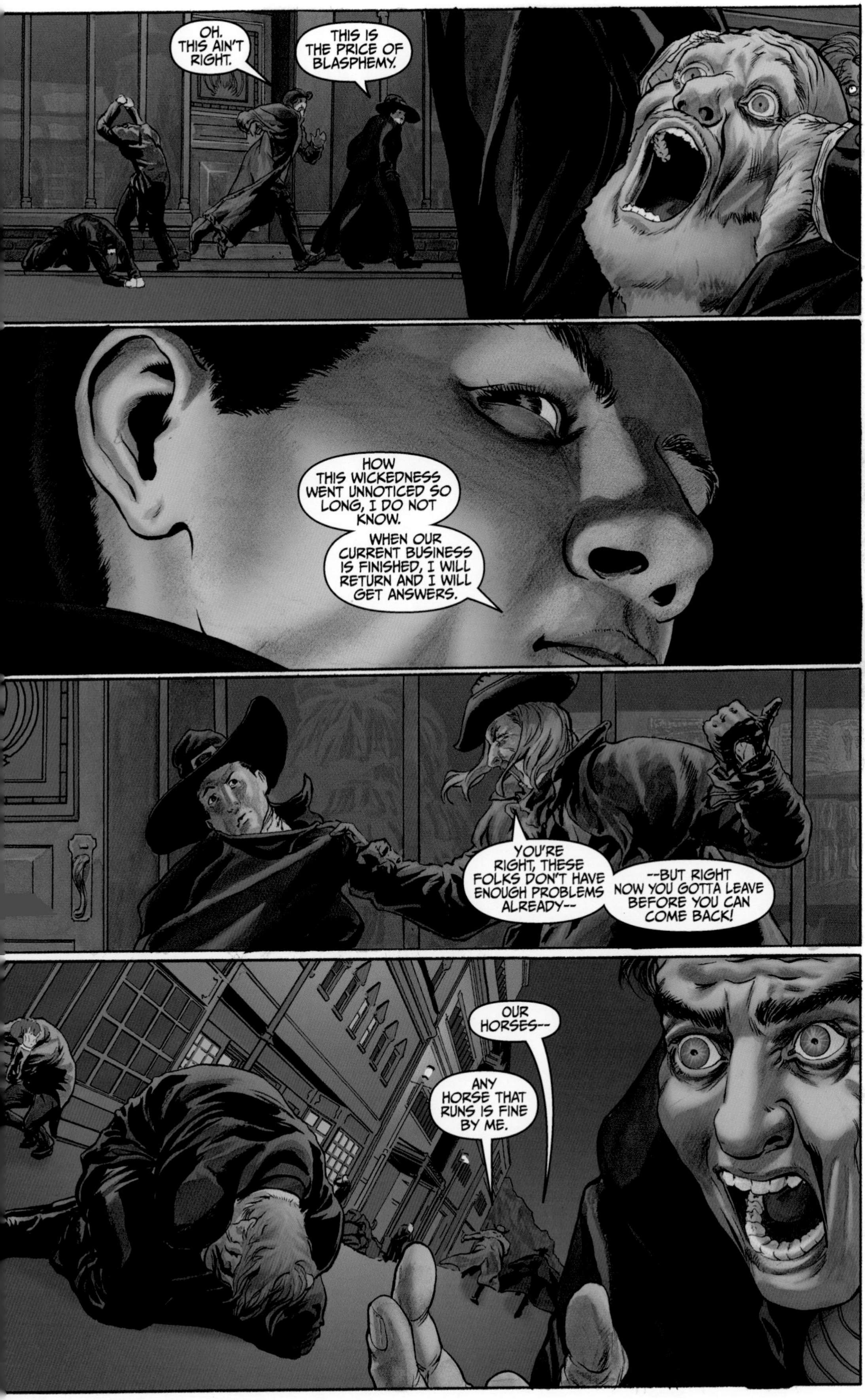
OH. THIS AIN'T RIGHT.
THIS IS THE PRICE OF BLASPHEMY.
HOW THIS WICKEDNESS WENT UNNOTICED SO LONG, I DO NOT KNOW.
WHEN OUR CURRENT BUSINESS IS FINISHED, I WILL RETURN AND I WILL GET ANSWERS.
YOU'RE RIGHT, THESE FOLKS DON'T HAVE ENOUGH PROBLEMS ALREADY--
--BUT RIGHT NOW YOU GOTTA LEAVE BEFORE YOU CAN COME BACK!
OUR HORSES--
ANY HORSE THAT RUNS IS FINE BY ME.

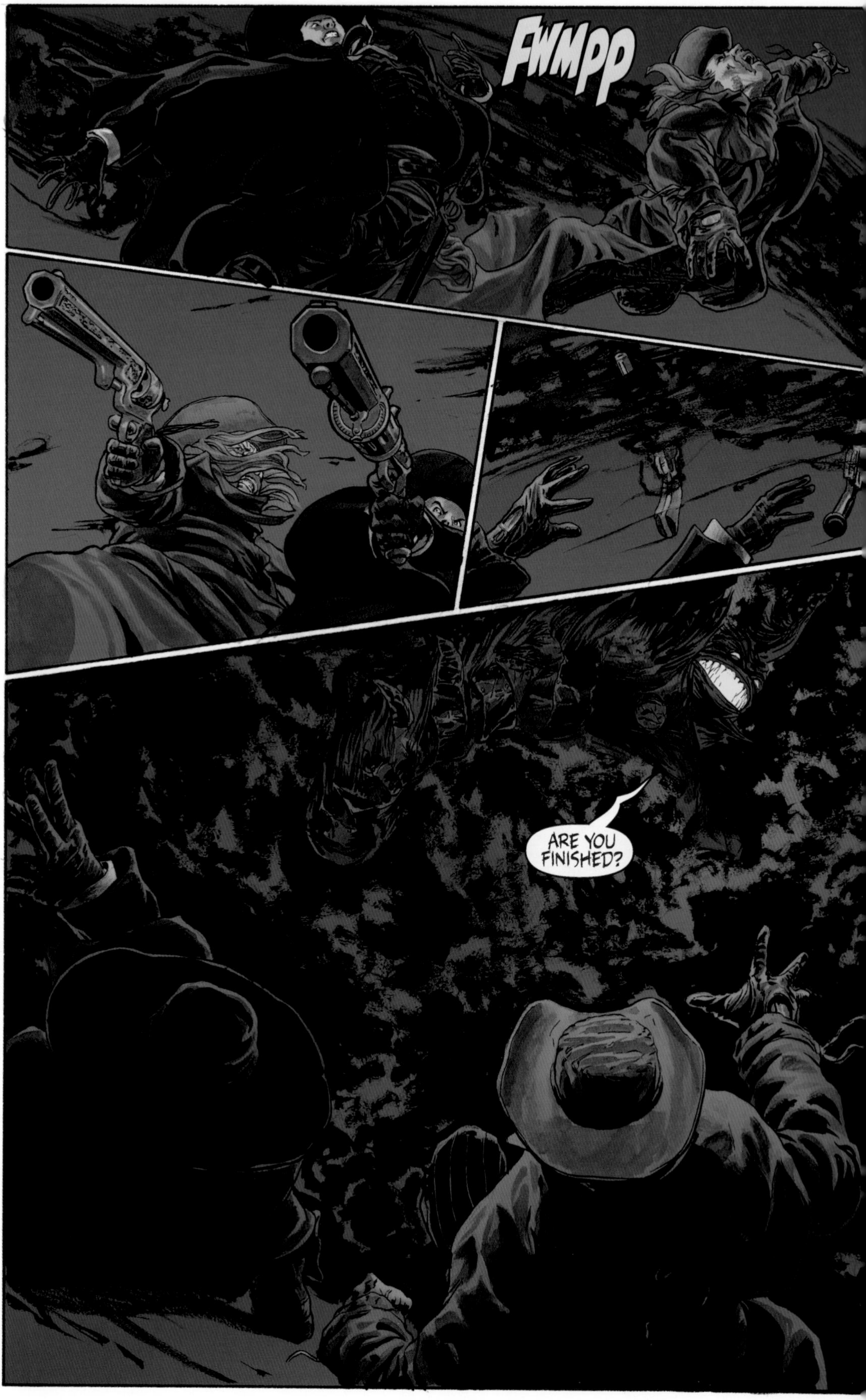
FWMPP
ARE YOU FINISHED?

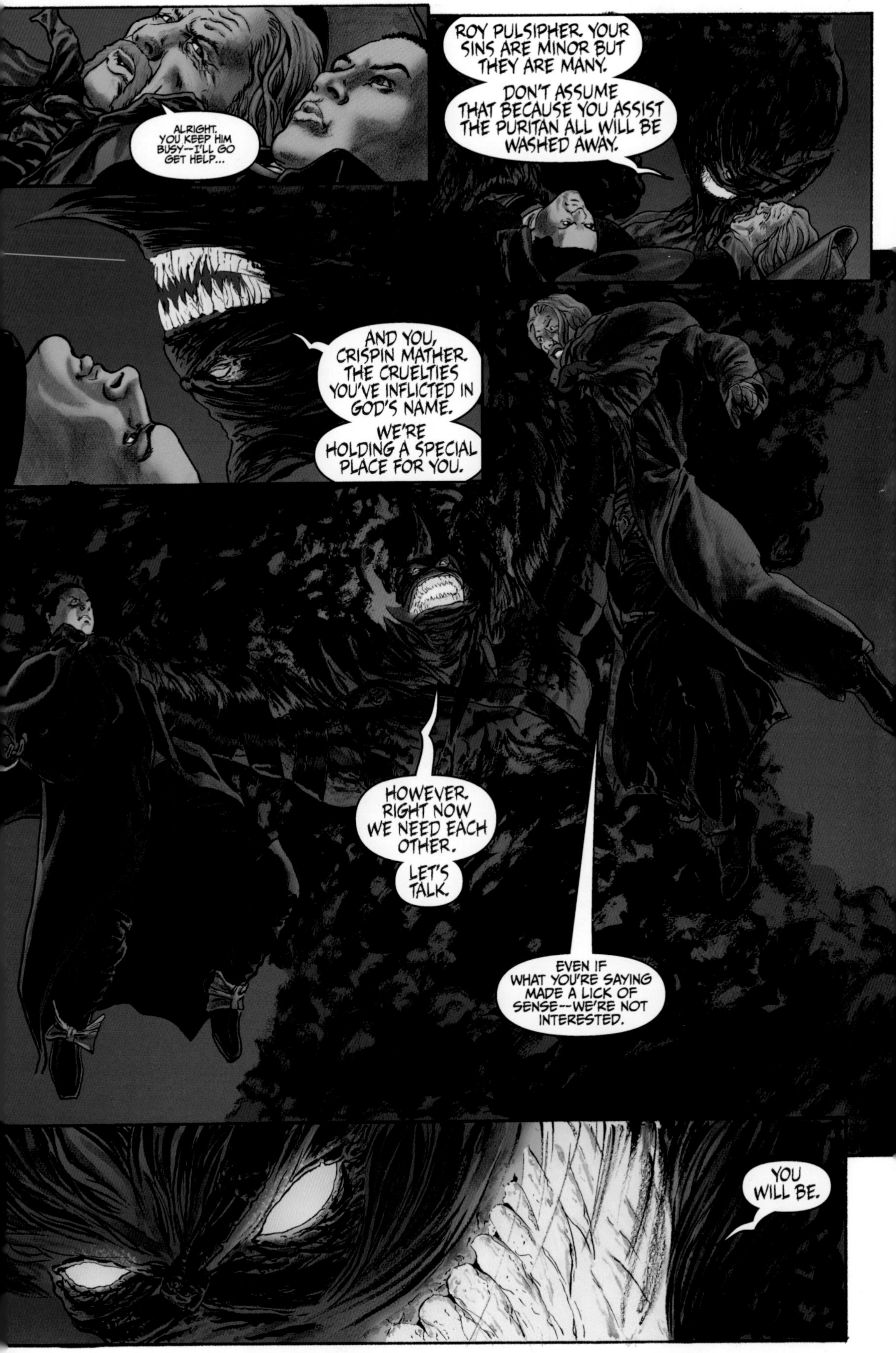
ALRIGHT. YOU KEEP HIM BUSY--I'LL GO GET HELP...
ROY PULSIPHER. YOUR SINS ARE MINOR BUT THEY ARE MANY.
DON'T ASSUME THAT BECAUSE YOU ASSIST THE PURITAN ALL WILL BE WASHED AWAY.
AND YOU, CRISPIN MATHER. THE CRUELTIES YOU'VE INFLICTED IN GOD'S NAME.
WE'RE HOLDING A SPECIAL PLACE FOR YOU.
HOWEVER. RIGHT NOW WE NEED EACH OTHER.
LET'S TALK.
EVEN IF WHAT YOU'RE SAYING MADE A LICK OF SENSE--WE'RE NOT INTERESTED.
YOU WILL BE.

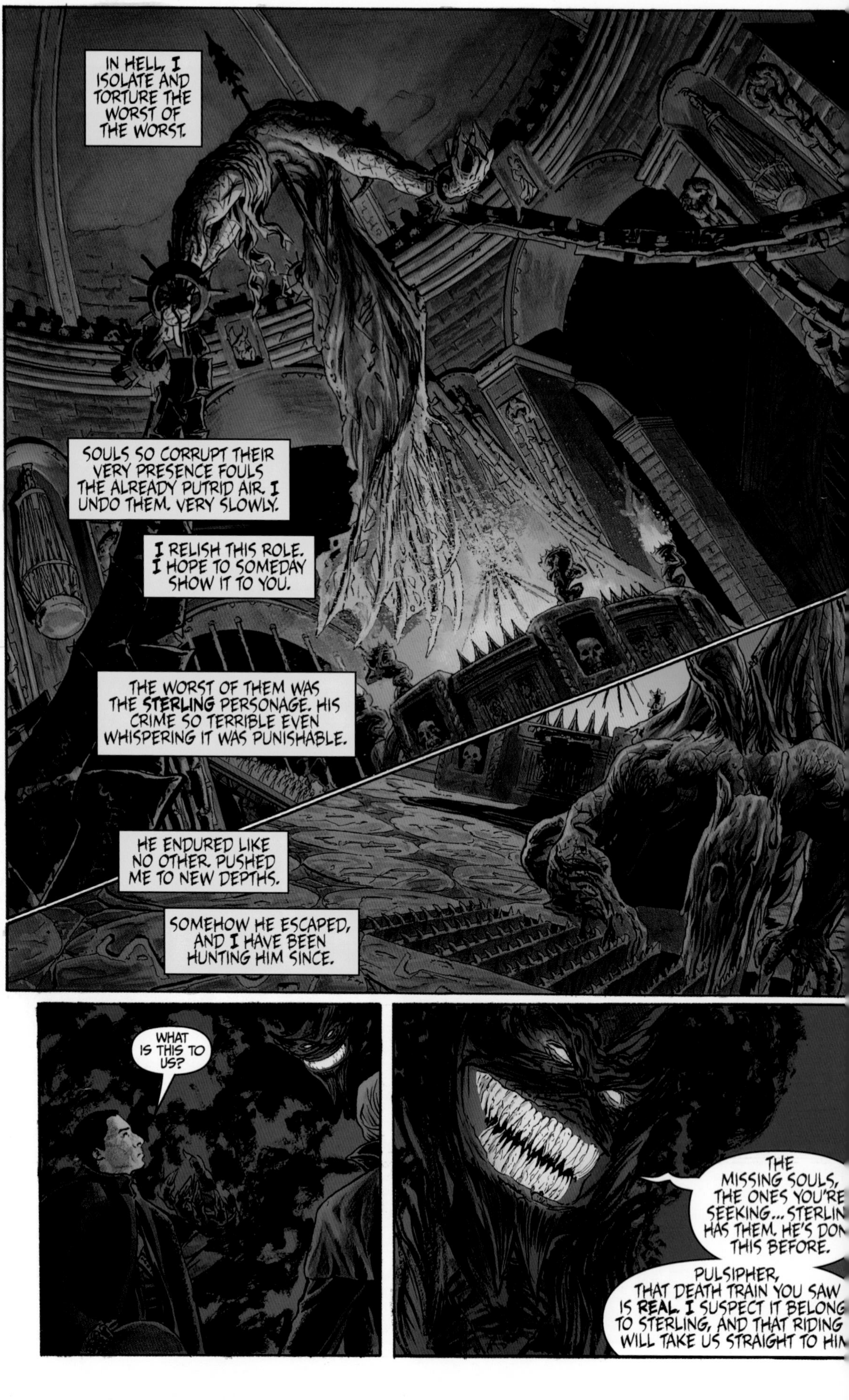

IN HELL, I ISOLATE AND TORTURE THE WORST OF THE WORST.
SOULS SO CORRUPT THEIR VERY PRESENCE FOULS THE ALREADY PUTRID AIR. I UNDO THEM. VERY SLOWLY.
I RELISH THIS ROLE. I HOPE TO SOMEDAY SHOW IT TO YOU.
THE WORST OF THEM WAS THE STERLING PERSONAGE. HIS CRIME SO TERRIBLE EVEN WHISPERING IT WAS PUNISHABLE.
HE ENDURED LIKE NO OTHER. PUSHED ME TO NEW DEPTHS.
SOMEHOW HE ESCAPED, AND I HAVE BEEN HUNTING HIM SINCE.
WHAT IS THIS TO US?
THE MISSING SOULS, THE ONES YOU'RE SEEKING... STERLIN HAS THEM. HE'S DON THIS BEFORE.
PULSIPHER, THAT DEATH TRAIN YOU SAW IS REAL. I SUSPECT IT BELONG TO STERLING, AND THAT RIDING WILL TAKE US STRAIGHT TO HIM

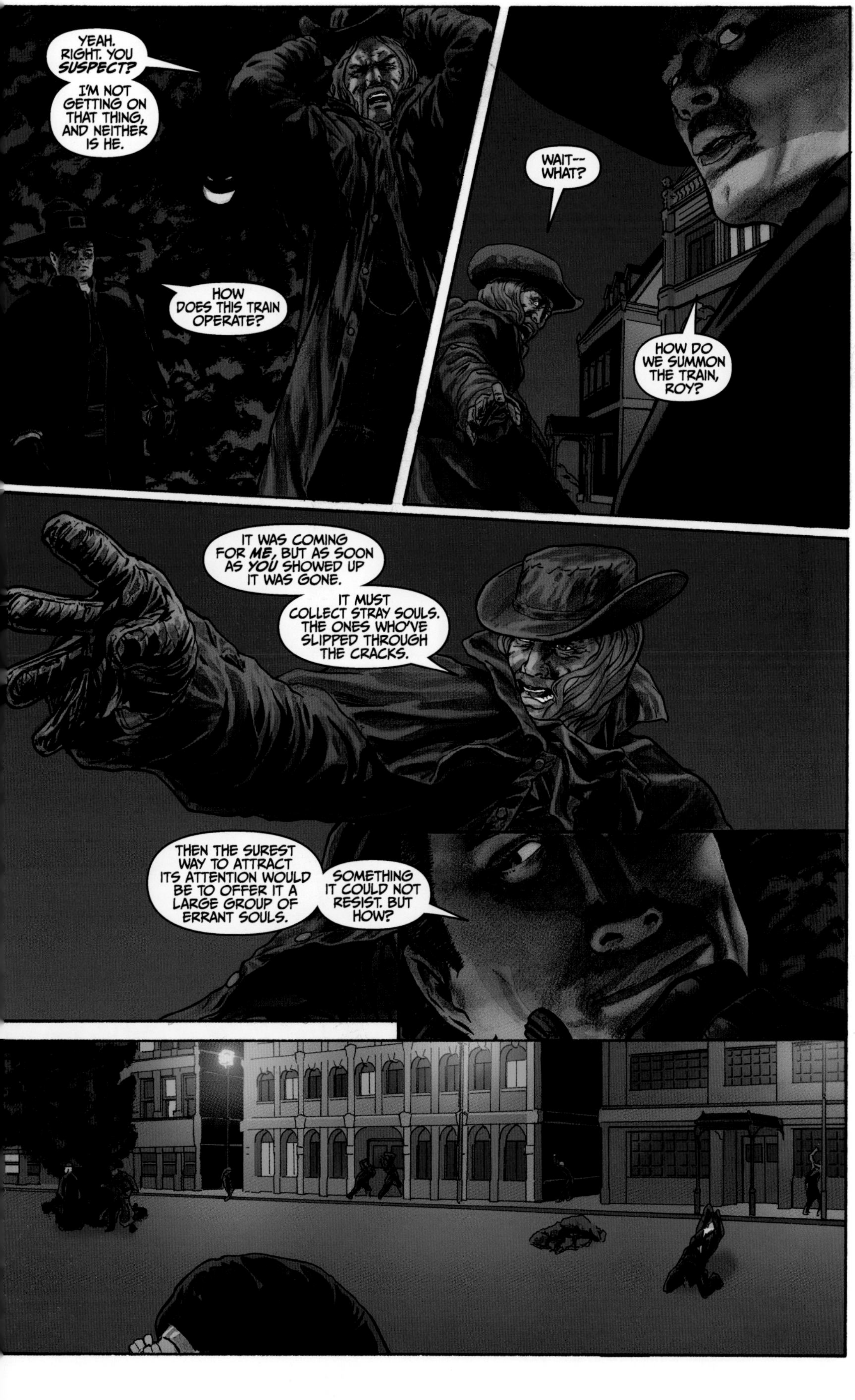
YEAH. RIGHT. YOU SUSPECT?
I'M NOT GETTING ON THAT THING, AND NEITHER IS HE.
HOW DOES THIS TRAIN OPERATE?
WAIT-- WHAT?
HOW DO WE SUMMON THE TRAIN, ROY?
IT WAS COMING FOR ME, BUT AS SOON AS YOU SHOWED UP IT WAS GONE.
IT MUST COLLECT STRAY SOULS. THE ONES WHO'VE SLIPPED THROUGH THE CRACKS.
THEN THE SUREST WAY TO ATTRACT ITS ATTENTION WOULD BE TO OFFER IT A LARGE GROUP OF ERRANT SOULS.
SOMETHING IT COULD NOT RESIST. BUT HOW?

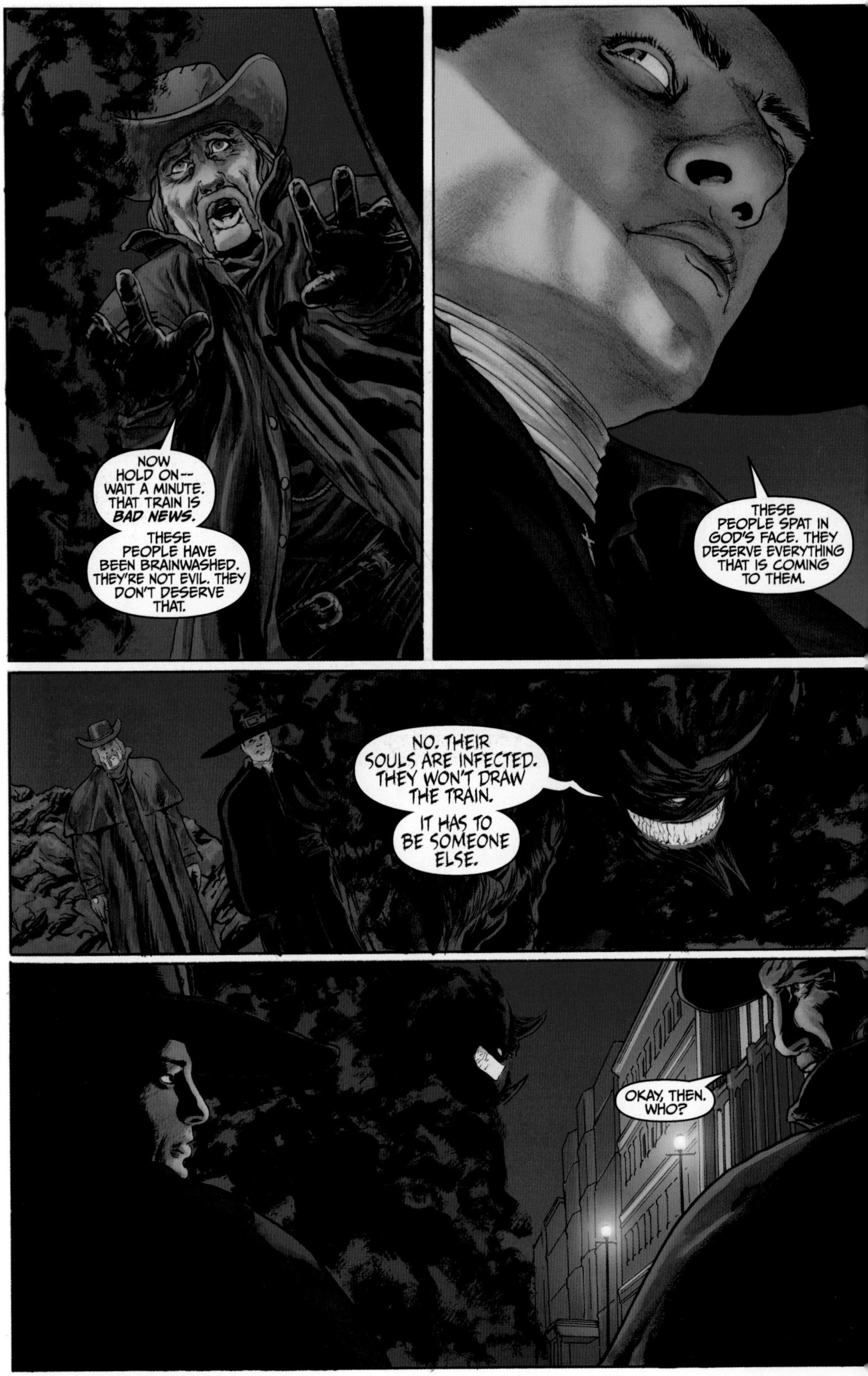
NOW HOLD ON-- WAIT A MINUTE. THAT TRAIN IS BAD NEWS.
THESE PEOPLE HAVE BEEN BRAINWASHED. THEY'RE NOT EVIL. THEY DON'T DESERVE THAT.
THESE PEOPLE SPAT IN GOD'S FACE. THEY DESERVE EVERYTHING THAT IS COMING TO THEM.
NO. THEIR SOULS ARE INFECTED. THEY WON'T DRAW THE TRAIN.
IT HAS TO BE SOMEONE ELSE.
OKAY, THEN. WHO?

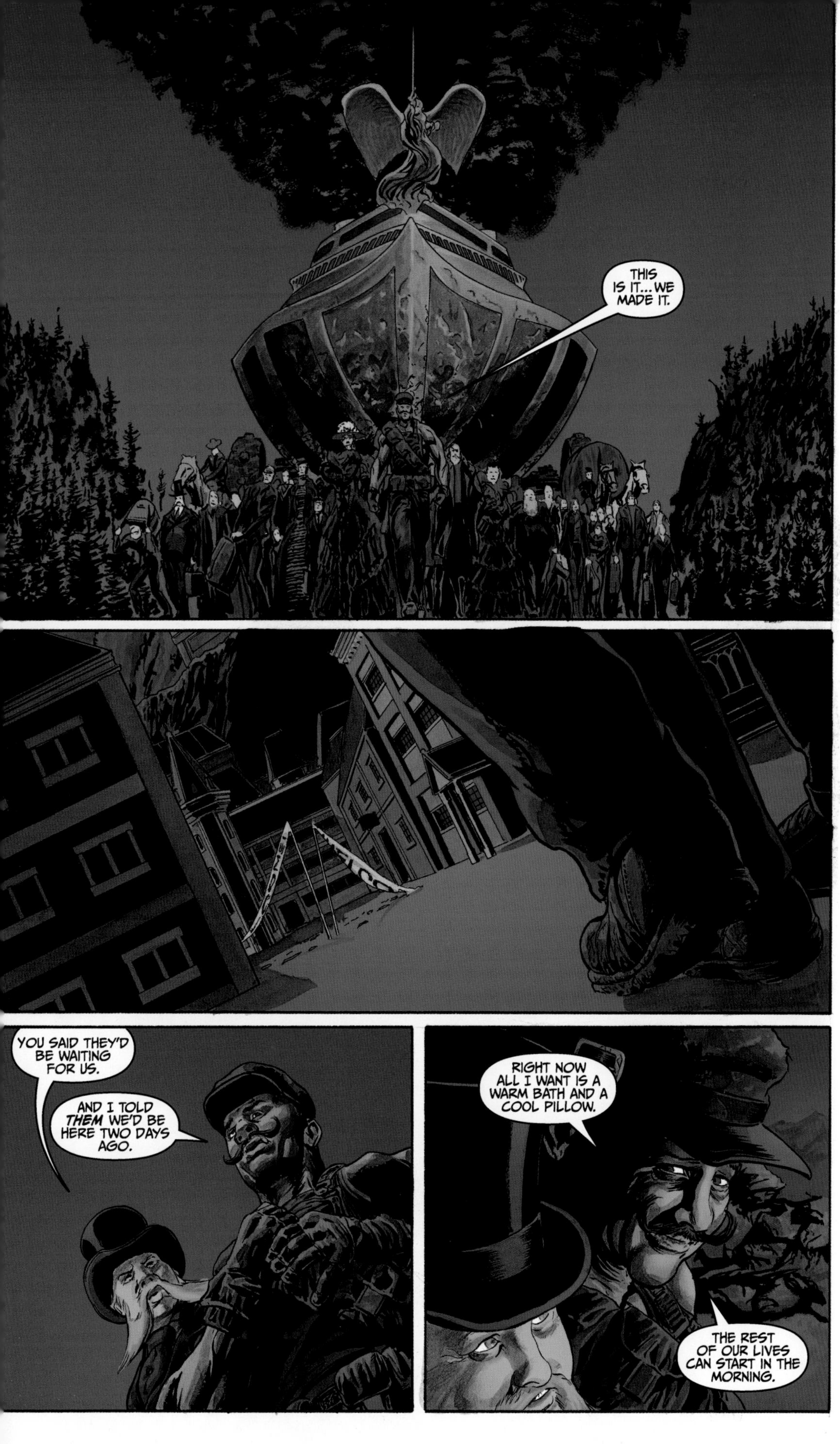
THIS IS IT... WE MADE IT.
YOU SAID THEY'D BE WAITING FOR US.
AND I TOLD *THEM* WE'D BE HERE TWO DAYS AGO.
RIGHT NOW ALL I WANT IS A WARM BATH AND A COOL PILLOW.
THE REST OF OUR LIVES CAN START IN THE MORNING.

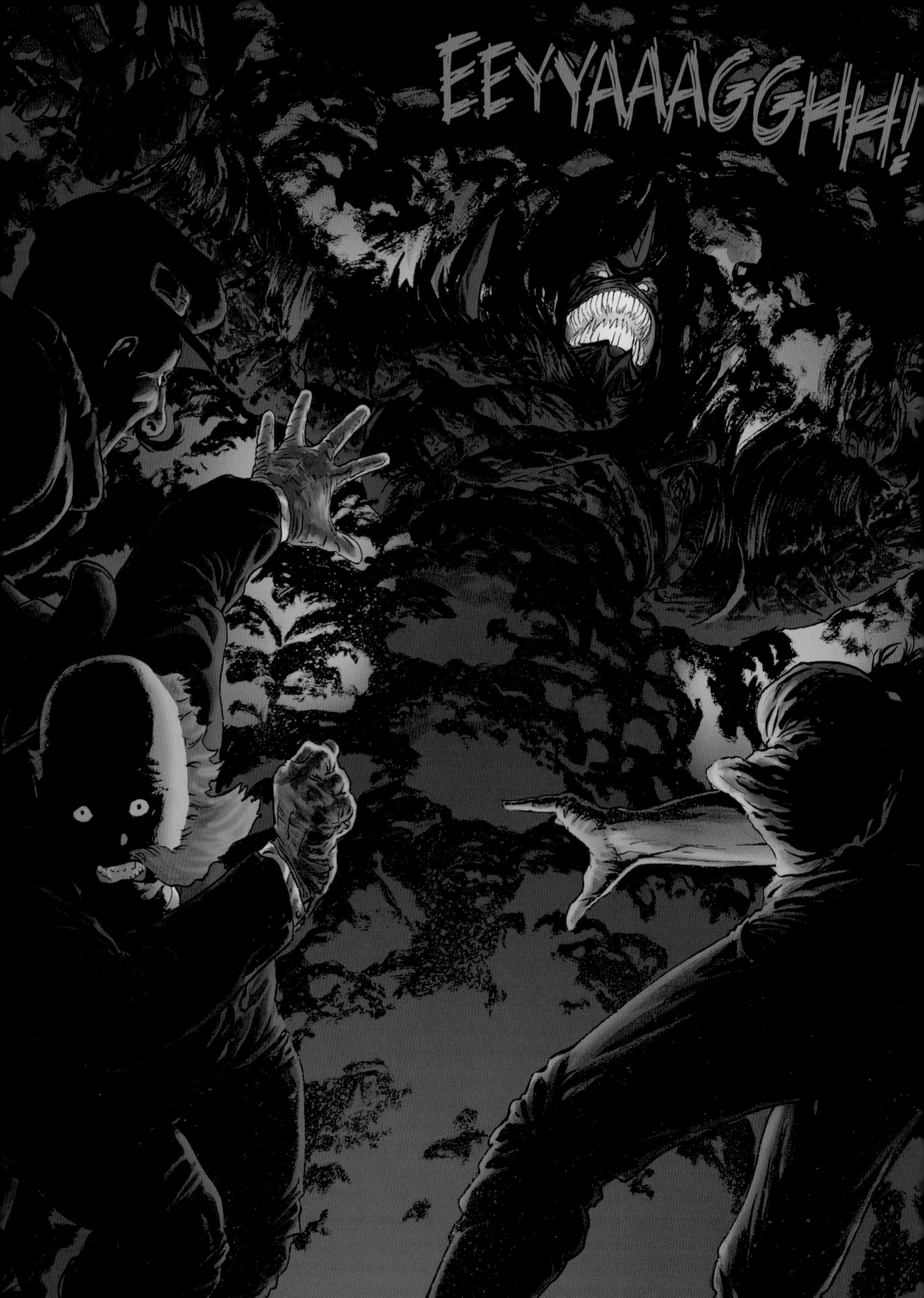
EEYYAAAGGHH!

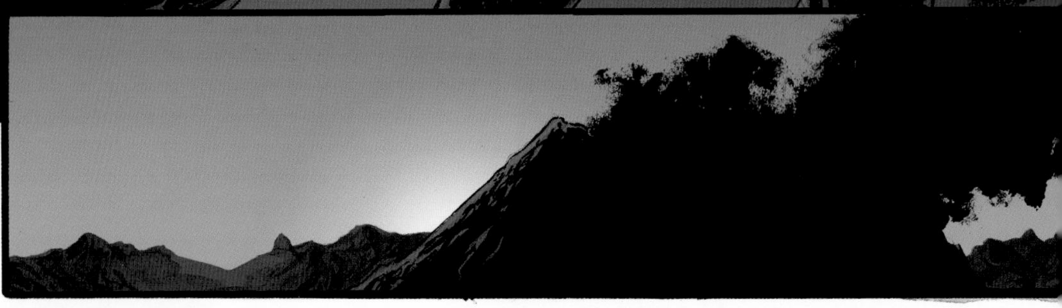

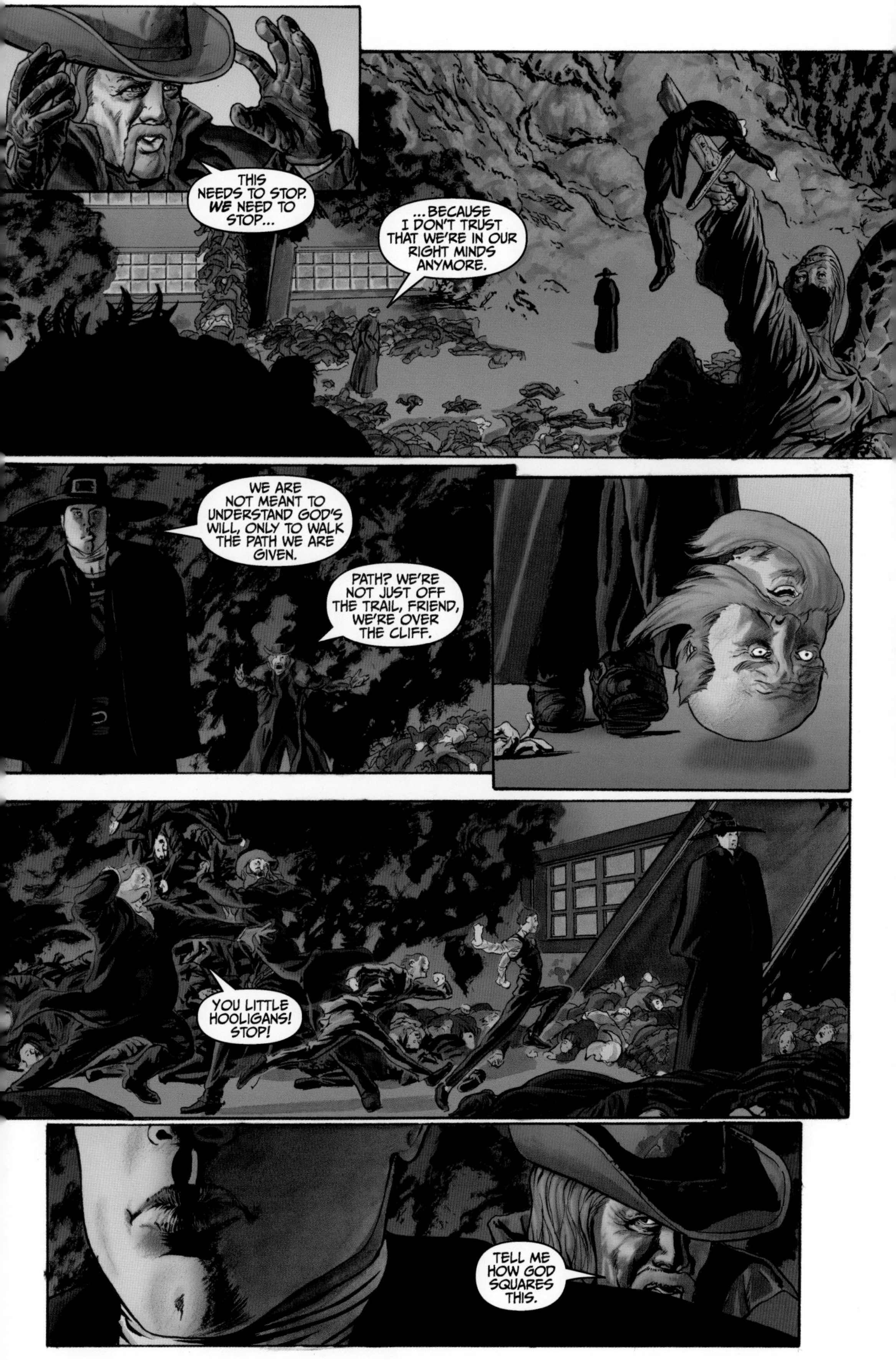
THIS NEEDS TO STOP. WE NEED TO STOP...
...BECAUSE I DON'T TRUST THAT WE'RE IN OUR RIGHT MINDS ANYMORE.
WE ARE NOT MEANT TO UNDERSTAND GOD'S WILL, ONLY TO WALK THE PATH WE ARE GIVEN.
PATH? WE'RE NOT JUST OFF THE TRAIL, FRIEND, WE'RE OVER THE CLIFF.
YOU LITTLE HOOLIGANS! STOP!
TELL ME HOW GOD SQUARES THIS.

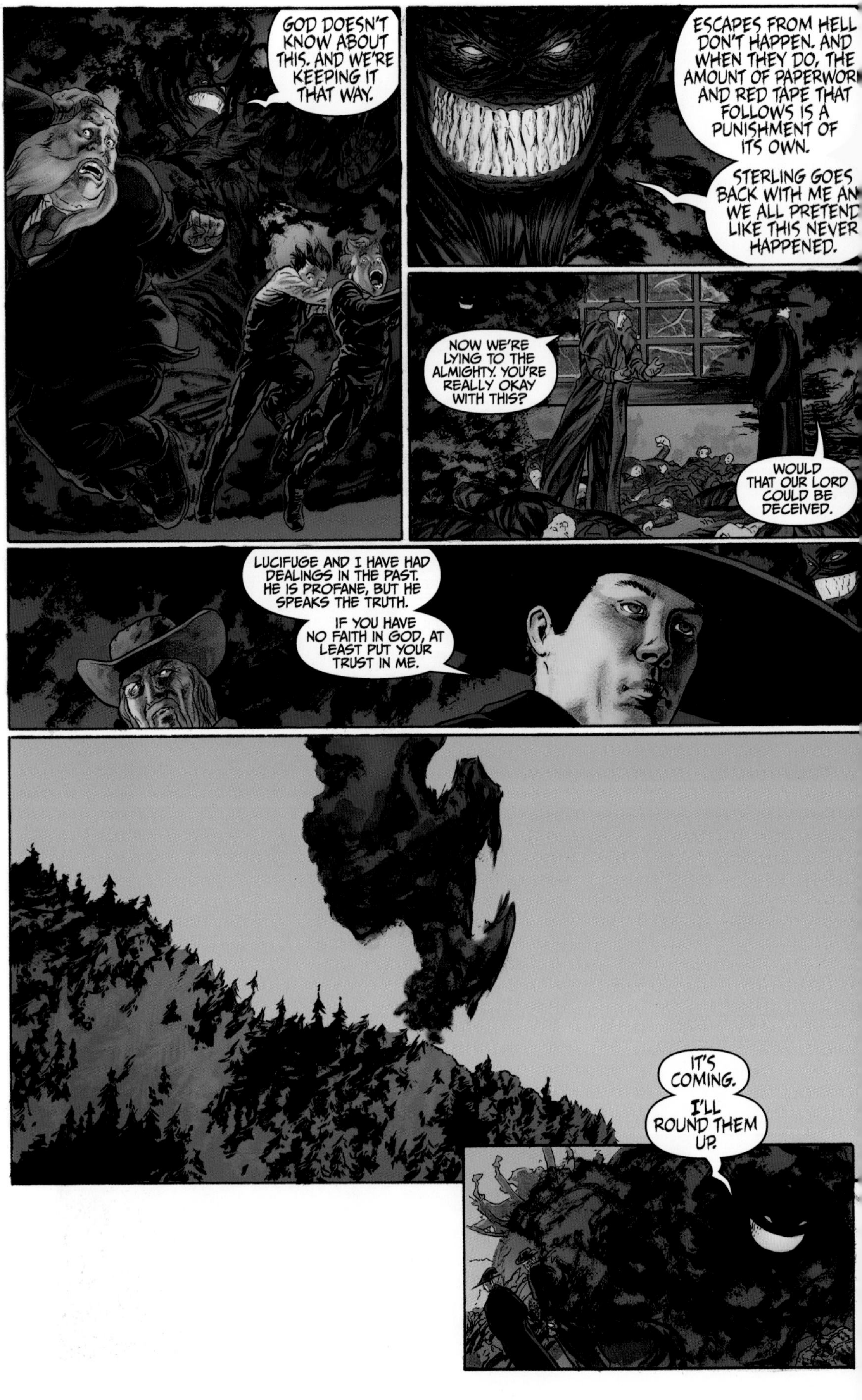
GOD DOESN'T KNOW ABOUT THIS. AND WE'RE KEEPING IT THAT WAY.
ESCAPES FROM HELL DON'T HAPPEN. AND WHEN THEY DO, THE AMOUNT OF PAPERWOR AND RED TAPE THAT FOLLOWS IS A PUNISHMENT OF ITS OWN.
STERLING GOES BACK WITH ME AN WE ALL PRETEND LIKE THIS NEVER HAPPENED.
NOW WE'RE LYING TO THE ALMIGHTY. YOU'RE REALLY OKAY WITH THIS?
WOULD THAT OUR LORD COULD BE DECEIVED.
LUCIFUGE AND I HAVE HAD DEALINGS IN THE PAST. HE IS PROFANE, BUT HE SPEAKS THE TRUTH.
IF YOU HAVE NO FAITH IN GOD, AT LEAST PUT YOUR TRUST IN ME.
IT'S COMING.
I'LL ROUND THEM UP.

REMOVE YOUR COAT AND HAT. LEAVE YOUR SIDEARM BEHIND.

I'M KEEPING MY HAT.

IF YOU ARE RIGHT ABOUT THE R.I.P.D.'S PRESENCE DRIVING AWAY THE MACHINE, WE MUST CONCEAL OUR IDENTITIES.

IF WE HAVE TO SNEAK ABOARD THAT THING, HOW'S LUCIFUGE CATCHING A RIDE?

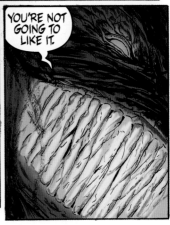

YOU'RE NOT GOING TO LIKE IT.

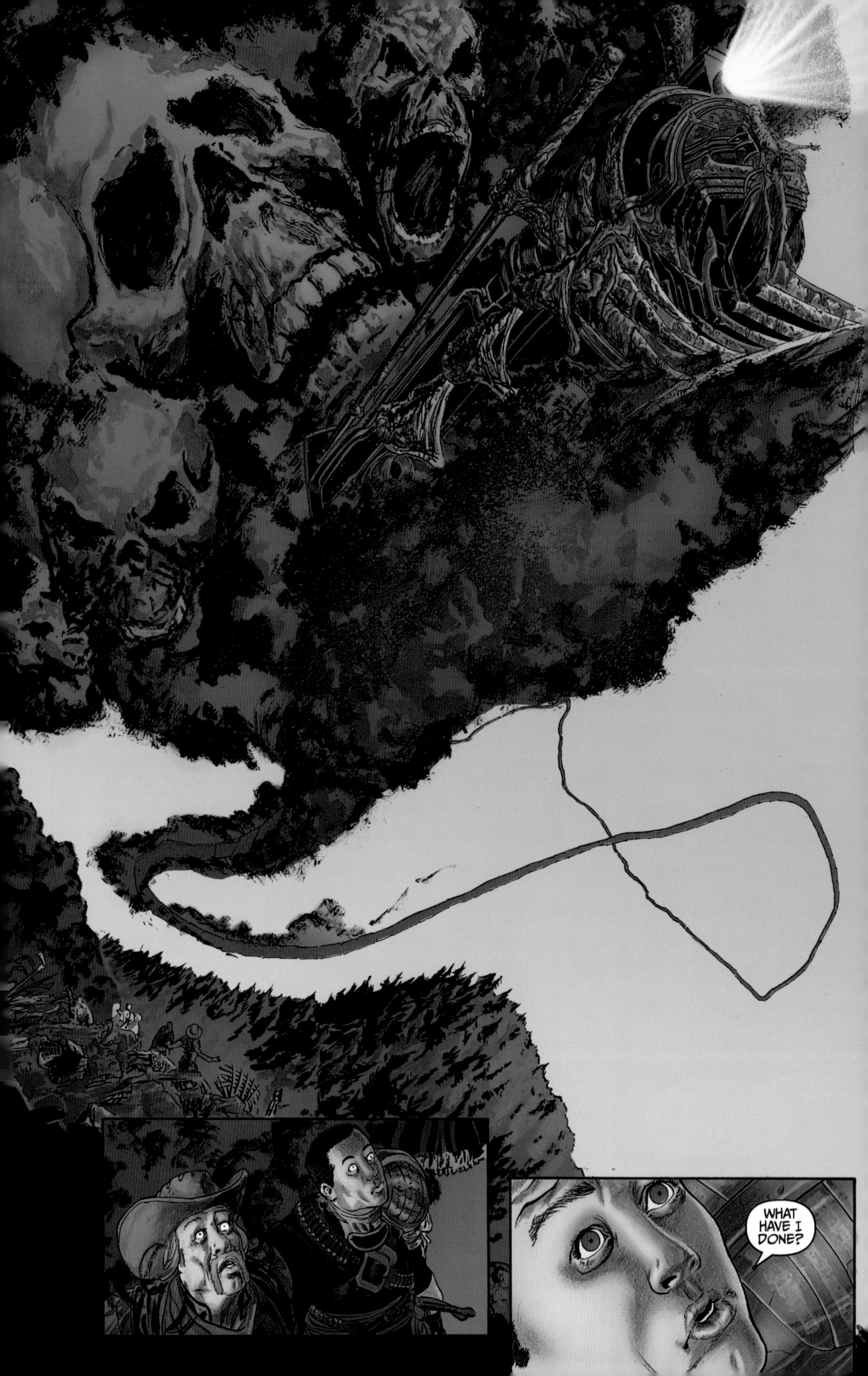
WHAT HAVE I DONE?

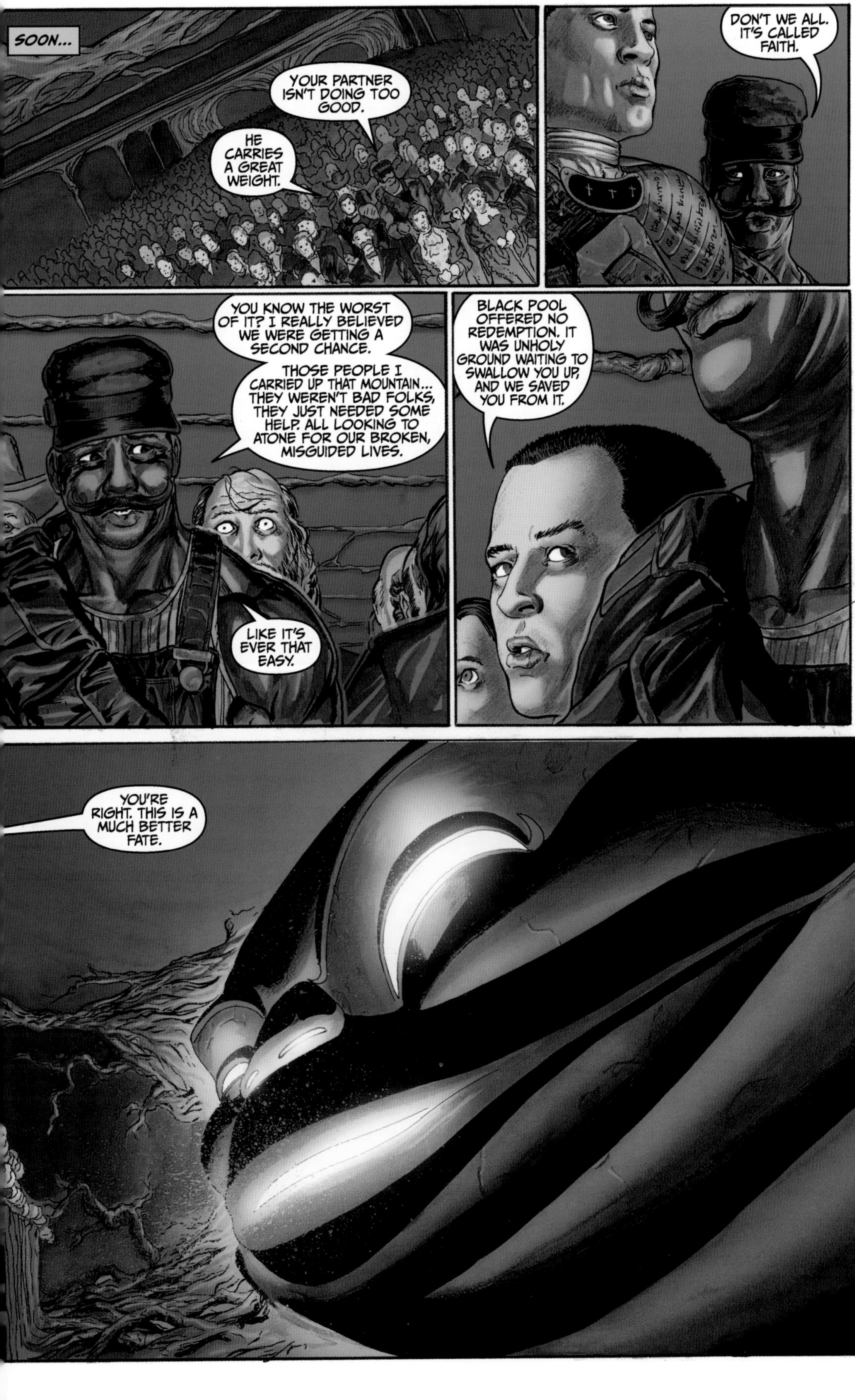
SOON...
YOUR PARTNER ISN'T DOING TOO GOOD.
HE CARRIES A GREAT WEIGHT.
DON'T WE ALL. IT'S CALLED FAITH.
YOU KNOW THE WORST OF IT? I REALLY BELIEVED WE WERE GETTING A SECOND CHANCE.
THOSE PEOPLE I CARRIED UP THAT MOUNTAIN... THEY WEREN'T BAD FOLKS, THEY JUST NEEDED SOME HELP. ALL LOOKING TO ATONE FOR OUR BROKEN, MISGUIDED LIVES.
LIKE IT'S EVER THAT EASY.
BLACK POOL OFFERED NO REDEMPTION. IT WAS UNHOLY GROUND WAITING TO SWALLOW YOU UP, AND WE SAVED YOU FROM IT.
YOU'RE RIGHT. THIS IS A MUCH BETTER FATE.

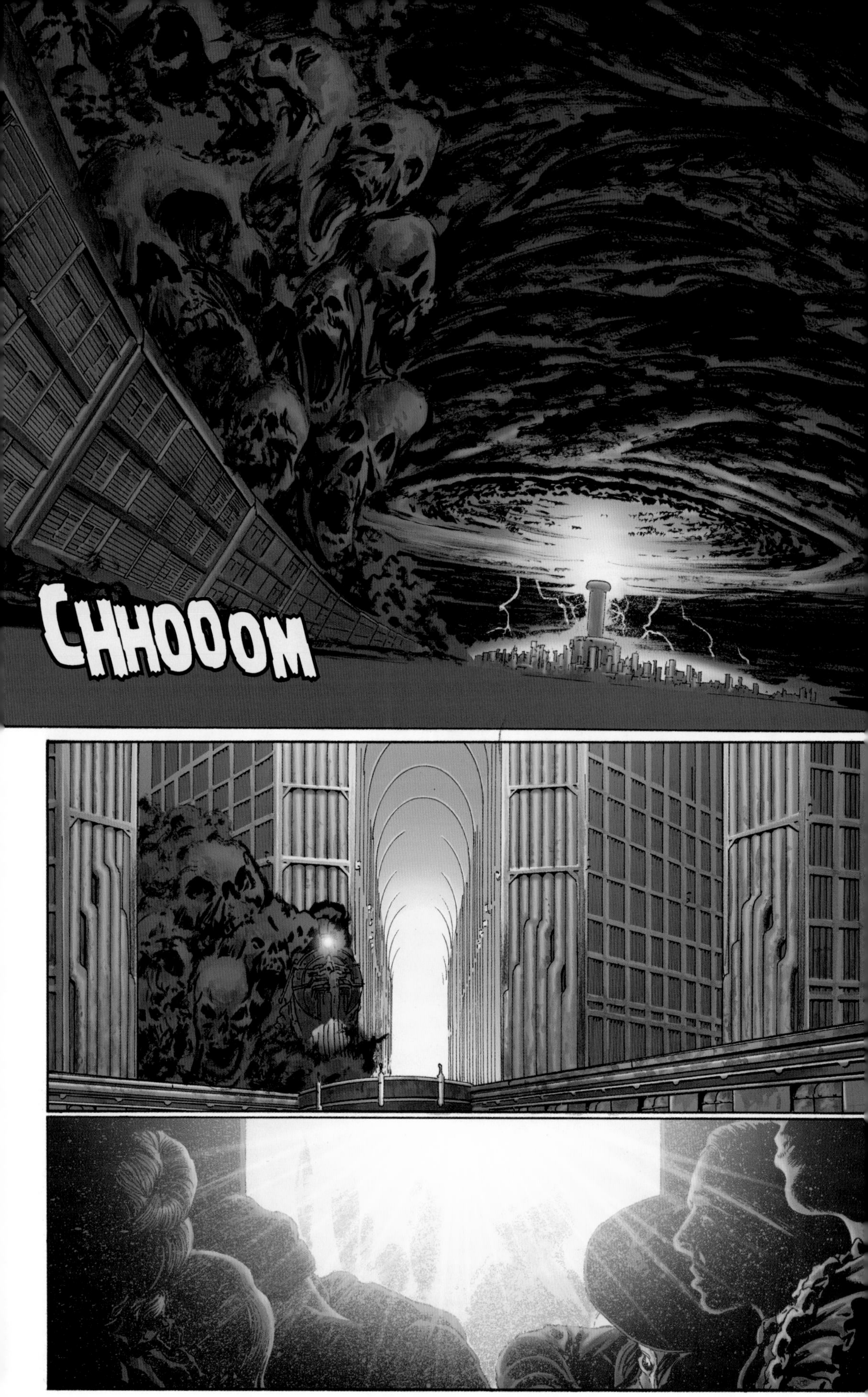
CHHOOOM

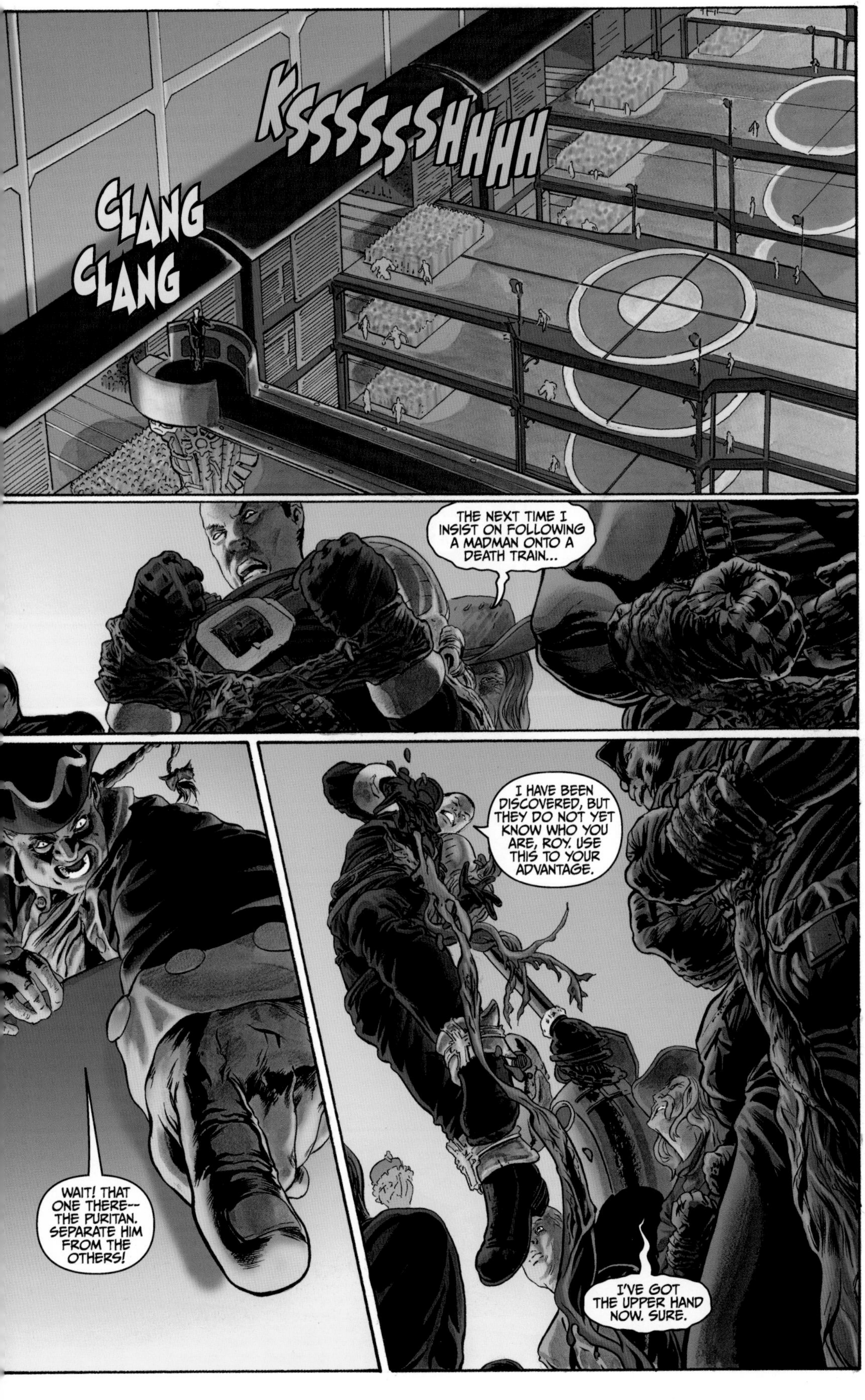
KSSSSSHHHH
CLANG CLANG
THE NEXT TIME I INSIST ON FOLLOWING A MADMAN ONTO A DEATH TRAIN...
WAIT! THAT ONE THERE-- THE PURITAN. SEPARATE HIM FROM THE OTHERS!
I HAVE BEEN DISCOVERED, BUT THEY DO NOT YET KNOW WHO YOU ARE, ROY. USE THIS TO YOUR ADVANTAGE.
I'VE GOT THE UPPER HAND NOW. SURE.

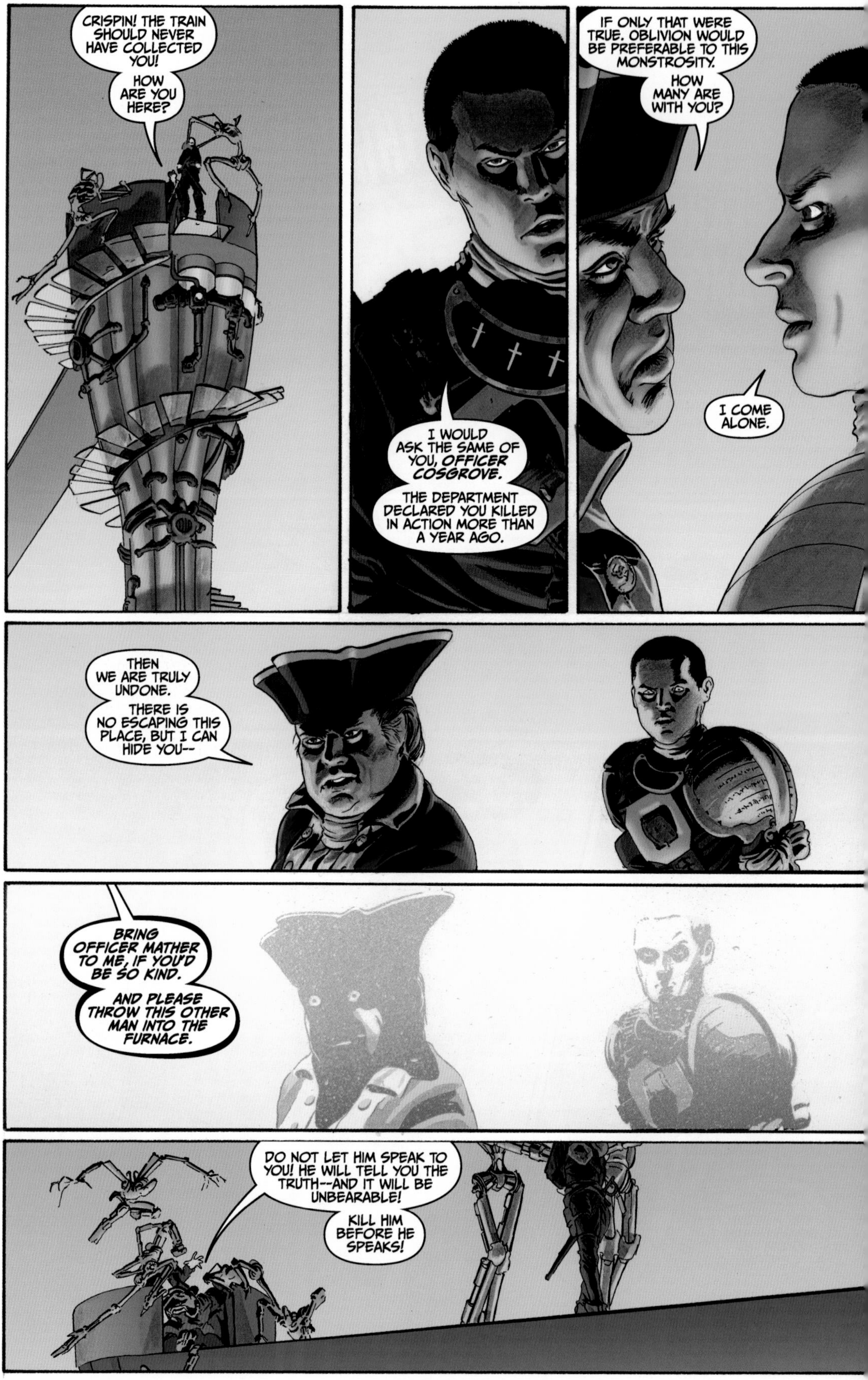
CRISPIN! THE TRAIN SHOULD NEVER HAVE COLLECTED YOU!
HOW ARE YOU HERE?
I WOULD ASK THE SAME OF YOU, *OFFICER COSGROVE.*
THE DEPARTMENT DECLARED YOU KILLED IN ACTION MORE THAN A YEAR AGO.
IF ONLY THAT WERE TRUE. OBLIVION WOULD BE PREFERABLE TO THIS MONSTROSITY.
HOW MANY ARE WITH YOU?
I COME ALONE.
THEN WE ARE TRULY UNDONE.
THERE IS NO ESCAPING THIS PLACE, BUT I CAN HIDE YOU--
BRING OFFICER MATHER TO ME, IF YOU'D BE SO KIND.
AND PLEASE THROW THIS OTHER MAN INTO THE FURNACE.
DO NOT LET HIM SPEAK TO YOU! HE WILL TELL YOU THE TRUTH--AND IT WILL BE UNBEARABLE!
KILL HIM BEFORE HE SPEAKS!

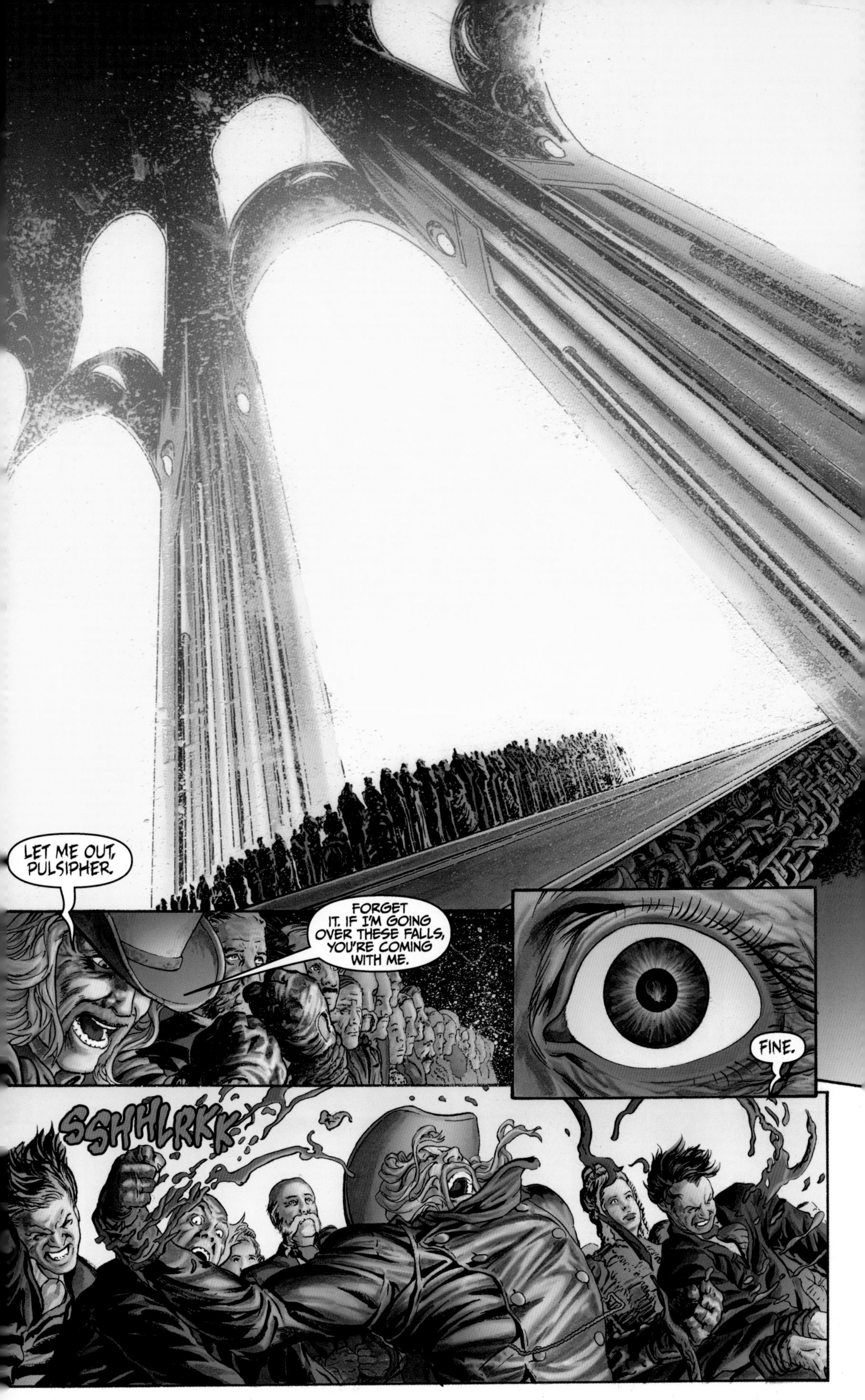
LET ME OUT, PULSIPHER.
FORGET IT. IF I'M GOING OVER THESE FALLS, YOU'RE COMING WITH ME.
FINE.
SSHHLRKK

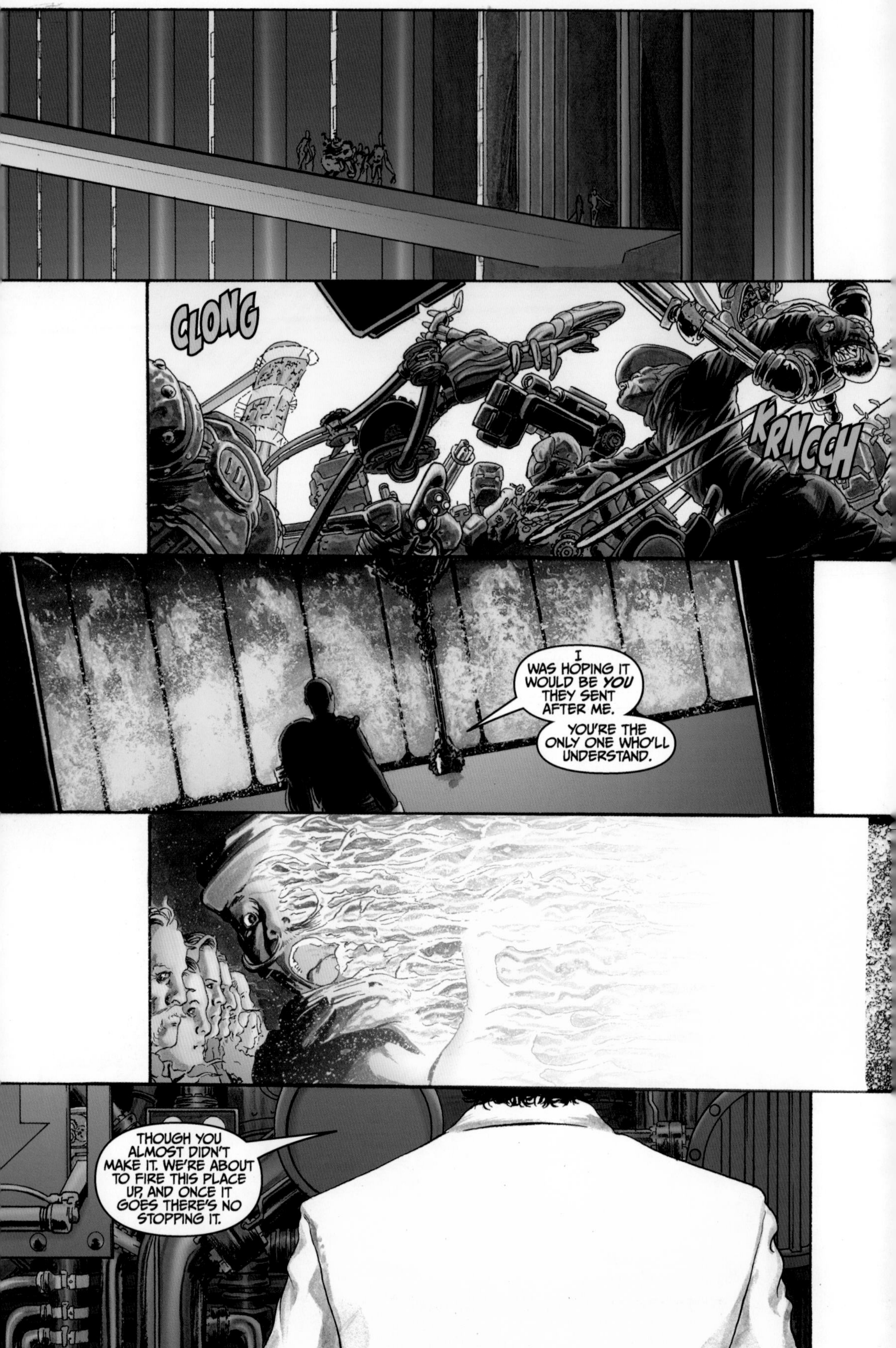

CLONG
KRNCCH
I WAS HOPING IT WOULD BE *YOU* THEY SENT AFTER ME.
YOU'RE THE ONLY ONE WHO'LL UNDERSTAND.
THOUGH YOU ALMOST DIDN'T MAKE IT. WE'RE ABOUT TO FIRE THIS PLACE UP, AND ONCE IT GOES THERE'S NO STOPPING IT.

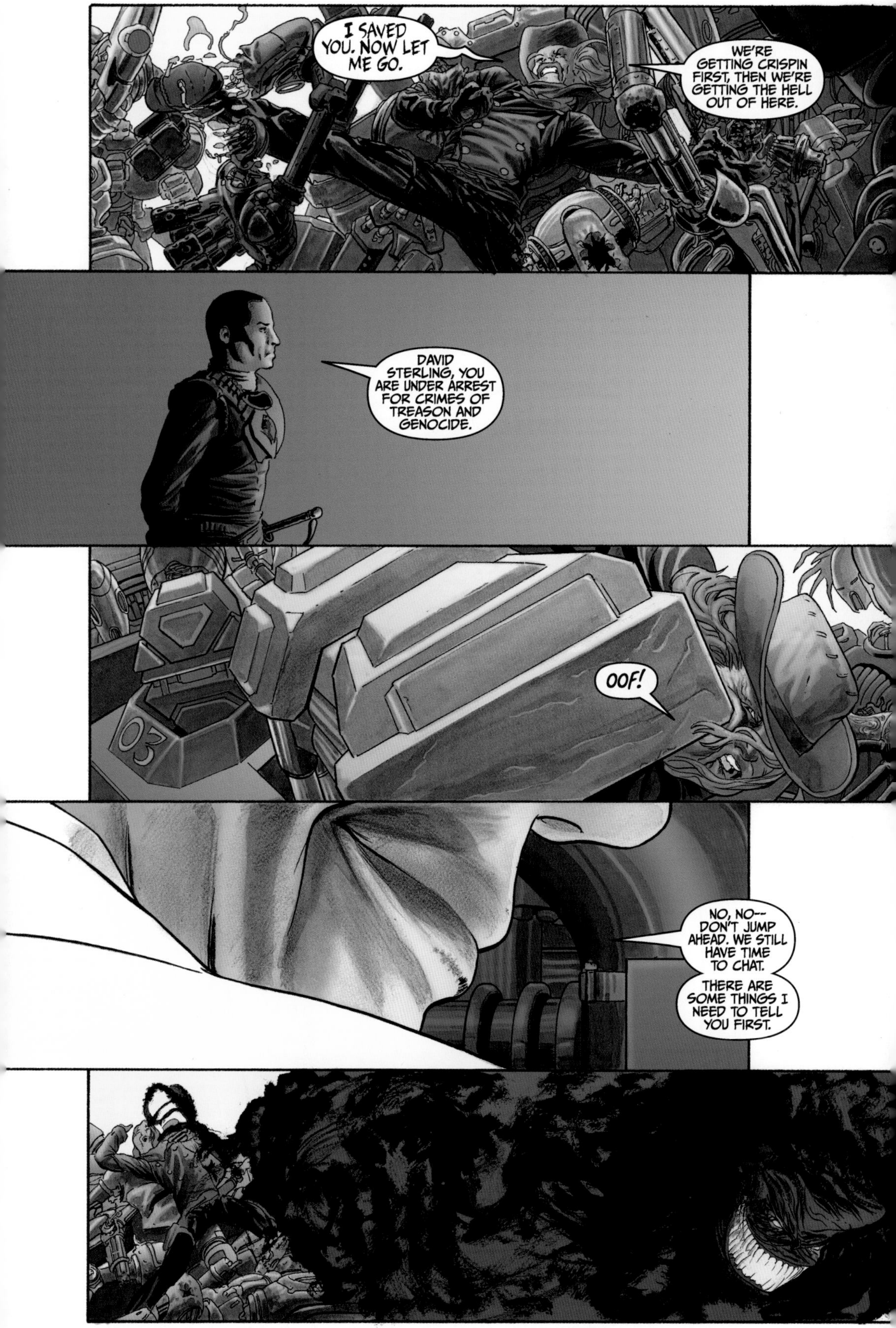

I SAVED YOU. NOW LET ME GO.
WE'RE GETTING CRISPIN FIRST, THEN WE'RE GETTING THE HELL OUT OF HERE.
DAVID STERLING, YOU ARE UNDER ARREST FOR CRIMES OF TREASON AND GENOCIDE.
03
OOF!
NO, NO-- DON'T JUMP AHEAD. WE STILL HAVE TIME TO CHAT.
THERE ARE SOME THINGS I NEED TO TELL YOU FIRST.

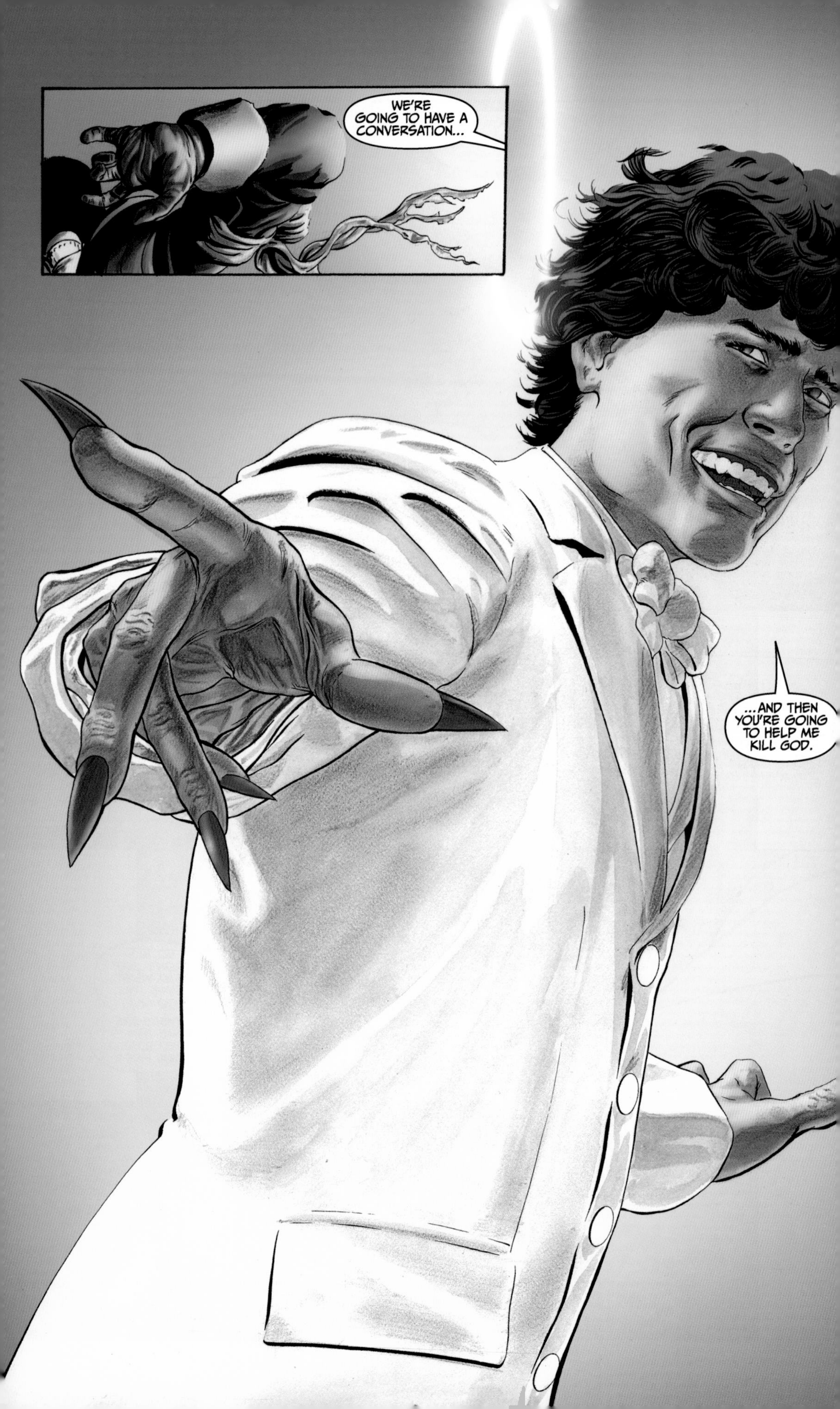
WE'RE GOING TO HAVE A CONVERSATION...
...AND THEN YOU'RE GOING TO HELP ME KILL GOD.

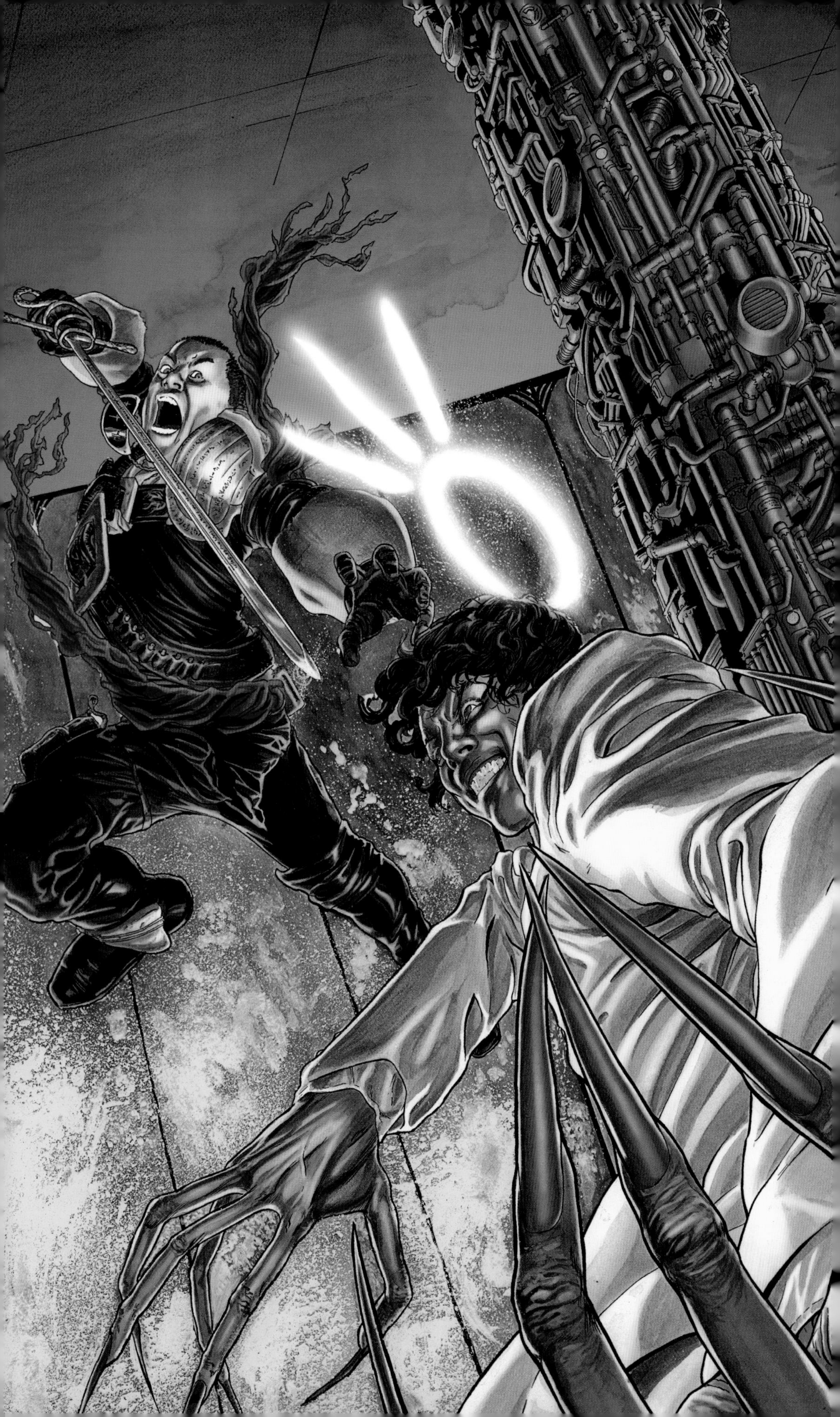

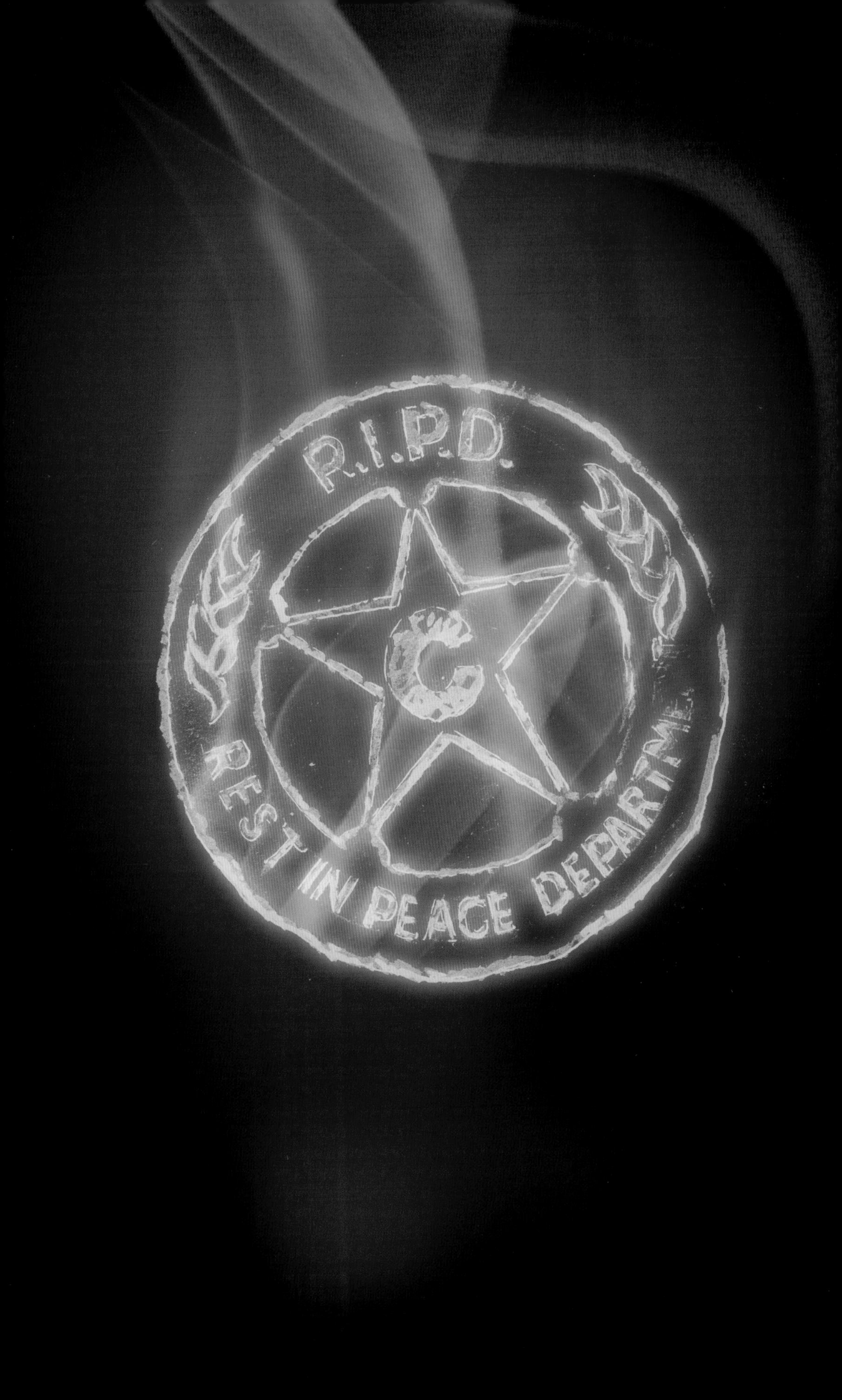
R.I.P.D.
C
REST IN PEACE DEPARTM

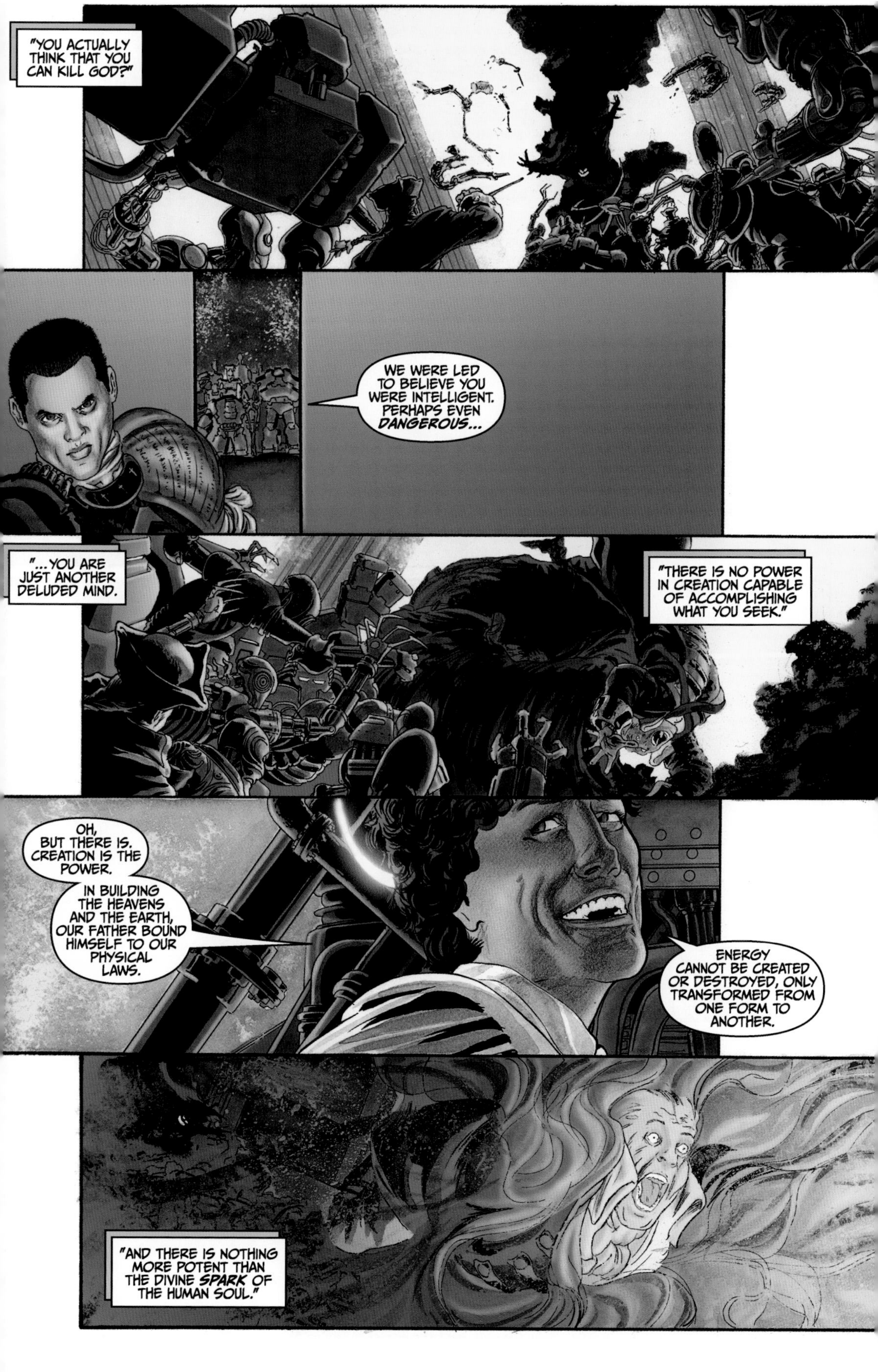
"YOU ACTUALLY THINK THAT YOU CAN KILL GOD?"
WE WERE LED TO BELIEVE YOU WERE INTELLIGENT. PERHAPS EVEN *DANGEROUS*...
"...YOU ARE JUST ANOTHER DELUDED MIND.
"THERE IS NO POWER IN CREATION CAPABLE OF ACCOMPLISHING WHAT YOU SEEK."
OH, BUT THERE IS. CREATION IS THE POWER.
IN BUILDING THE HEAVENS AND THE EARTH, OUR FATHER BOUND HIMSELF TO OUR PHYSICAL LAWS.
ENERGY CANNOT BE CREATED OR DESTROYED, ONLY TRANSFORMED FROM ONE FORM TO ANOTHER.
"AND THERE IS NOTHING MORE POTENT THAN THE DIVINE *SPARK* OF THE HUMAN SOUL."

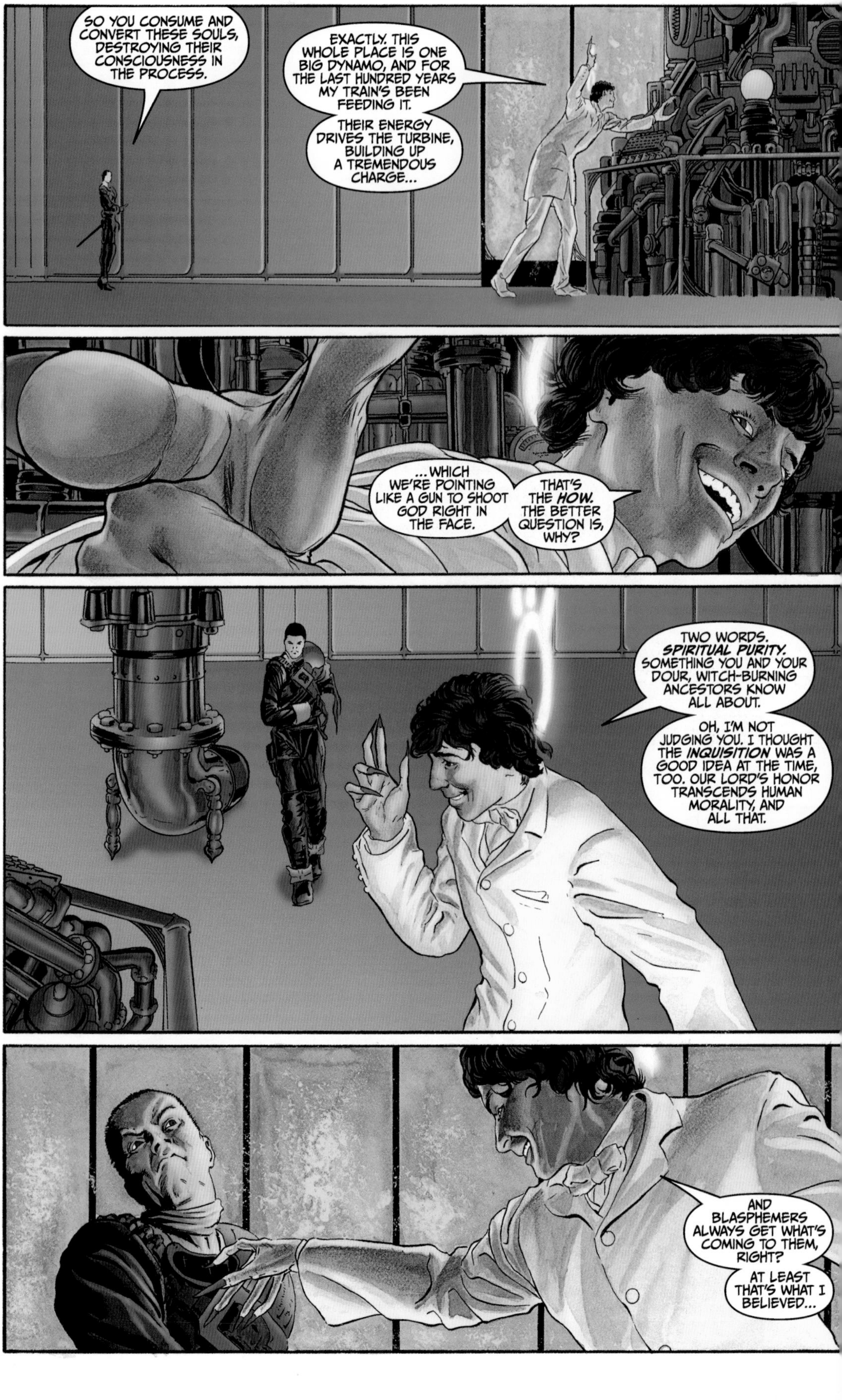
SO YOU CONSUME AND CONVERT THESE SOULS, DESTROYING THEIR CONSCIOUSNESS IN THE PROCESS.
EXACTLY. THIS WHOLE PLACE IS ONE BIG DYNAMO, AND FOR THE LAST HUNDRED YEARS MY TRAIN'S BEEN FEEDING IT.
THEIR ENERGY DRIVES THE TURBINE, BUILDING UP A TREMENDOUS CHARGE...
...WHICH WE'RE POINTING LIKE A GUN TO SHOOT GOD RIGHT IN THE FACE.
THAT'S THE *HOW*. THE BETTER QUESTION IS, WHY?
TWO WORDS. ***SPIRITUAL PURITY.*** SOMETHING YOU AND YOUR DOUR, WITCH-BURNING ANCESTORS KNOW ALL ABOUT.
OH, I'M NOT JUDGING YOU. I THOUGHT THE ***INQUISITION*** WAS A GOOD IDEA AT THE TIME, TOO. OUR LORD'S HONOR TRANSCENDS HUMAN MORALITY, AND ALL THAT.
AND BLASPHEMERS ALWAYS GET WHAT'S COMING TO THEM, RIGHT?
AT LEAST THAT'S WHAT I BELIEVED...

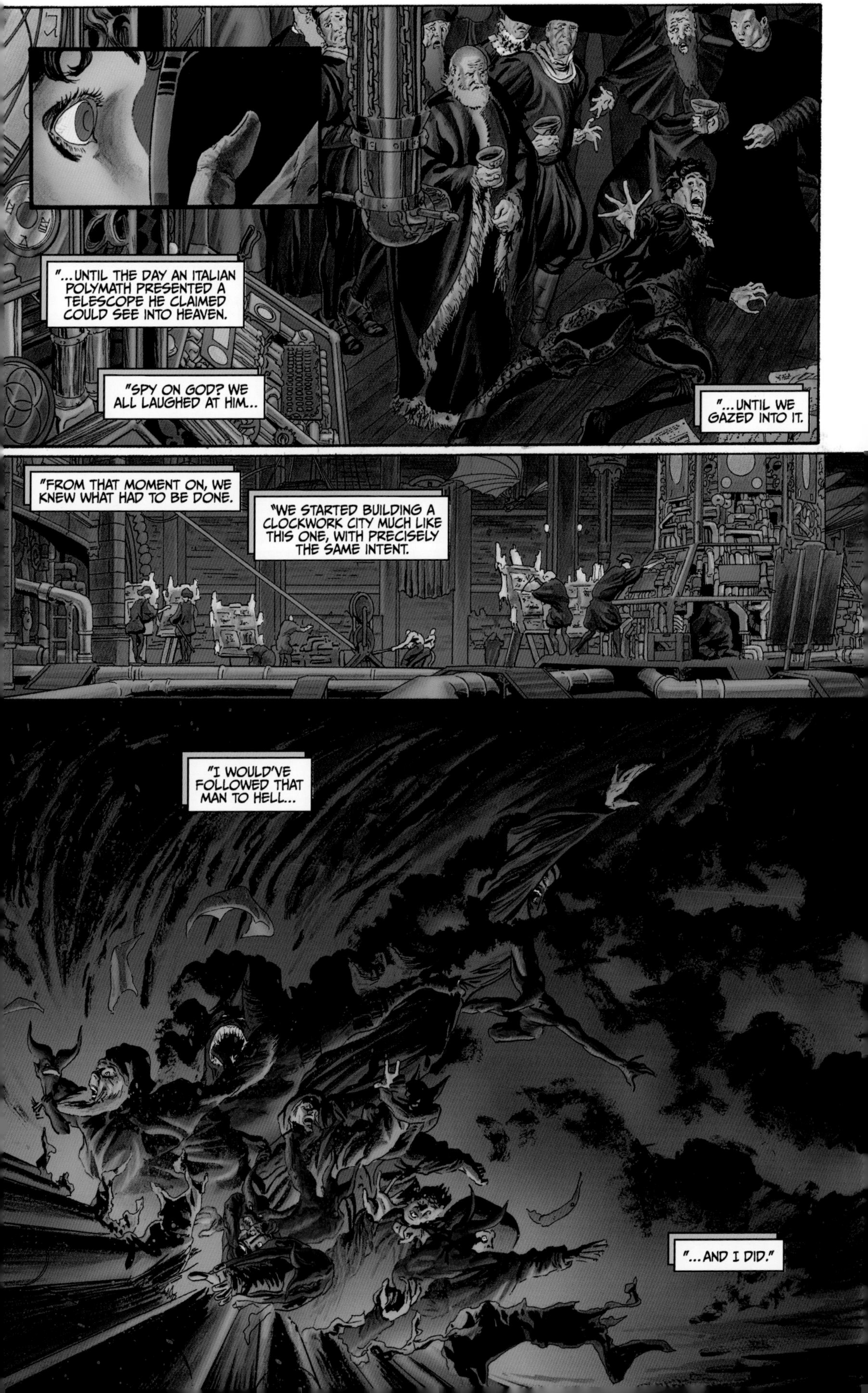
"...UNTIL THE DAY AN ITALIAN POLYMATH PRESENTED A TELESCOPE HE CLAIMED COULD SEE INTO HEAVEN.
"SPY ON GOD? WE ALL LAUGHED AT HIM...
"...UNTIL WE GAZED INTO IT.
"FROM THAT MOMENT ON, WE KNEW WHAT HAD TO BE DONE.
"WE STARTED BUILDING A CLOCKWORK CITY MUCH LIKE THIS ONE, WITH PRECISELY THE SAME INTENT.
"I WOULD'VE FOLLOWED THAT MAN TO HELL...
"...AND I DID."

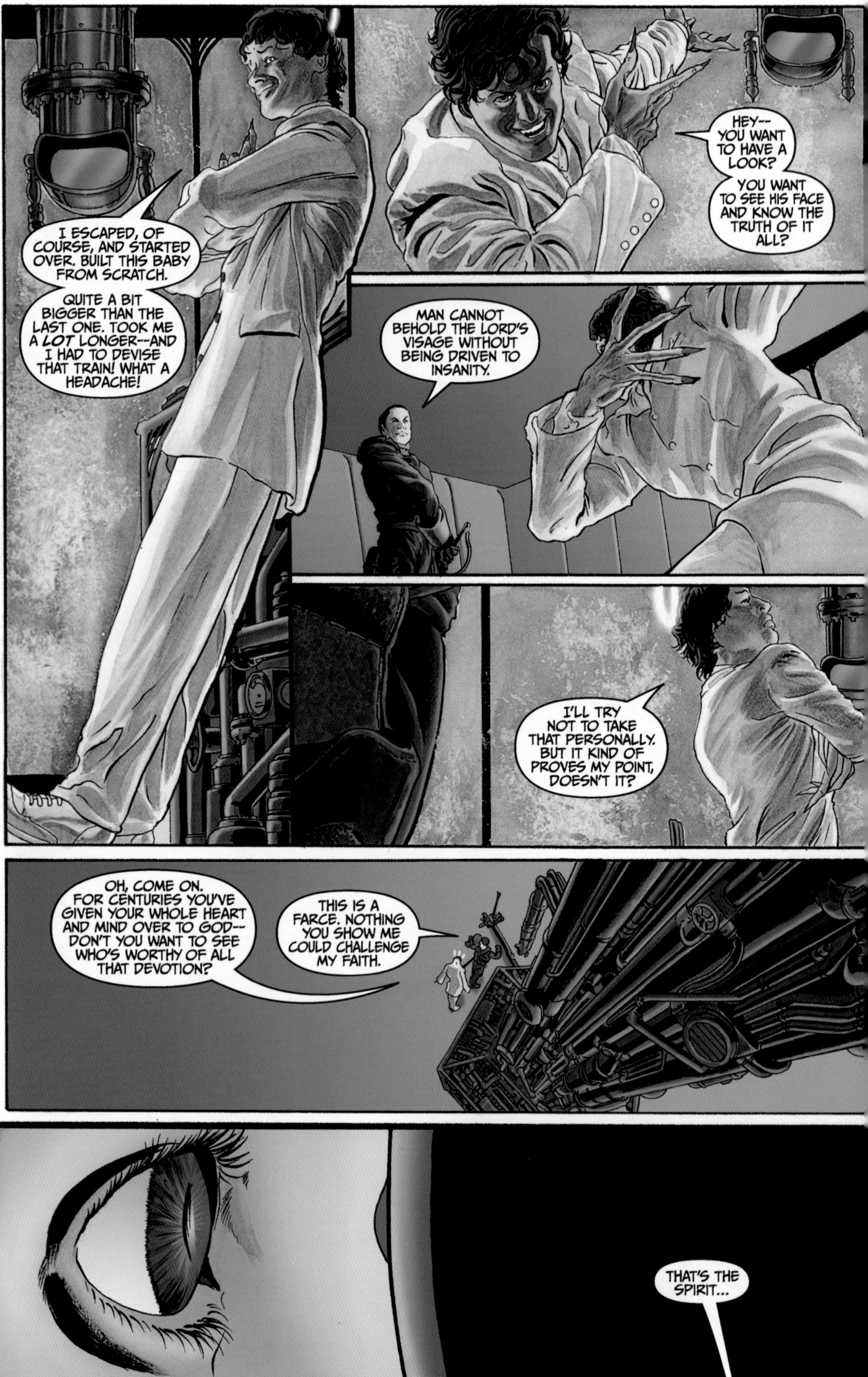
I ESCAPED, OF COURSE, AND STARTED OVER. BUILT THIS BABY FROM SCRATCH.
QUITE A BIT BIGGER THAN THE LAST ONE. TOOK ME A *LOT* LONGER--AND I HAD TO DEVISE THAT TRAIN! WHAT A HEADACHE!
HEY-- YOU WANT TO HAVE A LOOK?
YOU WANT TO SEE HIS FACE AND KNOW THE TRUTH OF IT ALL?
MAN CANNOT BEHOLD THE LORD'S VISAGE WITHOUT BEING DRIVEN TO INSANITY.
I'LL TRY NOT TO TAKE THAT PERSONALLY. BUT IT KIND OF PROVES MY POINT, DOESN'T IT?
OH, COME ON. FOR CENTURIES YOU'VE GIVEN YOUR WHOLE HEART AND MIND OVER TO GOD-- DON'T YOU WANT TO SEE WHO'S WORTHY OF ALL THAT DEVOTION?
THIS IS A FARCE. NOTHING YOU SHOW ME COULD CHALLENGE MY FAITH.
THAT'S THE SPIRIT...

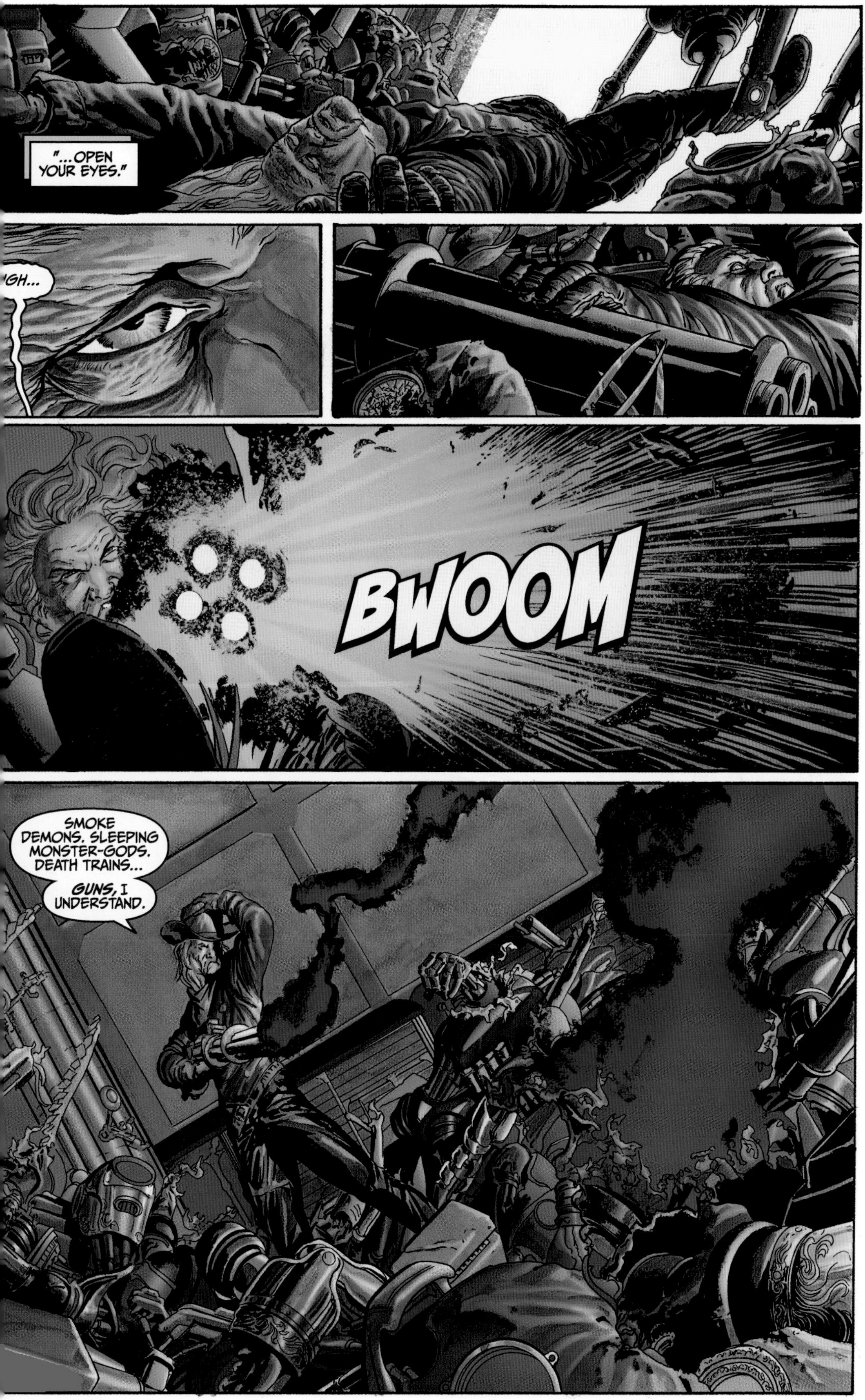
"...OPEN YOUR EYES."
GH...
BWOOM
SMOKE DEMONS. SLEEPING MONSTER-GODS. DEATH TRAINS...
GUNS, I UNDERSTAND.

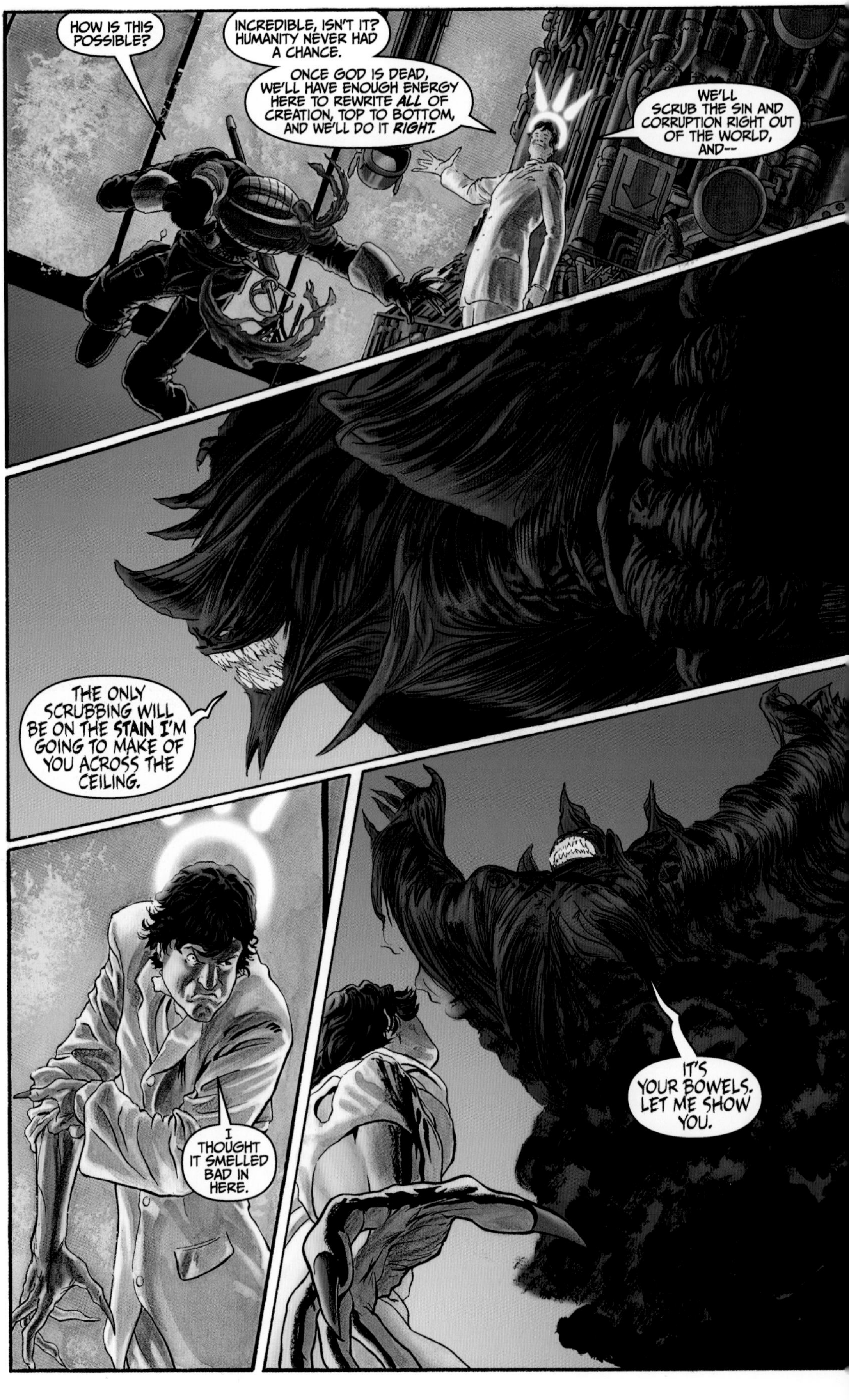
HOW IS THIS POSSIBLE?
INCREDIBLE, ISN'T IT? HUMANITY NEVER HAD A CHANCE.
ONCE GOD IS DEAD, WE'LL HAVE ENOUGH ENERGY HERE TO REWRITE ALL OF CREATION, TOP TO BOTTOM, AND WE'LL DO IT RIGHT.
WE'LL SCRUB THE SIN AND CORRUPTION RIGHT OUT OF THE WORLD, AND--
THE ONLY SCRUBBING WILL BE ON THE STAIN I'M GOING TO MAKE OF YOU ACROSS THE CEILING.
I THOUGHT IT SMELLED BAD IN HERE.
IT'S YOUR BOWELS. LET ME SHOW YOU.

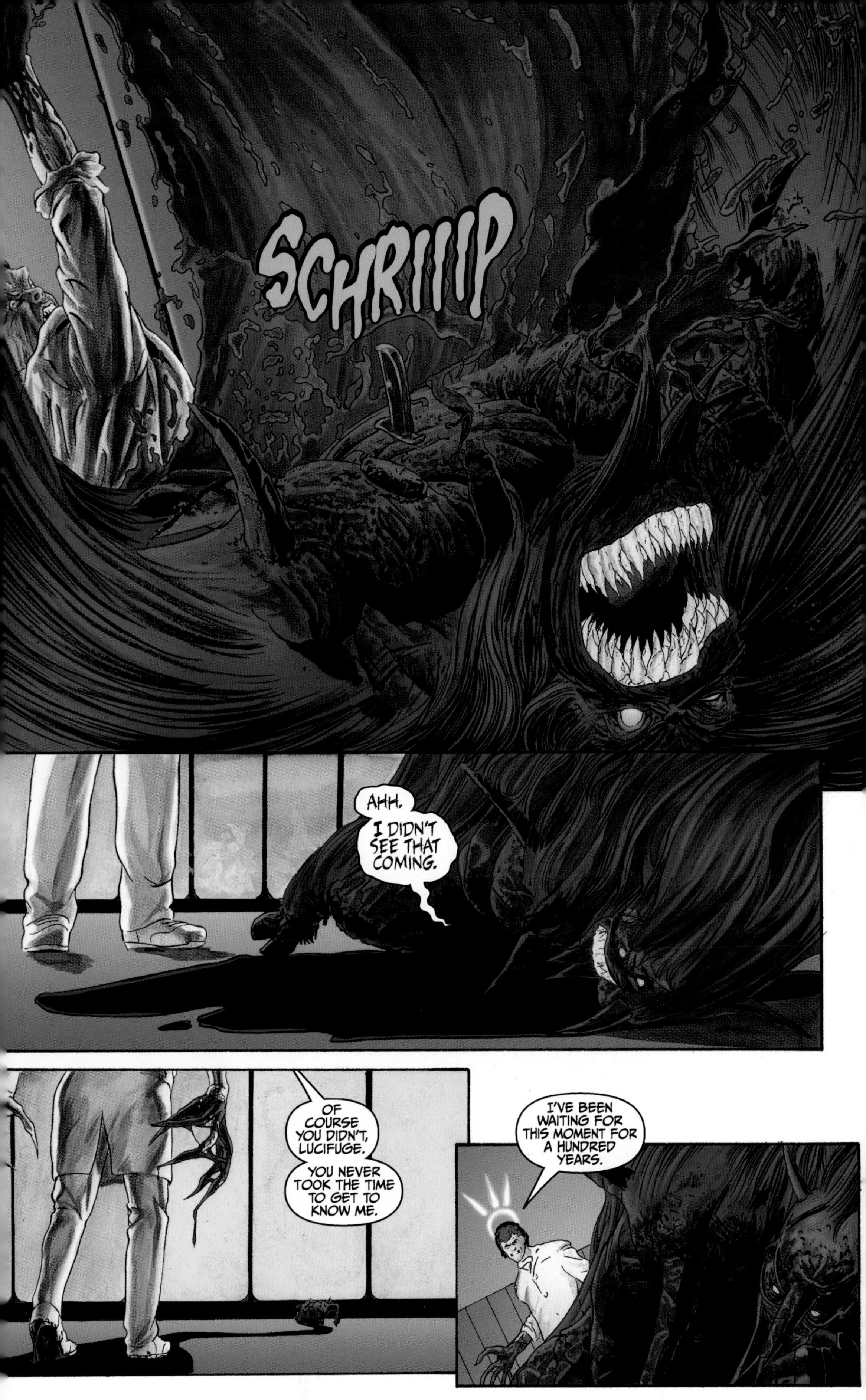
SCHRIIIP
AHH.
I DIDN'T SEE THAT COMING.
OF COURSE YOU DIDN'T, LUCIFUGE.
YOU NEVER TOOK THE TIME TO GET TO KNOW ME.
I'VE BEEN WAITING FOR THIS MOMENT FOR A HUNDRED YEARS.

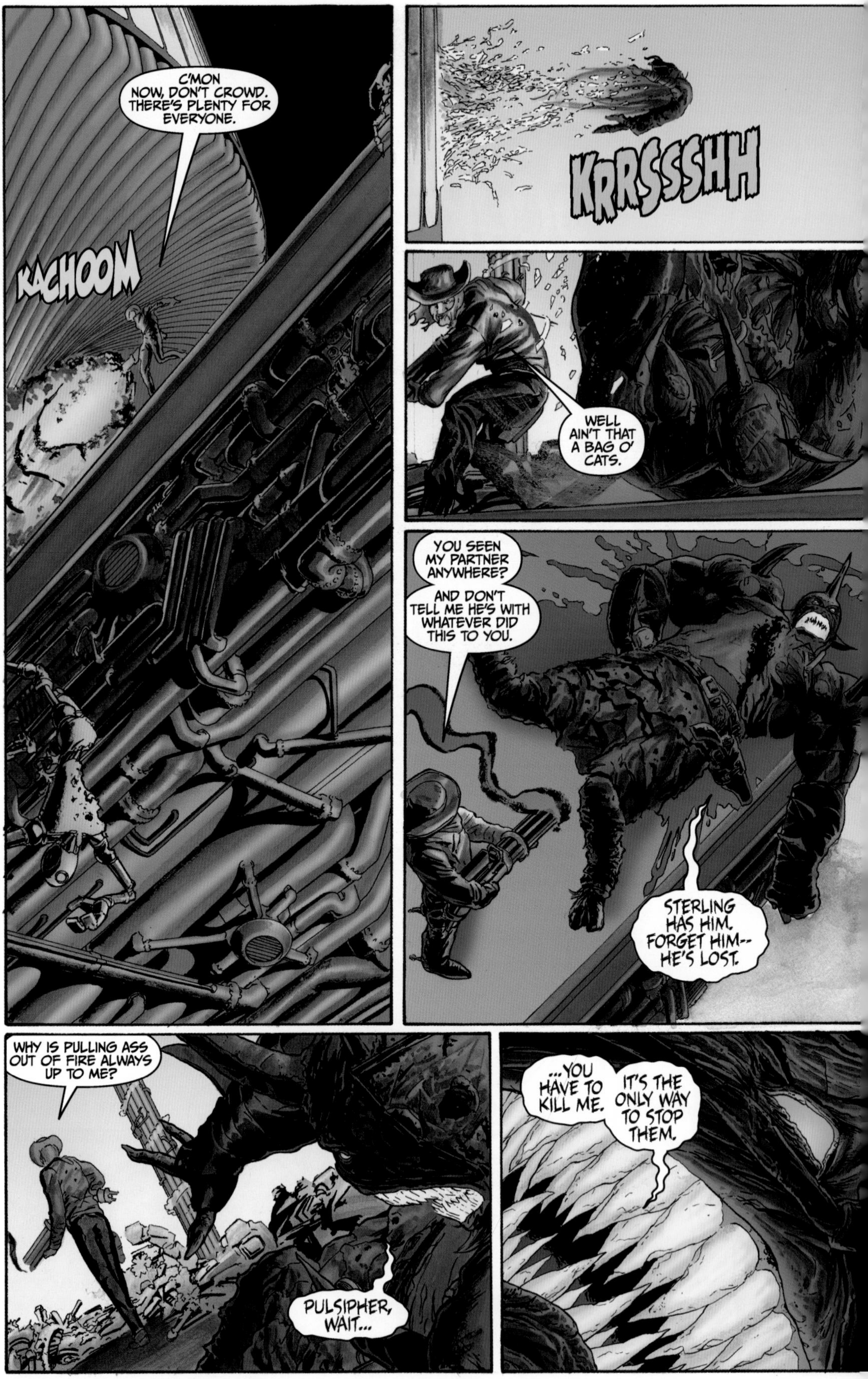
C'MON NOW, DON'T CROWD. THERE'S PLENTY FOR EVERYONE.
KACHOOM
KRRSSSHH
WELL AIN'T THAT A BAG O' CATS.
YOU SEEN MY PARTNER ANYWHERE?
AND DON'T TELL ME HE'S WITH WHATEVER DID THIS TO YOU.
STERLING HAS HIM. FORGET HIM-- HE'S LOST.
WHY IS PULLING ASS OUT OF FIRE ALWAYS UP TO ME?
PULSIPHER, WAIT...
...YOU HAVE TO KILL ME.
IT'S THE ONLY WAY TO STOP THEM.

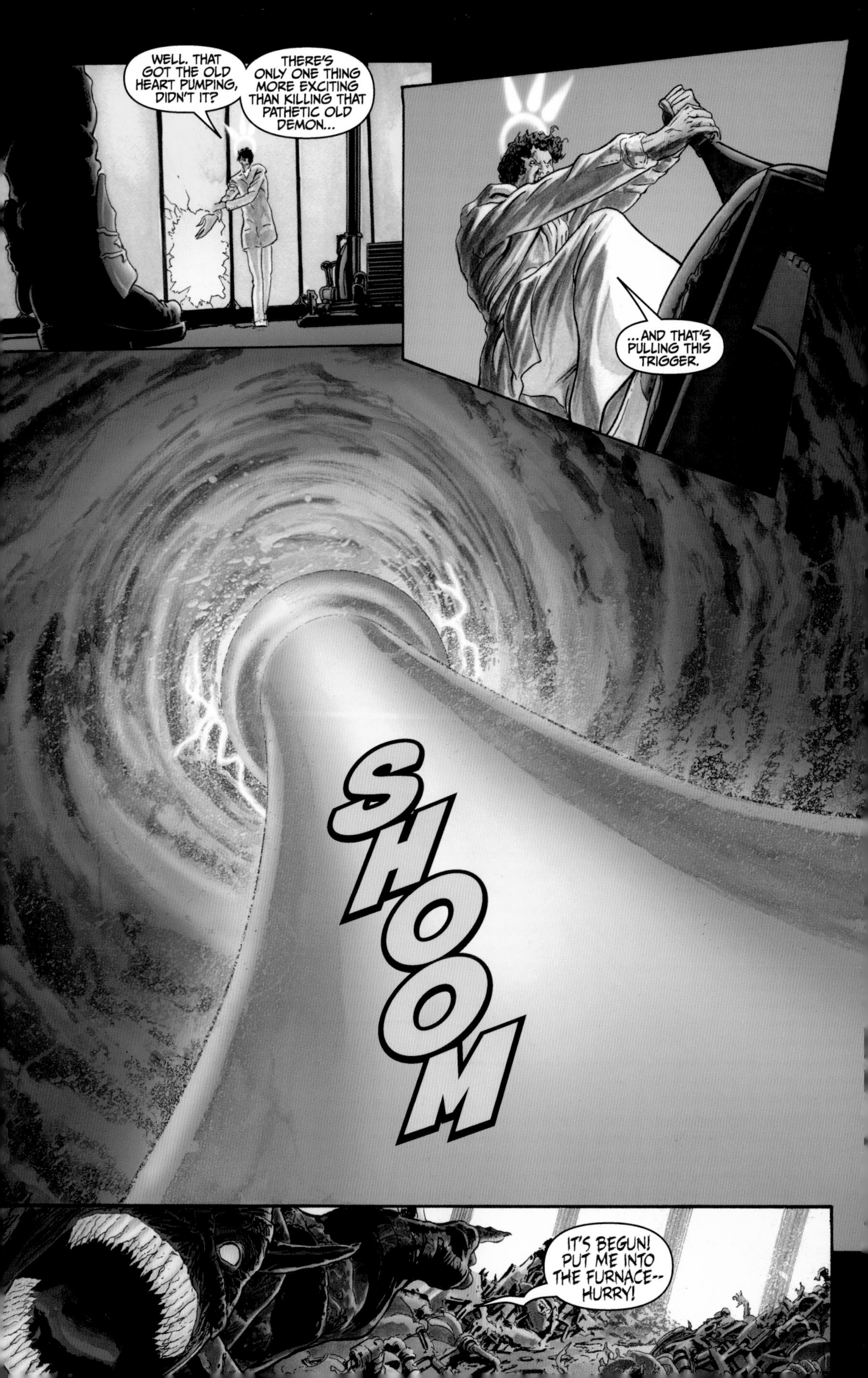
WELL. THAT GOT THE OLD HEART PUMPING, DIDN'T IT?
THERE'S ONLY ONE THING MORE EXCITING THAN KILLING THAT PATHETIC OLD DEMON...
...AND THAT'S PULLING THIS TRIGGER.
SHOOM
IT'S BEGUN! PUT ME INTO THE FURNACE-- HURRY!

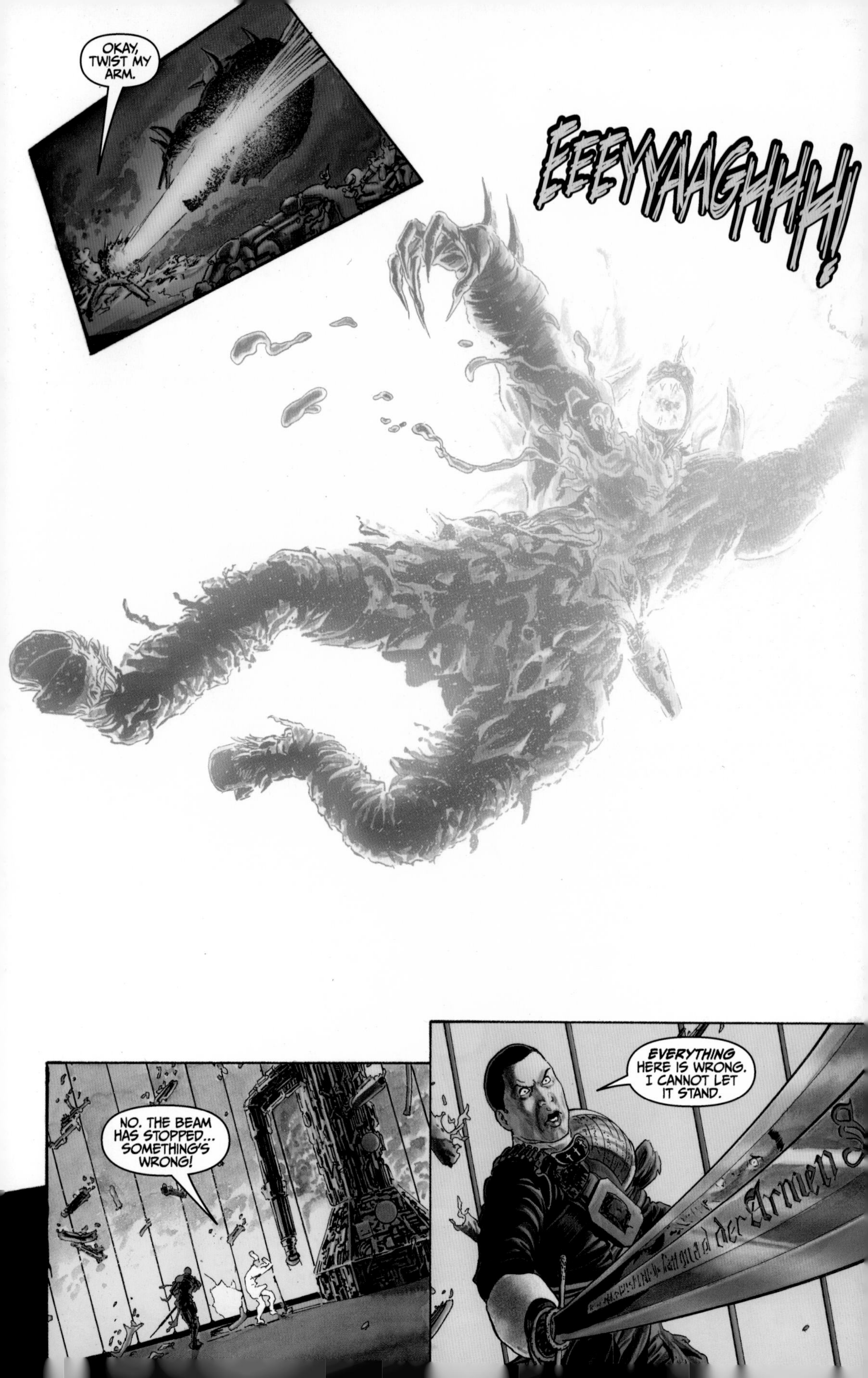
OKAY, TWIST MY ARM.
EEEYYAAGHHHH!
NO. THE BEAM HAS STOPPED... SOMETHING'S WRONG!
EVERYTHING HERE IS WRONG. I CANNOT LET IT STAND.

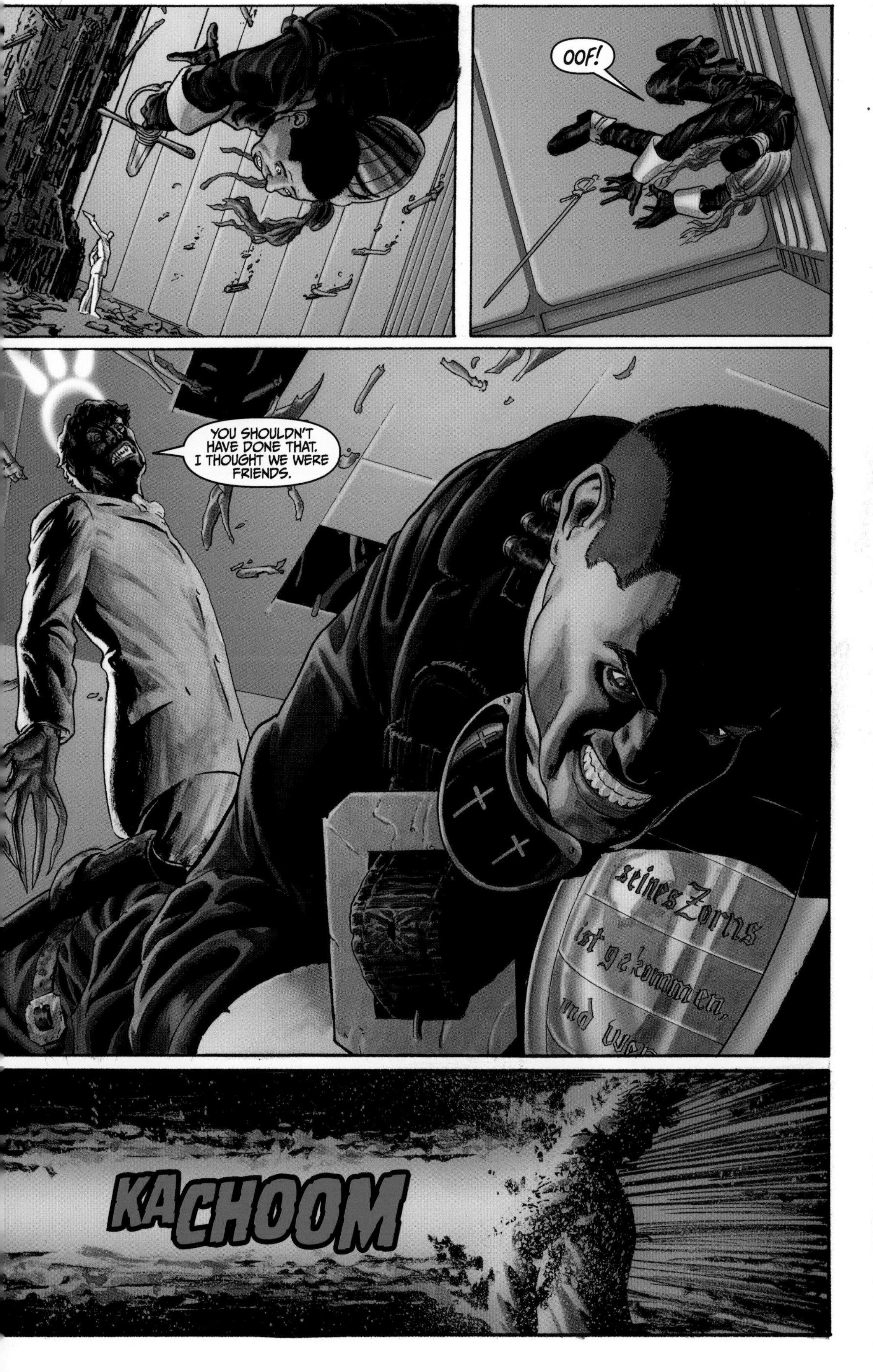
OOF!
YOU SHOULDN'T HAVE DONE THAT. I THOUGHT WE WERE FRIENDS.
seines Zorns
ist gekommen,
KACHOOM

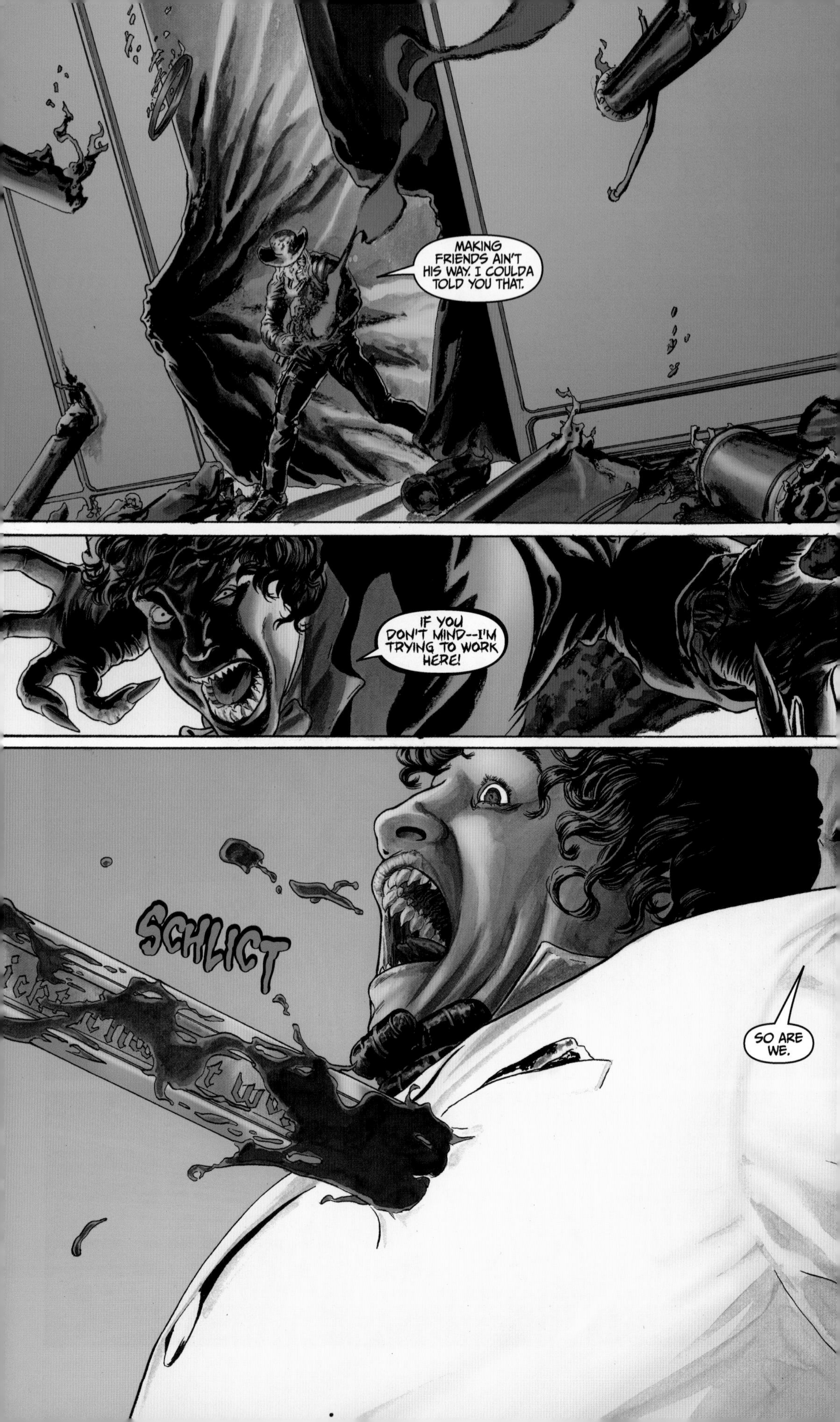
MAKING FRIENDS AIN'T HIS WAY. I COULDA TOLD YOU THAT.
IF YOU DON'T MIND--I'M TRYING TO WORK HERE!
SCHLICT
SO ARE WE.

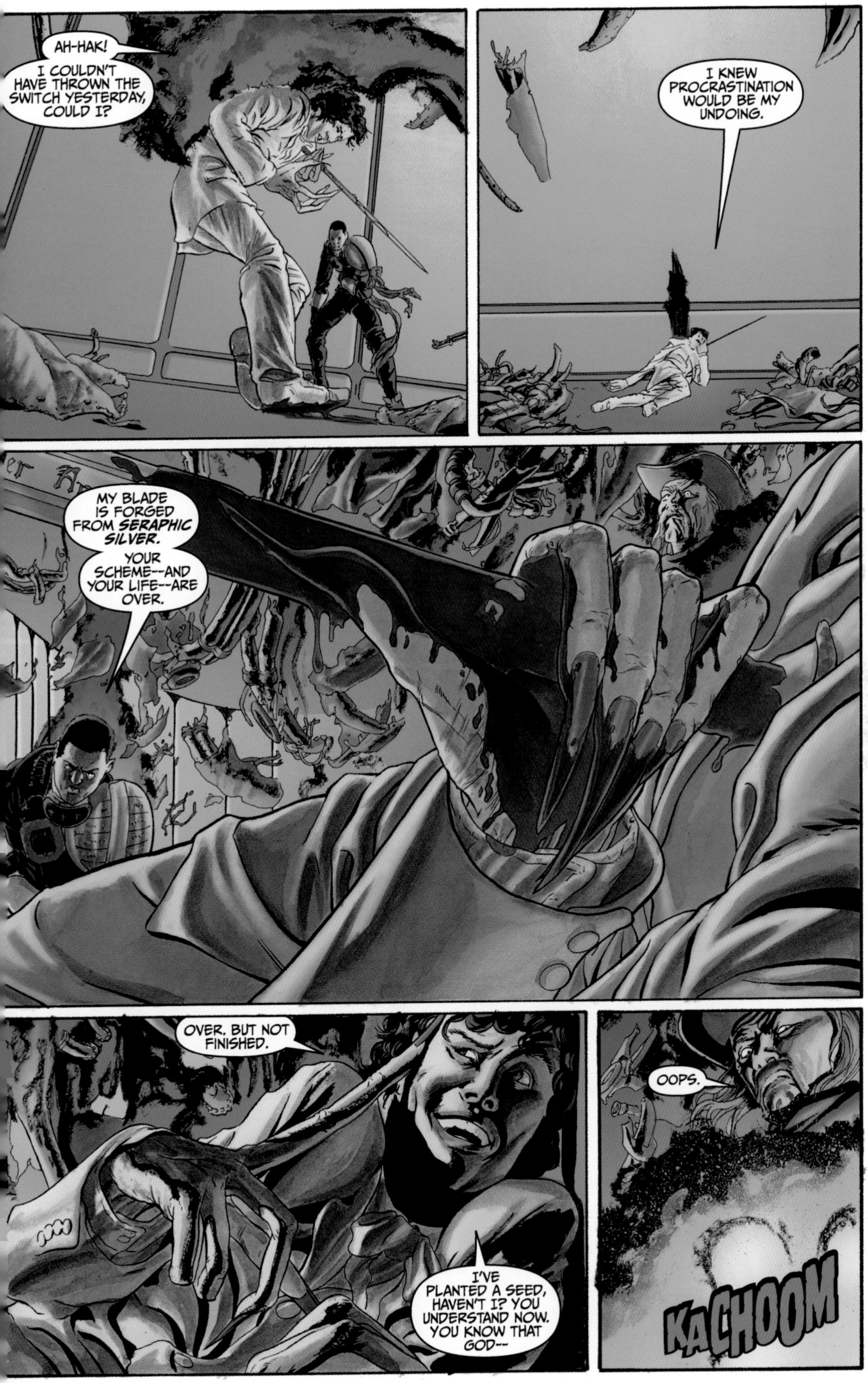
AH-HAK!
I COULDN'T HAVE THROWN THE SWITCH YESTERDAY, COULD I?
I KNEW PROCRASTINATION WOULD BE MY UNDOING.
MY BLADE IS FORGED FROM SERAPHIC SILVER.
YOUR SCHEME--AND YOUR LIFE--ARE OVER.
OVER. BUT NOT FINISHED.
I'VE PLANTED A SEED, HAVEN'T I? YOU UNDERSTAND NOW. YOU KNOW THAT GOD--
OOPS.
KACHOOM

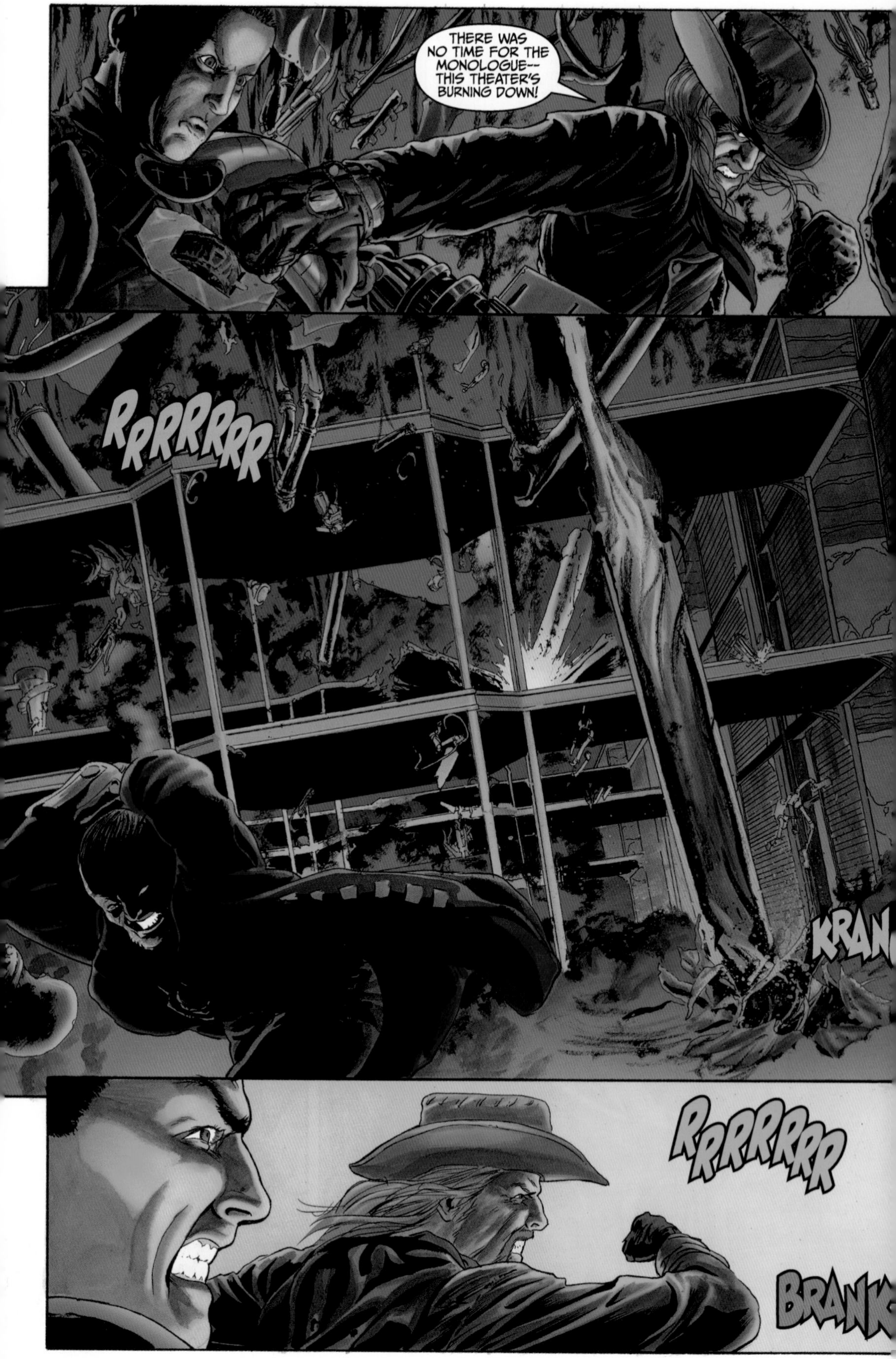
THERE WAS NO TIME FOR THE MONOLOGUE-- THIS THEATER'S BURNING DOWN!
RRRRRRR
KRAN
RRRRRRR
BRANK

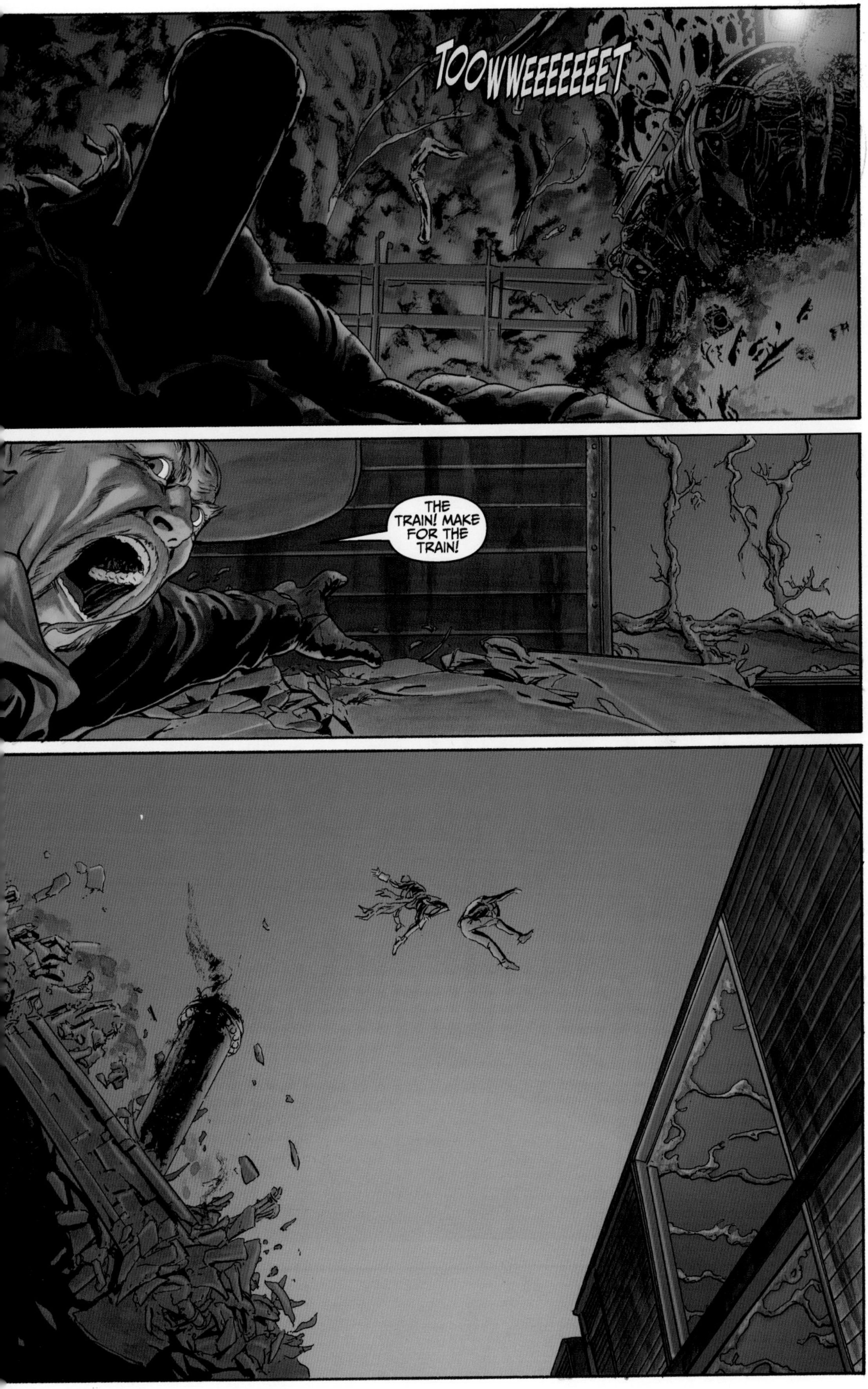
TOOWWEEEEEEET
THE TRAIN! MAKE FOR THE TRAIN!

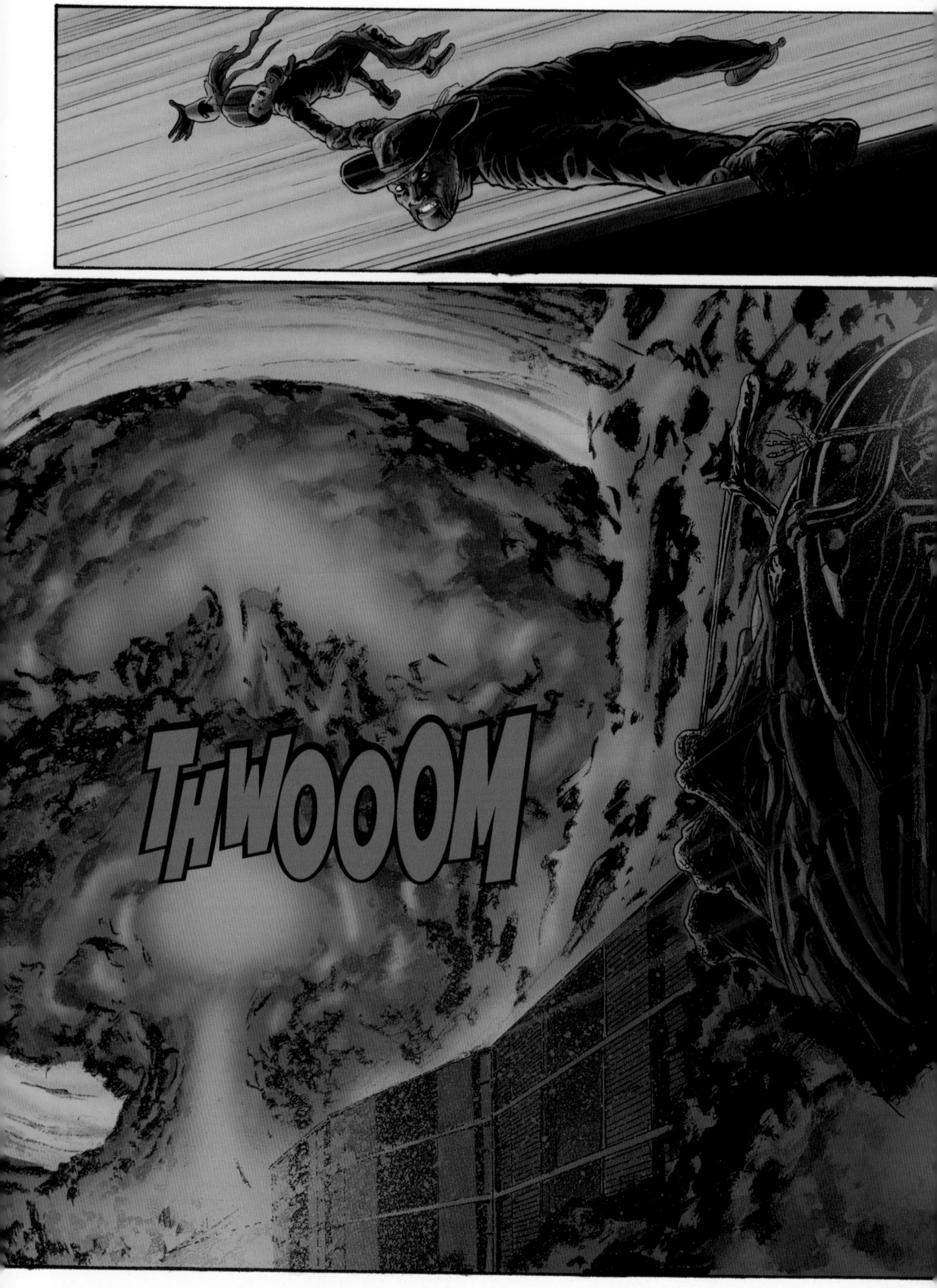
THWOOOM

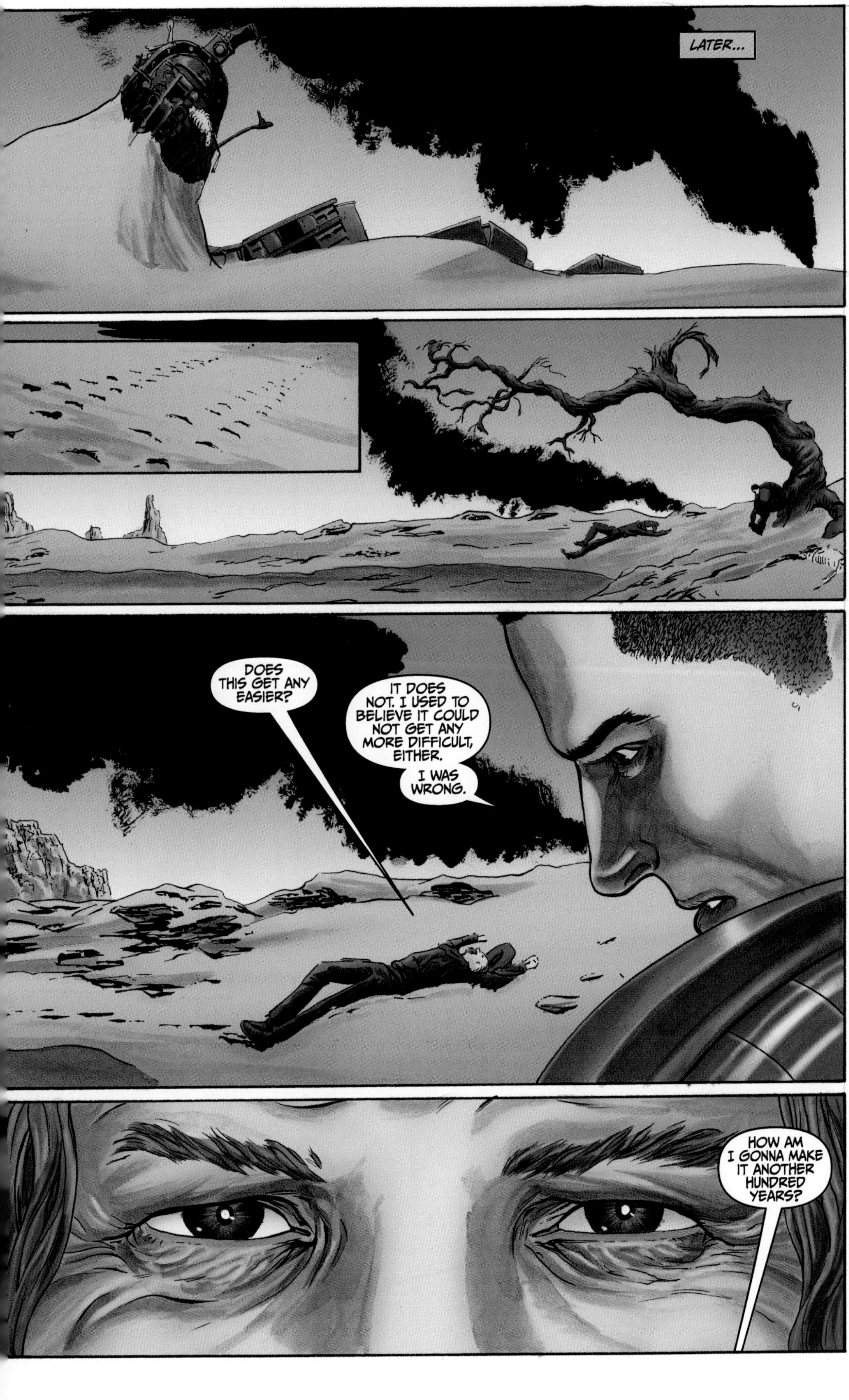
LATER...
DOES THIS GET ANY EASIER?
IT DOES NOT. I USED TO BELIEVE IT COULD NOT GET ANY MORE DIFFICULT, EITHER.
I WAS WRONG.
HOW AM I GONNA MAKE IT ANOTHER HUNDRED YEARS?

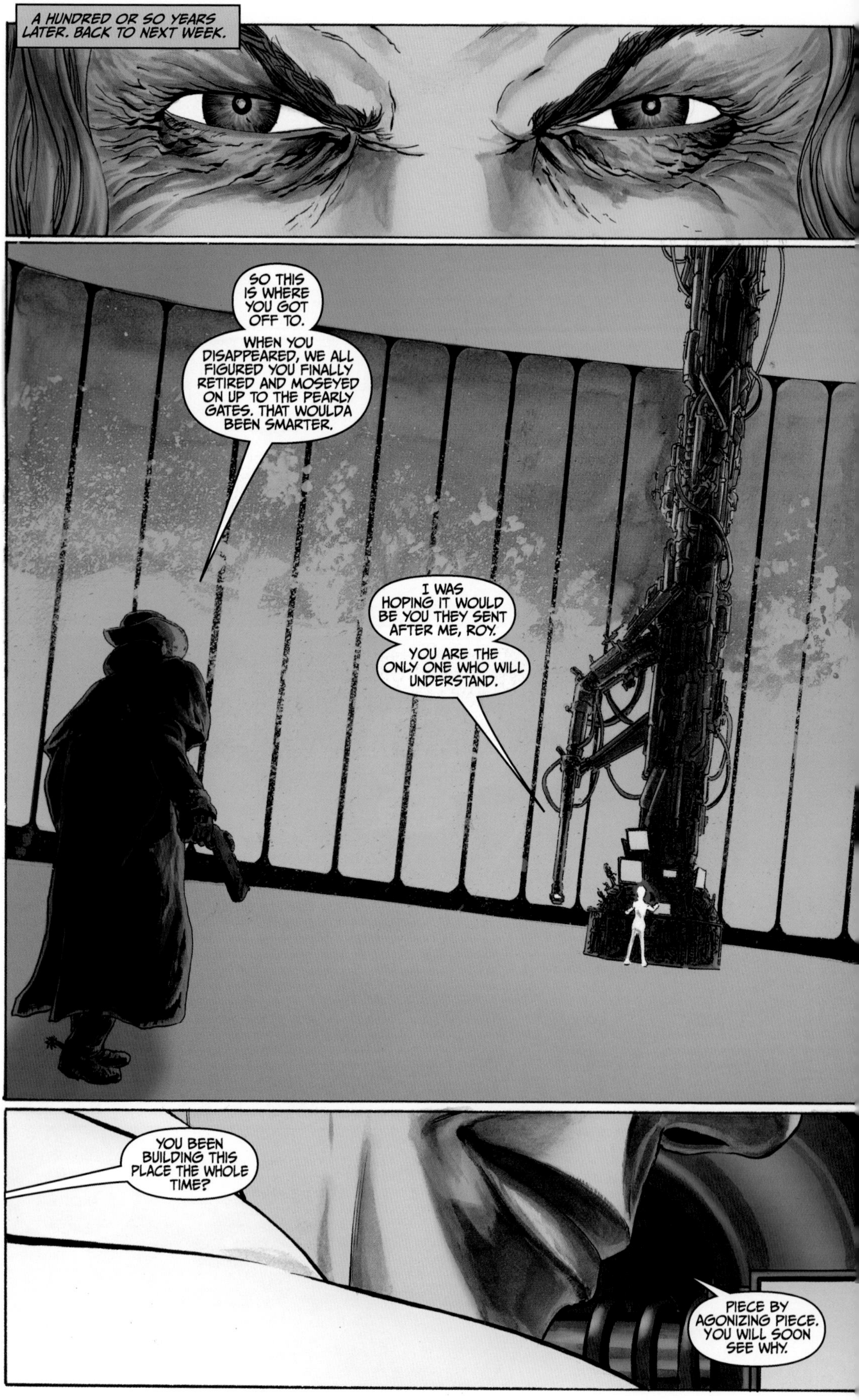
A HUNDRED OR SO YEARS LATER. BACK TO NEXT WEEK.
SO THIS IS WHERE YOU GOT OFF TO.
WHEN YOU DISAPPEARED, WE ALL FIGURED YOU FINALLY RETIRED AND MOSEYED ON UP TO THE PEARLY GATES. THAT WOULDA BEEN SMARTER.
I WAS HOPING IT WOULD BE YOU THEY SENT AFTER ME, ROY.
YOU ARE THE ONLY ONE WHO WILL UNDERSTAND.
YOU BEEN BUILDING THIS PLACE THE WHOLE TIME?
PIECE BY AGONIZING PIECE. YOU WILL SOON SEE WHY.

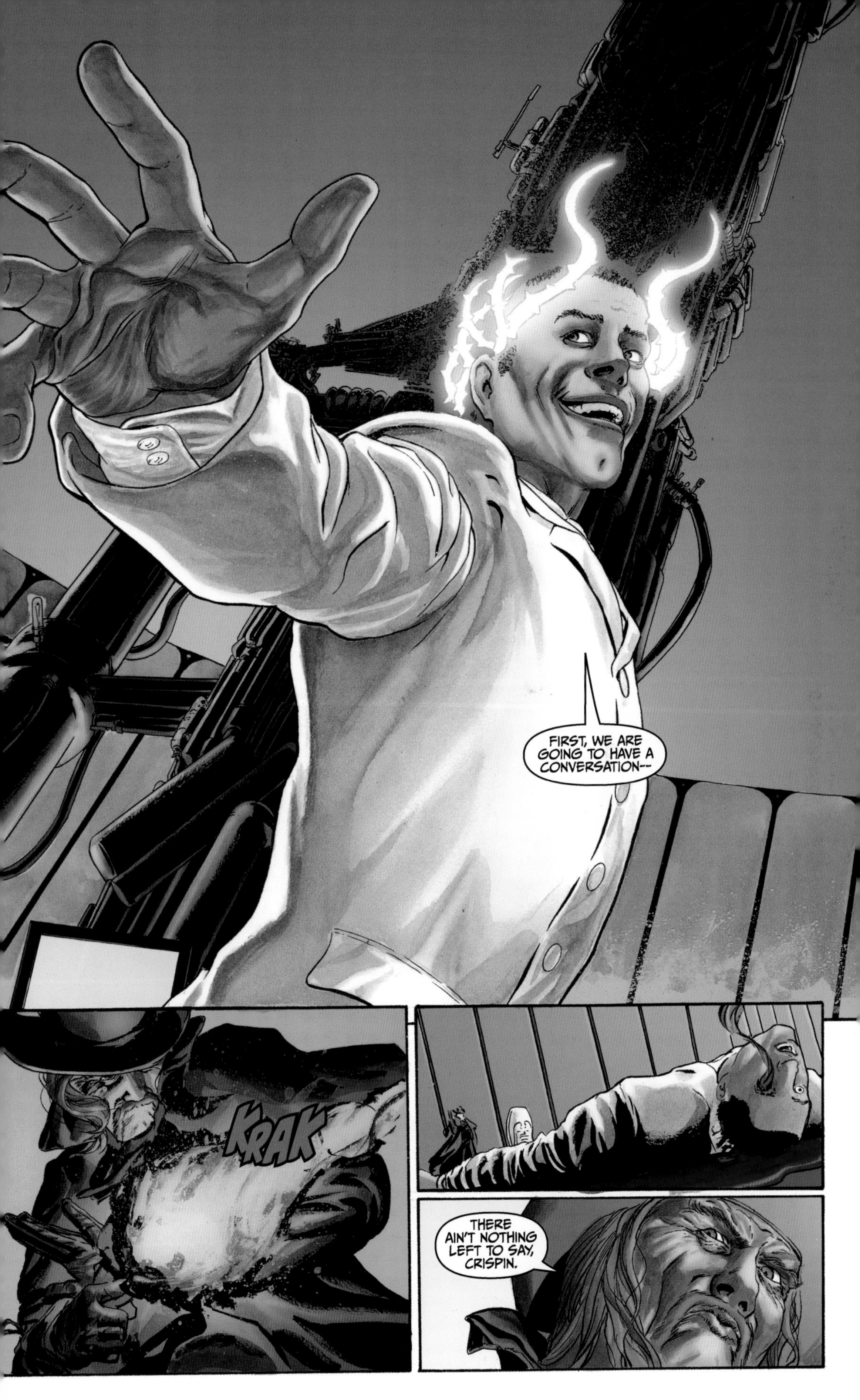

FIRST, WE ARE GOING TO HAVE A CONVERSATION--
KRAK
THERE AIN'T NOTHING LEFT TO SAY, CRISPIN.

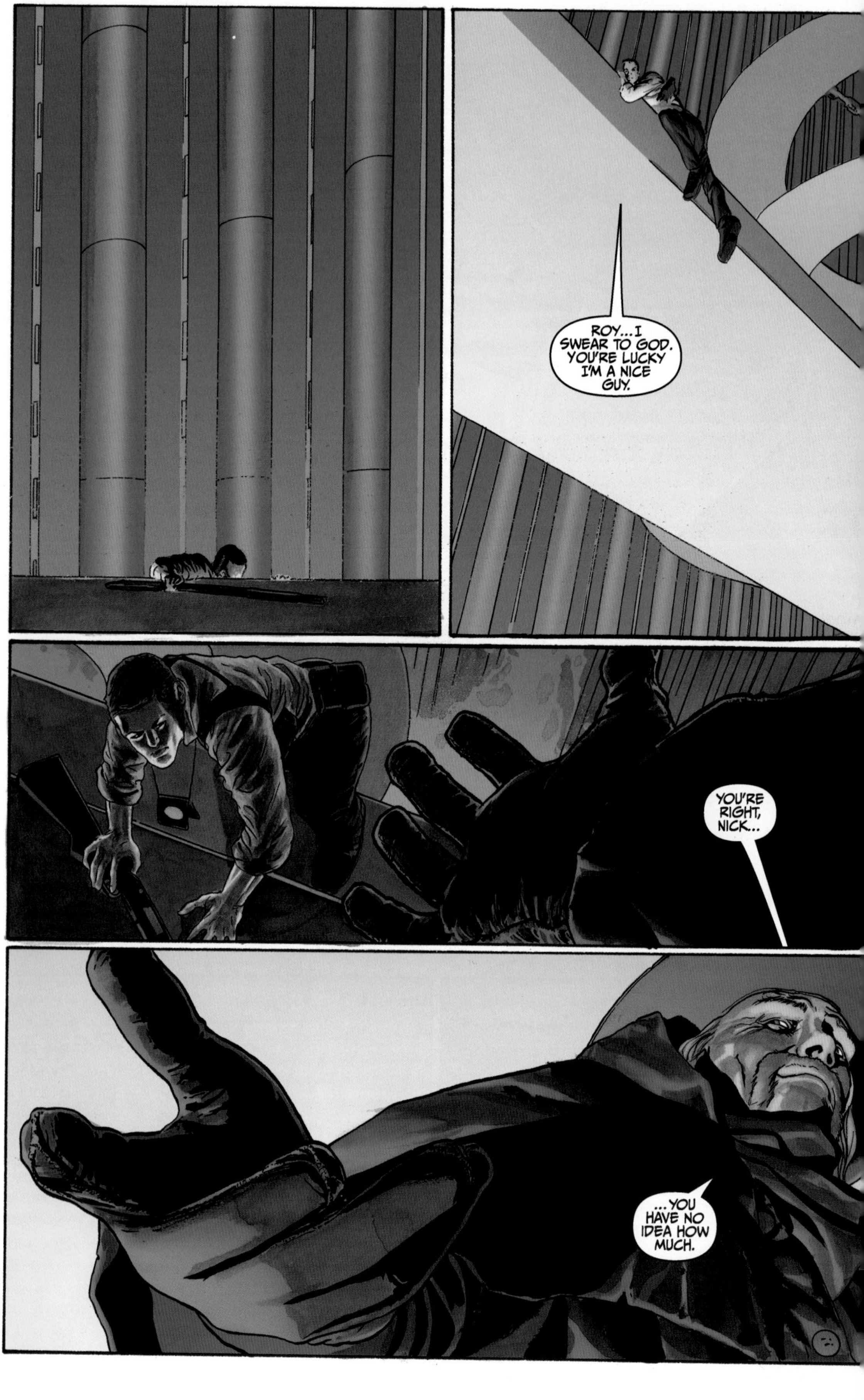
ROY... I SWEAR TO GOD. YOU'RE LUCKY I'M A NICE GUY.
YOU'RE RIGHT, NICK...
...YOU HAVE NO IDEA HOW MUCH.

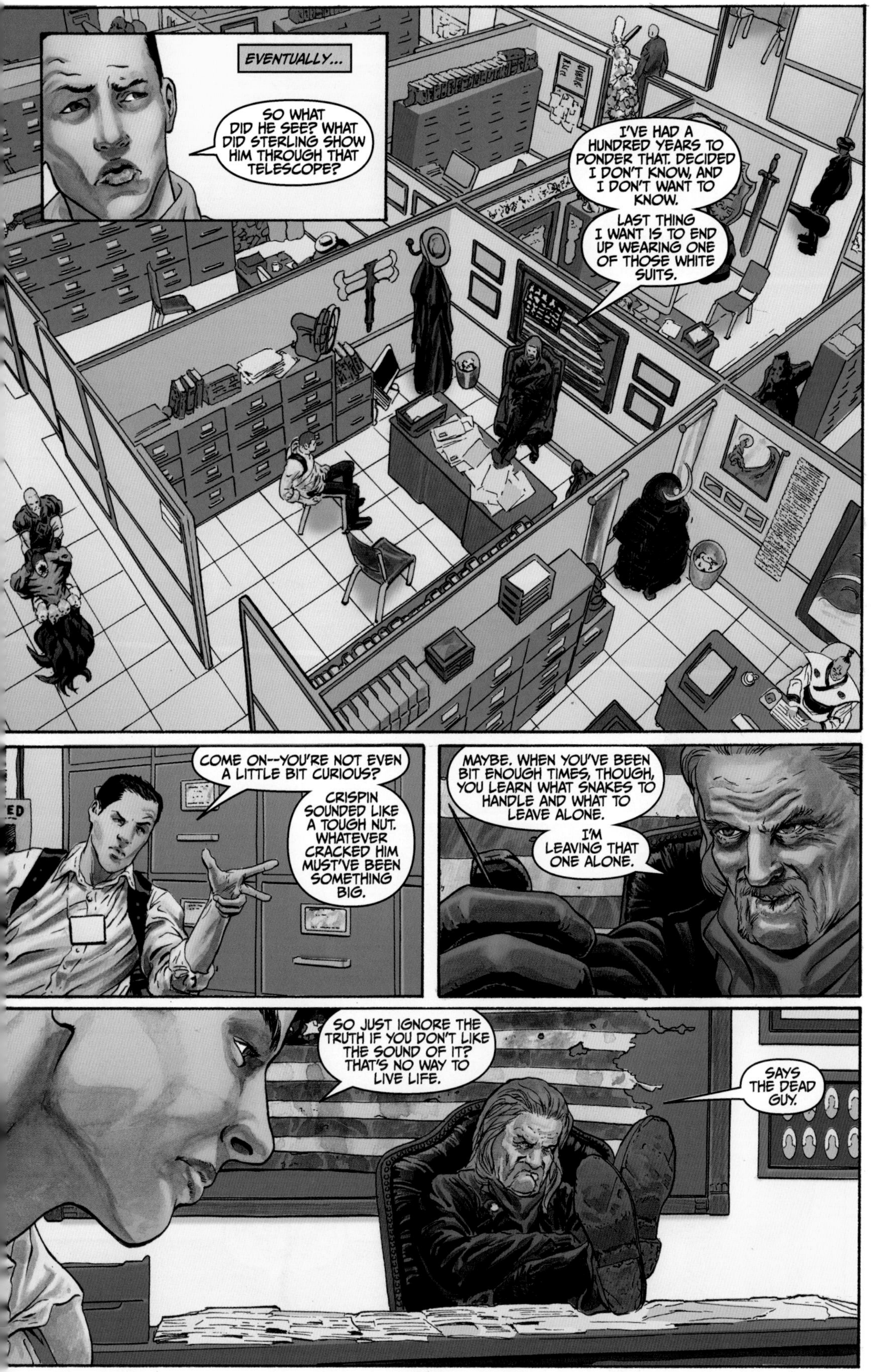

EVENTUALLY...
SO WHAT DID HE SEE? WHAT DID STERLING SHOW HIM THROUGH THAT TELESCOPE?
I'VE HAD A HUNDRED YEARS TO PONDER THAT. DECIDED I DON'T KNOW, AND I DON'T WANT TO KNOW.
LAST THING I WANT IS TO END UP WEARING ONE OF THOSE WHITE SUITS.
COME ON--YOU'RE NOT EVEN A LITTLE BIT CURIOUS?
CRISPIN SOUNDED LIKE A TOUGH NUT. WHATEVER CRACKED HIM MUST'VE BEEN SOMETHING BIG.
MAYBE. WHEN YOU'VE BEEN BIT ENOUGH TIMES, THOUGH, YOU LEARN WHAT SNAKES TO HANDLE AND WHAT TO LEAVE ALONE.
I'M LEAVING THAT ONE ALONE.
SO JUST IGNORE THE TRUTH IF YOU DON'T LIKE THE SOUND OF IT? THAT'S NO WAY TO LIVE LIFE.
SAYS THE DEAD GUY.

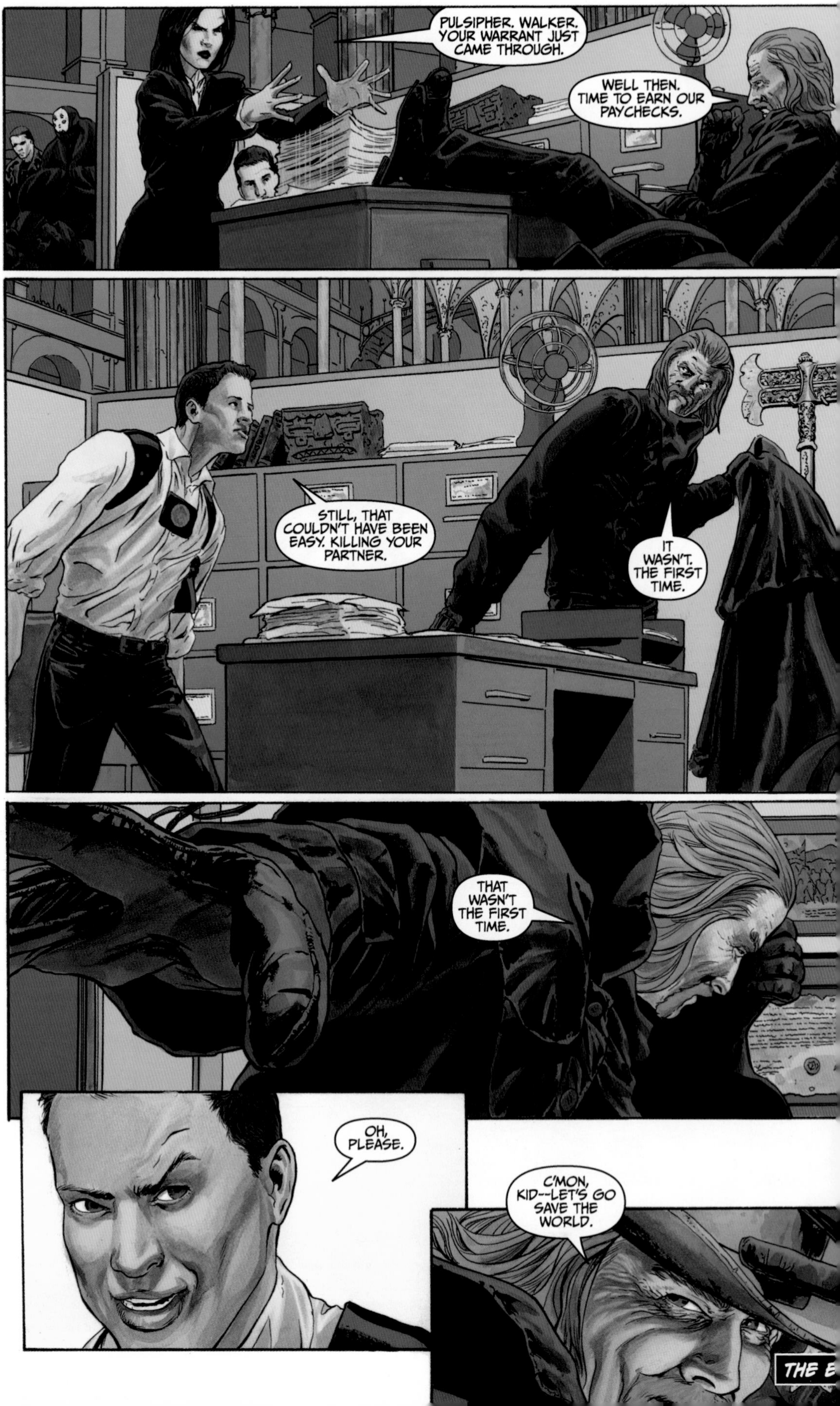
PULSIPHER. WALKER. YOUR WARRANT JUST CAME THROUGH.
WELL THEN. TIME TO EARN OUR PAYCHECKS.
STILL, THAT COULDN'T HAVE BEEN EASY. KILLING YOUR PARTNER.
IT WASN'T. THE FIRST TIME.
THAT WASN'T THE FIRST TIME.
OH, PLEASE.
C'MON, KID--LET'S GO SAVE THE WORLD.

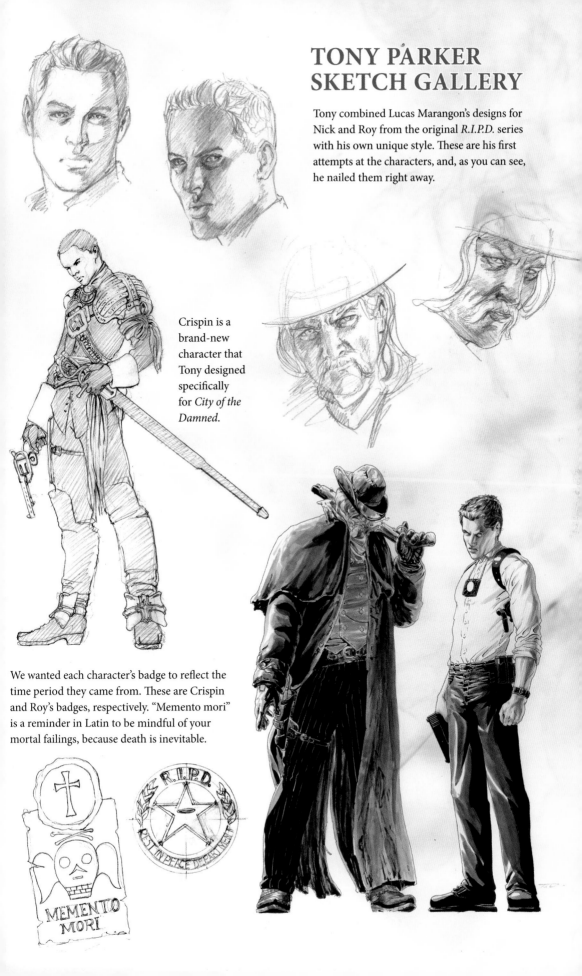

TONY PARKER SKETCH GALLERY

Tony combined Lucas Marangon's designs for Nick and Roy from the original *R.I.P.D.* series with his own unique style. These are his first attempts at the characters, and, as you can see, he nailed them right away.

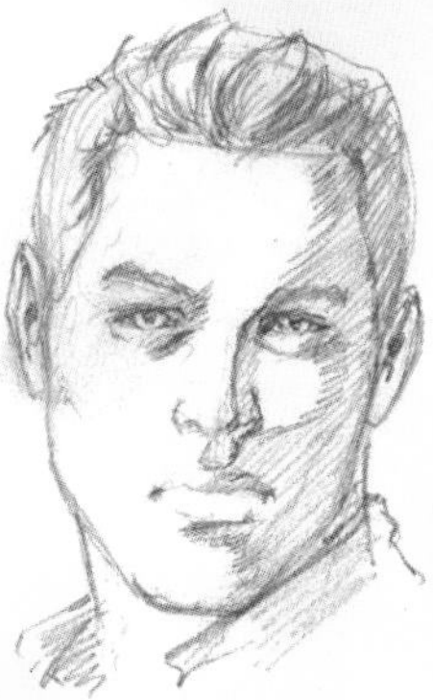

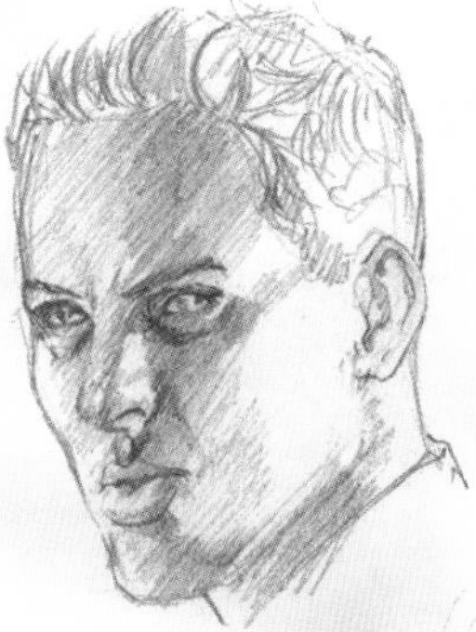

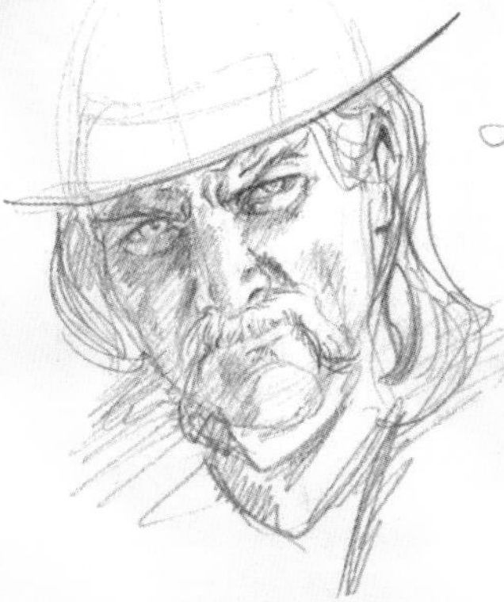

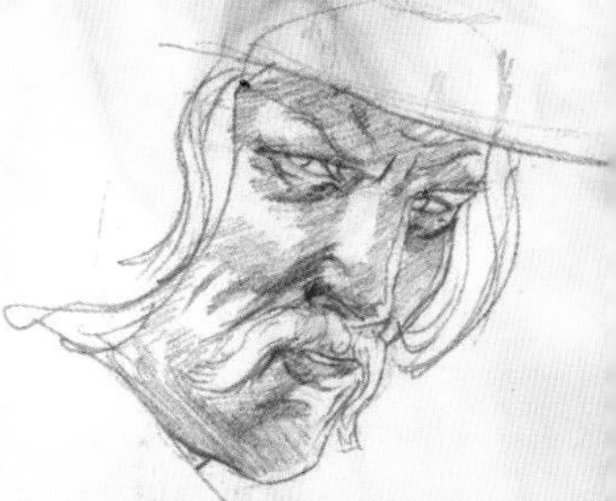

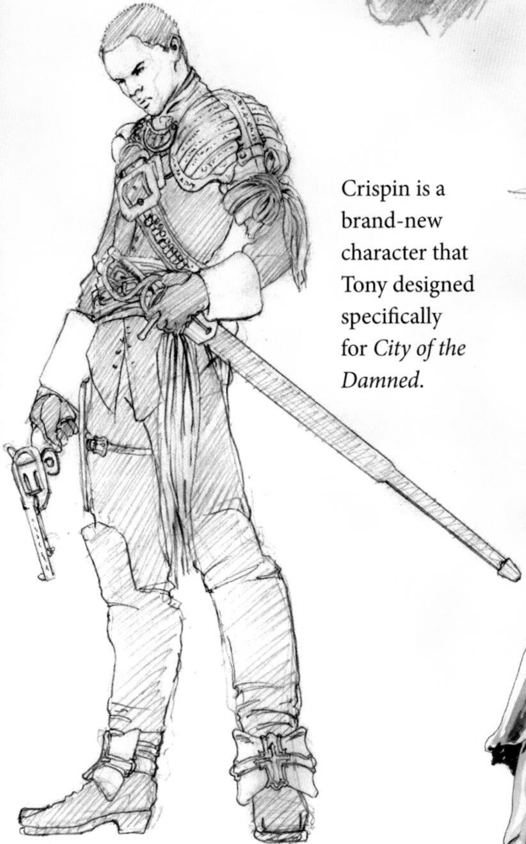

Crispin is a brand-new character that Tony designed specifically for *City of the Damned*.

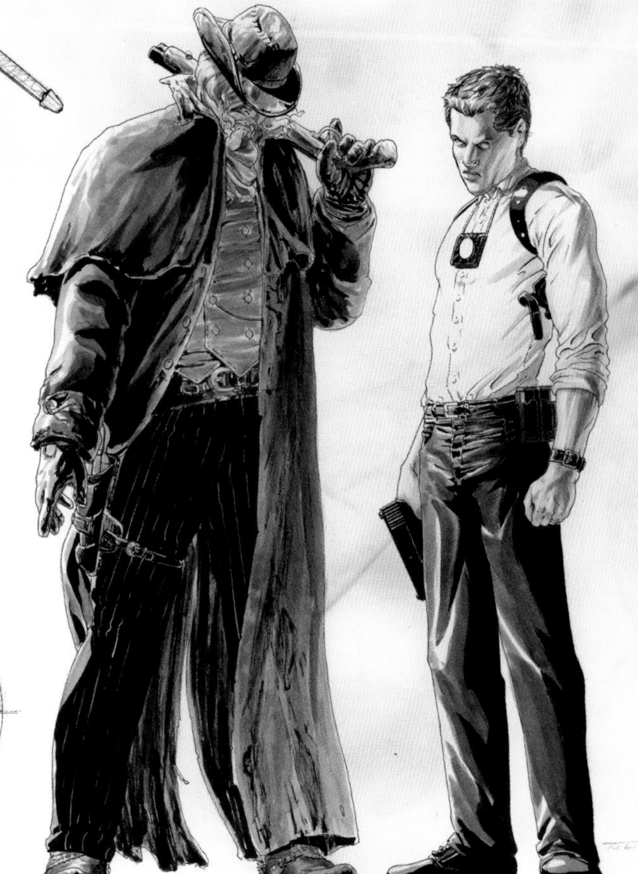

We wanted each character's badge to reflect the time period they came from. These are Crispin and Roy's badges, respectively. "Memento mori" is a reminder in Latin to be mindful of your mortal failings, because death is inevitable.

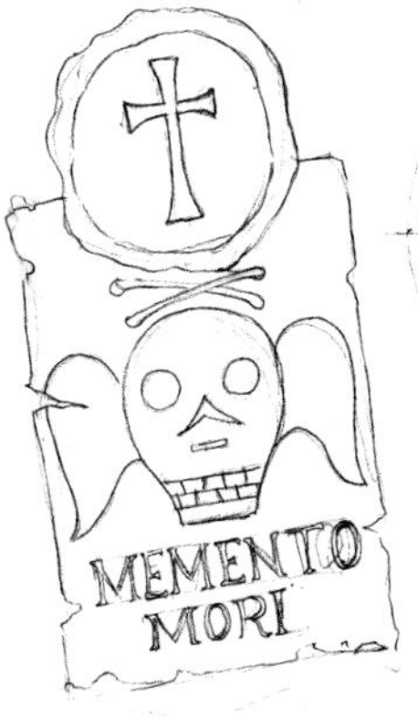
MEMENTO
MORI

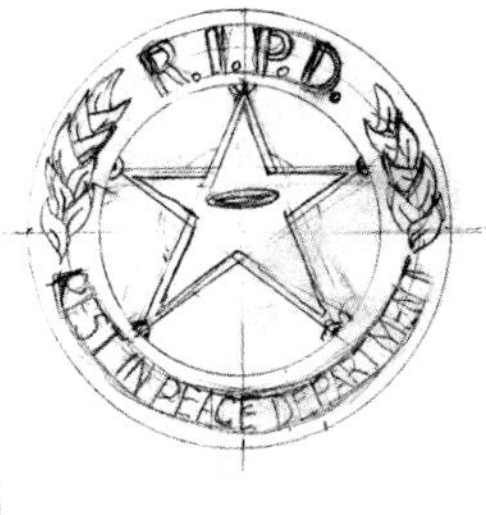
R.I.P.D.
REST IN PEACE DEPARTMENT

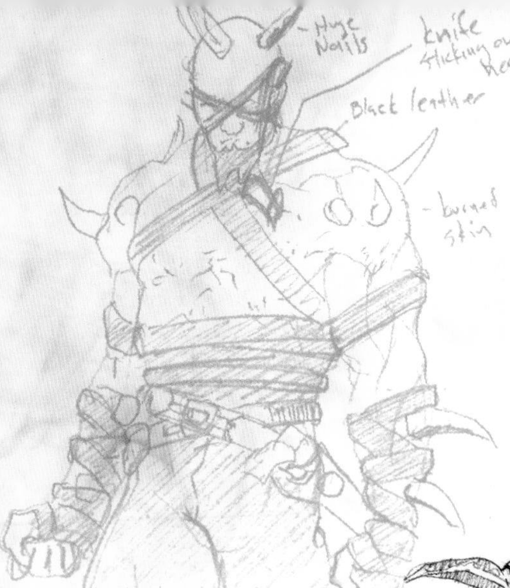

Huge Nails
knife sticking out of heart
Black leather
burned skin

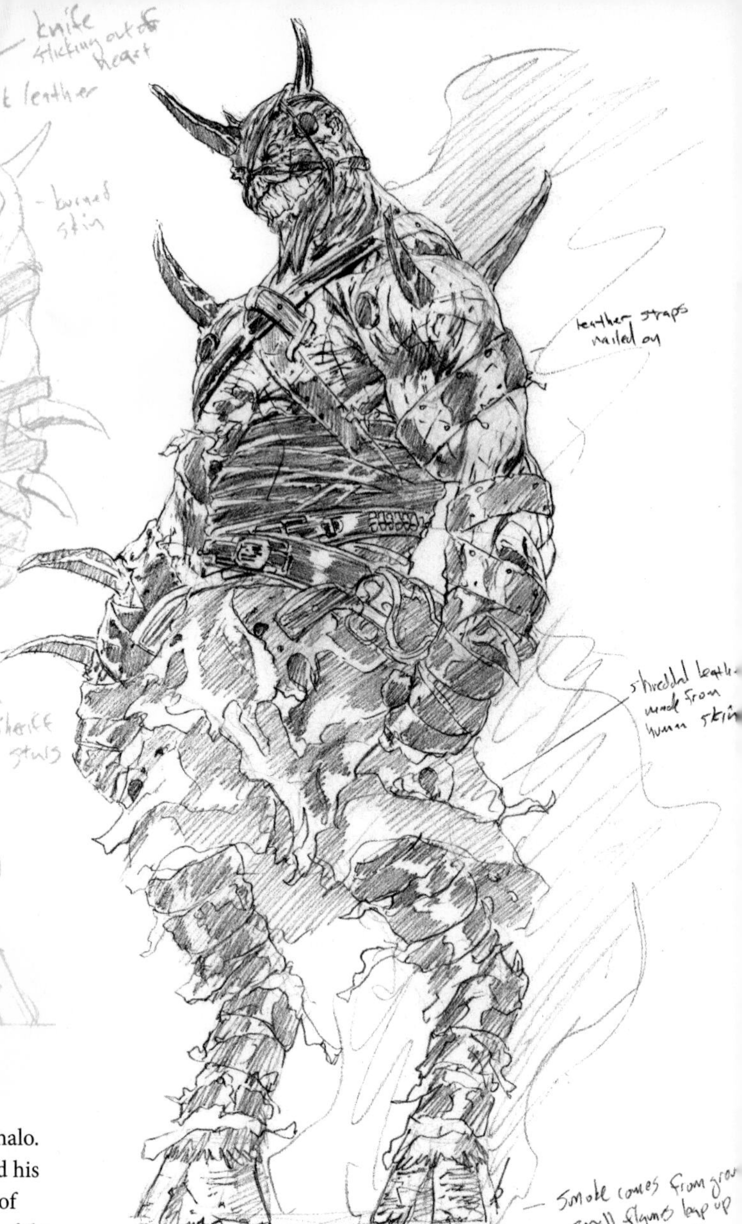

leather straps nailed on
Smoke comes from gro
small flames leap up
with each step

Enter the villains!

Lucifuge remains largely obscured in smoke throughout the comic. Here is the demon in all his monstrous glory!

As you can see, Sterling's appearance evolved quite a bit from a robed preacher to a sharply dressed man. A lot of thought went into the shape of his halo. We wanted something that reflected his personality, just as Crispin's crown of thorns halo from the closing pages of this collection reflects his.

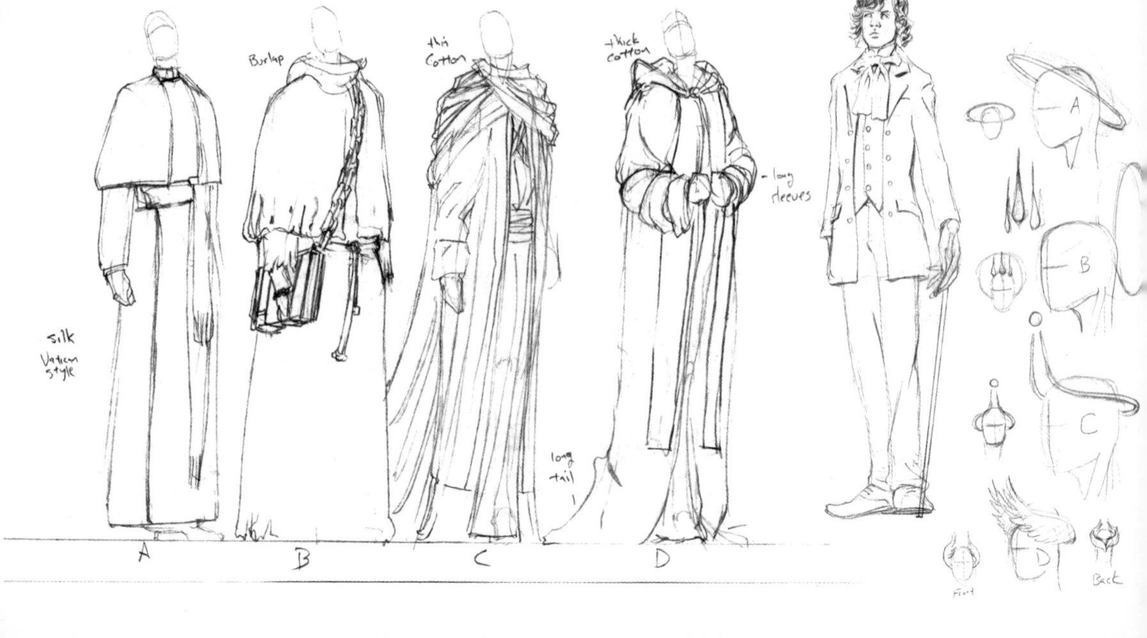

Burlap
thin Cotton
thick cotton
long sleeves
Silk
Vatican style
long tail
A
B
C
D
Front
Back

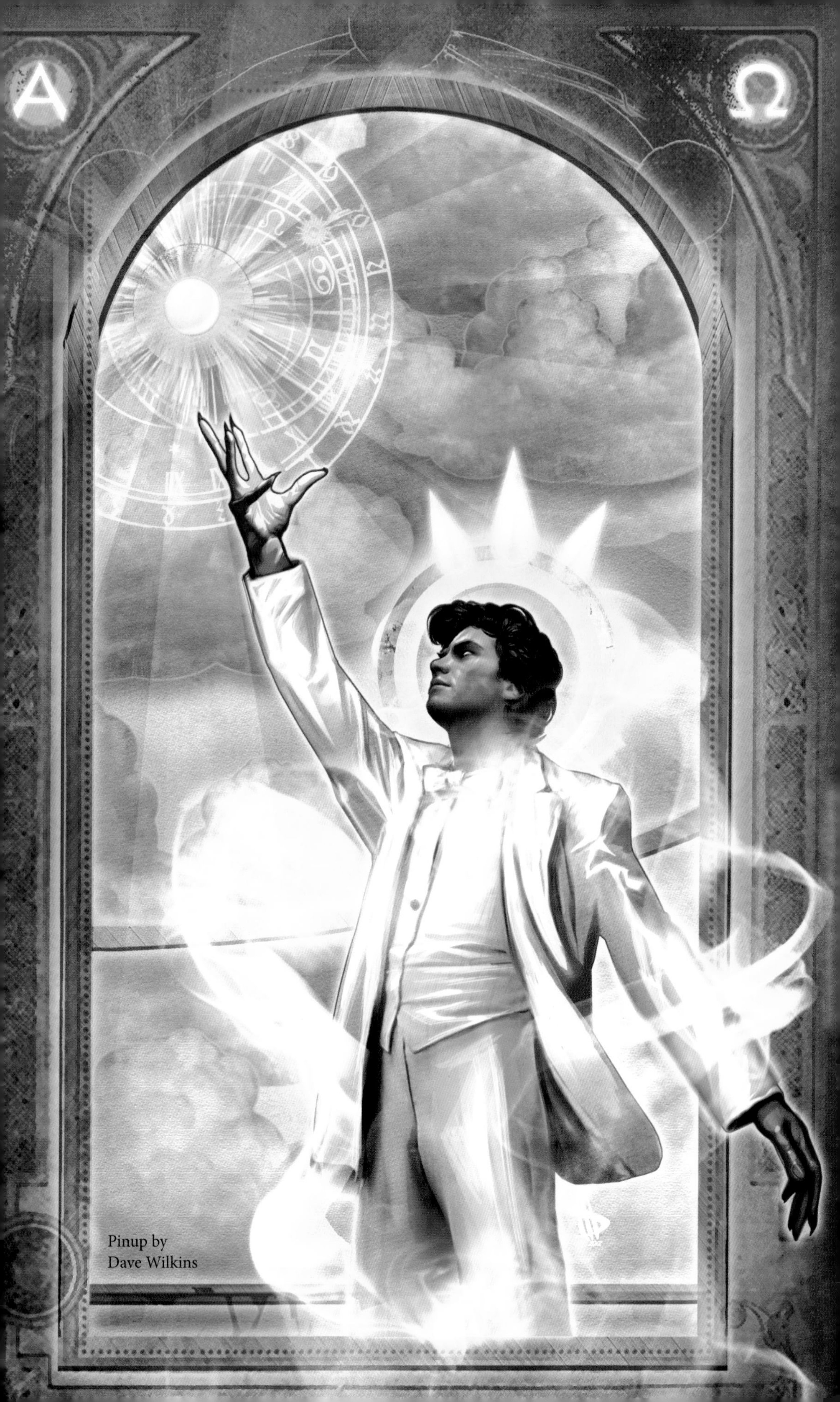
A
Ω
Pinup by
Dave Wilkins

WRITTEN BY PETER LENKOV • ART BY LUCAS MARANGON AND RANDY EMBERLIN

R.I.P.D.™

WELCOME TO THE REST IN PEACE DEPARTMENT—the devoted, yet dead, officers of divine law enforcement "patrolling the deadbeat . . . reporting to one boss." Yep—*that* boss. Nick Cruz was murdered by an unknown assailant at the height of his personal and professional life. Now he's traded a hundred years of service to the R.I.P.D. in exchange for a shot at finding who killed him. Unfortunately his search will take him to Hell and back—literally! Don't miss the postmortem mayhem, now a major motion picture!

978-1-61655-071-4 $12.99